Tony Really Loves Me

Tony Really Loves Me

STUART BELL

SpenView

First published in Great Britain in 2000 by
SpenView Publications Limited

The right of Stuart Bell to be identified as the Author of
the Work has been asserted by him in accordance with the
Copyright, Designs and Patents Act 1988.

10 9 8 7 6 5 4 3 2 1

A CIP catalogue record for this title is available
from the British Library

ISBN 0 953 86381 6

Typeset by Palimpsest Book Production Limited,
Polmont, Stirlingshire
Printed and bound in Great Britain by
Omnia Books Limited, Glasgow

SpenView Publications Ltd
One Old Burlington Street
London W1X 2NL

To Margaret and Malcolm

Contents

BOOK THREE

A Note on the Author

SpenView Publications Limited publishes this collection of short stories on the life of MP Stuart Bell entitled *Tony Really Loves Me*, describing his relations with Tony Blair and other leading figures within the New Labour Party and House of Commons; and also describing his early struggles to be a writer.

Stuart Bell is a Member of Parliament for Middlesbrough; he is a Barrister-at-law, and has been in the House of Commons since 1983. Born and bred in a pit village in North-West Durham, Mr Bell attended the local grammar school before beginning work in the colliery office; he subsequently became a newspaper reporter, free-lance journalist, copy-typist to *The Daily Telegraph*, and then typist and shorthand-typist in the city of London, before going to Paris to work for an American Lawyer.

He has published two novels and a chronicle of the Cleveland child abuse crisis of 1987. He read for the Bar to become a Barrister. He spent seventeen years in Paris before returning to enter British politics.

Stuart Bell lives in his Middlesbrough constituency with his wife Margaret.

Book One

Tony,

John Keats would die in Rome at the age of twenty-four, and on his tombstone he would have inscribed the words: Here lies one whose name was writ in water. *In fact, the poetry of John Keats lives on, and only his frail body has withered.*

You have not written your name on water but in the history books, not because of time and place, chance that happeneth to us all, but because you built New Labour on the traditions and values of the old; you built the future onto the past in the present.

It falls to few men or women to have such a vision, to be able to read in the runes of history what the present and future should mean, but by discipline, by detachment, by living one's life according to one's principles, by being the first Tony Blair rather than the second anyone-else, you have earned the right to be where you are today.

You have a right to be here, to savour this moment, to marvel at it, to be humble before it, to understand its reality, its frailty, that paths of glory lead but to the grave, but paths of glory they are nevertheless. In ancient Rome, when a General returned from his victories, with laurels around his head, crowds at his

3

feet, a slave would ride by his side in the chariot, below the sight of the crowd, whispering into his ear that all glory is fleeting.

When Winston Churchill became Prime Minister during the Second World War, he recalled how his worries had eased, burdens fell from him, there was relief because he now knew he had the authority and the will to do what he knew had to be done. He also had the backing of the nation behind him.

I hope the wonderment of this day will live forever in your mind, you have deserved your success, you have a right to it, you are entitled to it, and you will fashion and mould it not in your own self-interest but in the national interest. The future belongs to no-one, says a character in a play by Victor Hugo. No, *comes the response,* the future belongs to God.

Be that as it may, the future today belongs to you and the British people who have supported you.

Stuart

Letter to Tony Blair, sent to his home at Trimdon in his Sedgefield constituency, to be opened and read on Election Day 1997

Tony Blair Revisited

I had first met Tony Blair in the office of Tom Burlison in Newcastle when Tony had been looking for a seat in the House of Commons.

Tom had been made up to the Lords in the first session of the new 1997 Parliament; he had brought his family down from the North-East and I had met them briefly in the Members' Lobby of the Lords when the ceremony was over. Tom had been Regional Secretary of the General and Municipal Workers' Union, later to be joined by the Boilermakers'. He had become Treasurer of the Labour Party and had been made a life peer in his own right.

He would be appointed a government whip.

I had had the full support of the GMB when I stood for nomination as Prospective Parliamentary Labour Candidate for Middlesbrough. Seventeen candidates had put their names forward and one of the candidates had the support of the Electricians' and Plumbers' Union, better known then as the EETPU. I knew this particular candidate had no hope of winning the nomination and persuaded the GMB and the EETPU to switch their votes to whichever candidate stayed in the race.

As it happened, the EETPU candidate did not get short-listed and, true to their word, the EETPU delegates switched their vote to me at the selection conference. The young candidate not short-listed had been Tony Blair. He then stood for the neighbouring seat of Stockton, South and though on this occasion he was short-listed he was defeated by a candidate with similar colouring to my own, fair hair and blue eyes and a light complexion.

This turned out to be a blessing in disguise, since the Labour candidate did not win the seat and Tony went on to get the safe Sedgefield seat only a day or two before nominations closed for the 1983 General Election. The rest, as they say, is history except that each time I meet Cherie Booth, as Tony's wife prefers to be called, she reminds me how I beat Tony for the nomination for my seat. Having the same colouring as the Stockton, South candidate, it is an easy mistake to make, but I have not the heart to point out that it was not I who beat Tony for the nomination.

It had been someone else.

My wife Margaret and I had come to live in Middlesbrough from Newcastle and as a barrister I had gone into chambers with another son of a coal miner, Barry Stewart, who had opened new chambers in the town's Borough Road. Tony, also a barrister, would telephone me one day to say he was coming to Middlesbrough to represent a client before an industrial tribunal.

Could we meet?

We had lunch in the old law court in the town hall then converted into a restaurant, a noisy, friendly restaurant part-self-service, part-waitress, handy for the new Crown Court, the food simple and straightforward, the clatter lifting around us as we sat on the bench where judges in their robes and wigs might have sat, peering over their half-moon spectacles.

'Did you win your case?' I asked.

'Of course,' he said.

Years later, when Tony was Leader of the Opposition

on the verge of fighting the 1997 General Election, I took Tony Zivanaris to London to attend one of New Labour's fund-raising dinners. Tony owned the Vermont Hotel in Newcastle and the Baltimore in Middlesbrough; he also owned the Portland Hotel in Hull and had once been involved with Middlesbrough football club as a director. He followed closely business and politics and as once I had introduced him to John Smith, when John had been Leader of the Labour Party, I now introduced him to Cherie Booth.

Cherie was herself a barrister who would become Queen's Counsel and Recorder.

'Tony won't remember,' he said. 'I retained him years ago for an industrial tribunal in Middlesbrough.'

'And how did he get on?' Cherie asked.

'He won, of course,' I said.

Tony Blair and I would often lunch together in the members' dining room of the House of Commons.

We had lunch one day with Jim Callaghan, former Prime Minister, then a back-bencher. Jim had an office at the top of my corridor, he still maintained his chauffeur from the days he had been Prime Minister, and I would see him often as he came and went. Tony and I were thrilled to be lunching at the same table as a former Prime Minister and though I recall I would always call him Mr Callaghan Tony was bolder.

He called him Jim.

Jim wore what I called his JC suit.

He had brought Jimmy Carter, President of the United States, to Newcastle in 1976 when Carter had visited London for an international conference. Carter had been free for a day or two and his spin doctors had decided that it would be a good photo opportunity to have him visit the North-East and the legendary homestead of the ancestors of the first United States President, George Washington.

7

This had been a mighty event for Tyneside, the first and last time they would receive a visit from a President of the United States. Security would be a nightmare, thousands would gather before the Civic Centre and though in my vanity and vainglory, as Prospective Parliamentary Candidate for Hexham at the time, the President landing in my prospective constituency, I had put in a request to meet with him, this had fallen on stony ground.

It had been ignored.

I had stood with thousands of others before the Civic Centre when Jim Callaghan and Jimmy Carter had come onto a makeshift platform. Carter had endeared himself not only to thousands but millions of Geordies when he had begun his opening remarks by decrying: '*Howway the Lads!*' His reference to Newcastle United football club sent the cheers soaring beyond the steeple of the Cathedral and the towers of the Civic Centre through thin cloud to heaven itself.

Jim Callaghan had bought a gift for Jimmy Carter.

This was a dark suit with a neat white trim running through the suit; it had the look of a pin-stripe, but when you got close enough you found the initials were JC for Jim Callaghan. The Prime Minister of the day had had two suits made from the same cloth, with the same trim, the same initials running through them, linking forever the initials of the President of the United States with those of the Prime Minister of the United Kingdom.

One of the suits had been the gift for Jimmy.

Cutting through to the Commons from my office in Millbank, I would often avoid the cold by slipping along the red-carpeted corridors of the Lords. One day I would run into Jim Callaghan, now Lord Callaghan of Cardiff, and though at the age of eighty-seven he would have difficulty standing, nevertheless he would stop and talk and be as courteous as ever, eager for gossip and happy to swap tales of old. I had reminded him of the story of two suits and he told me that the suit had been patented and had sold well in Japan; but that Jimmy Carter, on leaving office and the White House, had been required to give up his suit to the United States Treasury because it had been a gift from a foreign dignitary.

Jim had been wearing his JC suit this day in the Commons dining room when Tony and I had lunched with him.

'Do you two hunt together?' he asked.

'Yes,' Tony replied.

Shortly after we became Members of Parliament, the Fishburn cokeworks closed in Tony's constituency with a loss of jobs. This was a dramatic local event, to be repeated often in the North-East, but it required a dramatic intervention on the floor of the House. Tony had moved to adjourn the proceedings under Standing Order Number Nine, as this procedural order had then been known; but it would be unusual for the Speaker to grant such an adjournment, since it would disrupt the government's business of the day.

It had been a useful mechanism, however, to draw attention to a grievance.

Tony would speak from the back of the Commons as far away from the front bench as he could get, just as he stood at the back of meetings of the Parliamentary Labour Party held on the Wednesday morning, and at the back of the meetings of the regional conferences the Party held at different venues in the North-East. He showed no eagerness to put himself forward.

He had a natural modesty.

On entering Parliament, he had joined neither the left-wing Tribune Group nor the right-wing Solidarity Group;

he certainly would not have joined the hard-left Campaign Group. Only two years after entering Parliament, upon the prompting of Derek Foster MP, then Parliamentary Private Secretary to Neil Kinnock, did he join the Tribune Group. He spent as little time as possible in the Commons' tea room, not hobnobbing with his colleagues, exchanging chit-chat, but sitting in an obscure corner, not drawing attention to himself, anxious at least to be seen.

He had appeared on a BBC *Newsnight* programme from Hartlepool, much to the irritation of the sitting Hartlepool MP, Ted Leadbitter, who had not been aware of this intrusion into his constituency. There had been another *Newsnight* programme, with Tony on constituency duty, meeting his constituents in his surgery at Trimdon, smiling all the way, reassuring, already marked out by the media as a man to watch.

I had congratulated him on the programme.

'Don't tell everyone,' he said.

He had shown no clear ideological bent when, on entering Parliament, he had been required to choose between Neil Kinnock and Roy Hattersley as future Leader of the Labour Party. As someone who was both pro-European and anti-nuclear disarmament, positions held by Roy Hattersley though not by Neil Kinnock, I had no difficulty not only signing up for Roy Hattersley but offering to speak on his behalf in his campaign to become Leader of the Labour Party.

I had canvassed, too, for votes within the Parliamentary Labour Party.

'Will you vote for Neil Kinnock or Roy Hattersley?' I asked Tony.

'I've not made up my mind,' Tony said.

'Bloody lawyers!' Neil Kinnock said, when I reported

10

the conversation to him, since this was a friendly election between him and Roy Hattersley. 'You're all alike!'

In fact, like the rest of the 1983 Labour intake, except myself, he voted for Neil Kinnock. But this day, standing at the back of the Commons, against the ingrained panelling, he made his three-minute plea for the adjournment of the House so that it could debate the proposed closure of the Fishburn cokeworks. He spoke with style and grace and without notes; he had memorised his speech; and it was an effective if unsuccessful performance.

I chided him afterwards for not using notes.

'This is not a memory test,' I said.

I was fearful that he might find himself as Winston Churchill had once found himself at the onset of his career, when he had memorised a speech for the floor of the House, only to discover that it fled when he had caught the Speaker's eye. The author Somerset Maugham had a similar experience. From then on, whenever speaking in public, both Churchill and Maugham would not only memorise their speeches but makes notes, although Maugham who suffered from a stammer preferred not to speak publicly at all.

When Tony became front-bench spokesman, responsible for winding-up a debate for the Opposition, he would sit through the entire proceedings, listening to all the contributions, modifying his own original speech so that when he stood at the Dispatch Box he would respond to the points made by other members rather than reading from the speech prepared days earlier.

At his first Question Time as Prime Minister he would respond to questions without a note, but having moved from two Question Times a week, each a quarter of an hour, to once a week on the Wednesday for a half-hour, prudence and common sense pushed him to entering the

11

Commons with two large wine-red books under his arm, that he would lay before him at the Dispatch Box and delve into when responding to questions.

At the beginning of his Parliamentary career, he had both nerve and confidence, intervening at a Minister's question time, turning to his colleagues, demanding to know why there were not free television licences for our senior citizens, a pledge he would fulfil for those over seventy-five. When opening a debate for the Opposition he would turn now to the left, now to the right, a tall man, using his full height, using his hands too with grace, not crouched with diffidence, nor gripping the sides of the Dispatch Box to hide his nervousness.

He would speak with great clarity, not swallowing his words, nor even his syllables, and it became plain that he would be a formidable debater and a great asset to the Party. There were those even in those early days who saw Tony as a future Party leader, but this had not been my view; he lacked the traditional Trade Union base, the block vote would never take to him, even though sponsored by the Transport & General Workers' Union; but few would have foreseen then how this would change when Labour moved to a one-member-one-vote system for choosing its leaders.

'He's good news for Labour.'

These had been the words of Jack Cunningham, MP for Copeland, former Minister in the Callaghan government and Minister again under Tony Blair. Conservatives, too, recognised not only his qualities as one of the future leaders of the Party but also on the floor of the House. Geoffrey Dickens, a Conservative MP whose career would be cut short by illness leading to his death in office, remarked to me one day on coming out of the chamber as Tony was speaking, that from the Opposition benches:

'He's making a good fist of it!'

12

I would spend the first five weeks as a new MP simply finding my way around, to the Vote Office and Table Office and Post Office, the Central and Members' Lobby. I would wander the corridors, upstairs to committee rooms, across Westminster Hall to the so-called Grand Committee Room, finding washrooms in nooks and crannies, even a changing room with bath and shower next to the barber's shop. There were so many restaurants and bars and lifts manned by senior servants of the House, some of them bent and gnarled, as if they had been there since the Victorian era, crashing shut the iron gates as if locking you into eternity.

I had met Tony outside the members' cloak room.

The cloak room has its own eccentricity in that there hangs a strand of red tape from each name plate. There are two red stripes across the floor on either side of the House. An MP is not allowed to cross these when participating in a debate. The benches are at least two sword lengths' apart. The swords were to be left in the members' cloak room, hanging from the tapes. The swords may now be gone but the tapes are still there, frail red ribbons, useless and forlorn.

Tony asked me the way to the library.

I told him he should go through the doors from the cloak room, up a narrow flight of winding stairs to the right, past the washroom, up some marble steps into the Members' Lobby, down the green-carpeted corridor with lockers on each side, tall chandeliers above, through more wooden doors with decorated glass windows, across another wide corridor leading to the Speaker's quarters, more lockers to either side.

13

And there before him would be the library.

'Blimey!' he said. 'You've been in the House only as long as I have. And you know your way around already!'

He and I went onto the front bench together after only a year in the House.

I had been Parliamentary Private Secretary to Roy Hattersley and he had taken me aside to say that it was time I went onto the front bench. This would indeed have been a great honour. It meant that I would speak on behalf of the Opposition on a specific portfolio; I would become a Shadow Minister, *ministre fantôme* as the French would say. The front bench was somewhat hallowed in Parliamentary terms, it was lèse-majesté to settle yourself on the comfortable green leather with your feet up on the desk unless you were authorised to sit there by the Leader of the Opposition; and if you were a Shadow Cabinet member you were not allowed at all to speak from the back benches.

Once on the front bench, you would not be expected to make speeches from the benches behind and would end last on any Speaker's list to be called in any debate, on the presumption you had the privilege of speaking on behalf of the Opposition from the front bench, with your hands on the solid Dispatch Box with its heavy gold trimming, leaning over if you liked to get closer to the microphone, imposing your will on the House, government Ministers only a few feet away on other green benches behind another Dispatch Box.

'I don't want to go on the front bench,' I said. 'I want to stay working with you.'

'If Neil Kinnock asks,' Roy said. 'You can hardly refuse.'

Parliamentary Private Secretary might have been bag carrier to the Deputy Leader of the Labour Party, since

Kinnock had won the election for Leader, but it meant too preparing speeches that Roy would make as Shadow Chancellor of the Exchequer on the floor of the House, visiting by-elections with him, preparing Prime Minister's questions when he was standing in for Neil, and essentially being at the centre of influence, if not of power, within the Labour team.

'If I go on the front bench,' I said. 'Tony Blair should go too.'

'Young Tony'll be all right,' Roy assured.

I saw Tony at about eleven o'clock the following morning outside the library.

'You're looking pleased with yourself,' he said.

'You will too,' I said. 'Shortly.'

He gave me a quizzical look.

'It's too early,' he said.

'Not for you and me it isn't.'

We went for a coffee in the smoking room and I told him that it was Neil Kinnock's intention to put him, me and Gordon Brown on the front bench. Gordon had come into the House at the same time. The intention would wobble in the days ahead, Roy Hattersley would say that Neil had changed his mind, and I had to take Tony aside and say that it might not come about after all. As it happened, Gordon Brown wished to stay on the back benches to specialise in social security, and notwithstanding my own wish to stay with Roy Hattersley I was appointed junior spokesman for Northern Ireland.

Tony would be appointed to work with Roy Hattersley in the shadow Treasury team.

I had seen John Smith, then Trade and Industry spokesman for the Party, and he had congratulated me on my appointment. I indicated that Neil Kinnock had called with good news and bad news. The good news had been my appointment to the front bench; the bad news that it had been to Northern Ireland. I had gone, too, to the library to begin studying the subject when Tony had come along to invite Margaret and me for dinner with him and Cherie at his new home in Trimdon.

'Are you studying Northern Ireland already?' he asked.

'No,' I joked 'I'm studying a map to see where it is!'

Margaret and I had difficulty finding the house at Trimdon and arrived late, but it hardly mattered, these were moments to celebrate, two MPs only in the House for a year and now on the front bench. André Maurois, in his biography of Victor Hugo, author of *The Hunchback of Notre-Dame* and *Les Misérables*, would talk of Hugo as standing on the threshold of life, with the full expectation of fame, filled with confidence in the future.

'*How does one call it,*' Maurois mused. '*When the senses are on fire and the heart is pure, when genius asks only to leap like a fountain by the quiet pool, and a man knows not how to reach that liquid and refreshing surface?*'

It is called *youth.*

How does one call it when two young politicians, with their beautiful and eager wives, in a house in Trimdon, celebrate their elevation to the front bench, each holding a glass to the light, holding the glass so high the wine glows ruby and the light flecks gold from the crystal, the ruby and gold reflecting the enthusiasm to their eyes, their joy, their certain knowledge that the future belonged to them; that they would imprint their names in the history books as surely as footprints in damp sand; and as they did so, as they wove their own magic carpets of integrity and high duty and national interest, so too they would enjoy every minute?

How is it called, you may ask.

It is called *ambition.*

16

Tony Goes to Carlisle

'I can't believe it,' Tony said.

A year ago, he had been looking for a seat in the House of Commons and now he was a member of the front-bench Treasury team. He had come to Carlisle to attend the Northern Regional Conference of the Labour Party and such was the iron to the soul of Old Labour it had chosen Cup Final Day to have its annual meeting.

I had dinner with Tony on the Friday evening.

Roy Hattersley, Deputy Leader and Shadow Chancellor, would make the keynote speech the following day and he and I had dined with Joe Mills and his wife Larena. Joe had been Regional Secretary of the TGWU, responsible for Tony's sponsorship, but he was also Chairman of the Northern Regional Labour Party. He had arranged for Tony and me, Cherie and Margaret and Roy Hattersley, to join him at the top table.

Hattersley would always have a special affection for Tony; he would say to Derek Foster MP when he was chief whip that Tony would go to the very top; 'not the top you and I understand,' he would say. 'The very top.' And when running for the leadership of the Party, Tony who had his office not far from that of Roy in the Parliament building would always call in for advice.

Roy had been electioneering in Scotland when he had

17

heard that Tony had been nominated for Sedgefield. He had been wakened at midnight by his lady minder whom he had found standing in the corridor in her dressing gown, excited if not agitated at the news, as if she too had understood its significance. Roy was always worried at late-night knocks on the door since he feared there might be news of illness in the family at the other side of the knock.

'Young Blair!' his minder said. 'He's been chosen for Sedgefield!'

I had made up my mind to vote for Roy Hattersley in the leadership election on the Sunday after the General Election, notwithstanding my high regard for Neil Kinnock. Neil had visited the Middlesbrough constituency to attend a fund-raising dinner. He had flown up in the late afternoon and I had met him at the airport. This would be our first meeting, he had laughed and cracked jokes all the way into town, showing his ebullient nature. He had spoken at the Irish Club before the dinner and I had remarked upon his high sense of humour.

'My wife says I'll die laughing!' he said.

He had so impressed Margaret and me that it would take several days to come down from the high of having a future Leader of the Labour Party in our prospective constituency. He had not flown back to London but taken the night sleeper from Darlington because there was a meeting of the National Executive Committee of the Party the following day which he could not miss. He had a copy of our Programme, thought by some to be the longest suicide note in history, though this would later be attributable to the Manifesto on which Labour fought the Election; but the Programme was as lengthy and as closely printed as a Tolstoy novel, and Neil was about to try and get into it on the sleeper.

I mentioned that he was due to put together a book about

18

Nye Bevan, one of his heroes, both from the Welsh valleys; I believe he had in mind to compile a book of his essays and writings; but I pointed out what subsequently came to be true, that he would be far too busy. At the time he was Education spokesman for the Party but it was clear with his wit, his political erudition, his feeling for the people that had come out in his speech at the Irish Club, that his destiny lay beyond his Shadow Education post.

After the 1983 Election when I had comfortably held Middlesbrough with a majority of just less than ten thousand against what turned out to be a massive anti-Labour swing, *The Sunday Times* had called to ask if I would be voting for Kinnock or Hattersley in the forthcoming leadership election, since it was evident that Michael Foot, the present leader, would stand down. I had replied without hesitation:

'Probably Neil Kinnock!'

'All the new MPs are saying that,' the reporter remarked.

I would meet Neil again at Southampton University when I had attended an education conference and Roy Hattersley would also come to Middlesbrough, although to a neighbouring constituency, so that I would know both contenders before the General Election. When I had lunched with Neil Kinnock he had asked for a glass of white wine, when with Roy Hattersley he had asked for a pint of bitter.

Which, I wondered, was a true man of the people?

But notwithstanding my high admiration for Neil Kinnock, he appeared on the Sunday television news after the Election to say that he believed in unilateral nuclear disarmament, and since this was far beyond what I could accept I immediately told Margaret there was no question about it. I would be supporting Roy Hattersley.

I had left Middlesbrough to take my seat in the House of

19

Commons, feeling a sense of relief that so much effort over so many years, not to mention the effort of fighting a General Election, had come to an end. In fact, I would learn that nothing comes to an end in politics, not even to this day, the task is uphill all the way, but the goals must be worthy of the journey; or rather, quoting Browning, *'a man's reach should exceed his grasp, Or what's a heaven for?'*

When I first entered the famous smoking room of the House of Commons I found Roy Hattersley talking to John Smith, who would be his campaign manager in the election. They had been standing by the corner where first Nye Bevan and then Michael Foot would sit, regaling their entourage with political stories, sharing their wit and wisdom with fellow MPs. The Thames ran grey and turgid beyond the windows and the light flooded stark and white through the tall narrow windows.

Roy Hattersley and John Smith fell silent.

They looked at me.

'Not only shall I vote for you, Roy,' I said. 'I'll campaign for you too.'

Arthur Bottomley, whom I had succeeded in Middlesbrough, advised me to swear the oath of allegiance early so that, in years to come, I might be Father of the House. Arthur had great prescience and when such a time came to choose the Father, not only the year of intake would be taken into account but also the order of swearing the oath. I had taken his advice but it may be some years yet before I can tell whether it will yield fruit.

John Silkin, formerly a Minister under Jim Callaghan, had taken new MPs under his wing by offering them drinks and canapés in his room off Speaker's Court. He gave me two pieces of advice: Lloyd George had made his name on Friday speeches; and get your maiden speech out the way early.

There was little prospect of my making a name on Friday speeches, since no-one listened, they were rarely reported, and besides I was on my way back to the constituency; but I did get my maiden speech in early, unlike many of the 1997 intake who had still to make their maiden speeches months after a General Election. This was through no fault of their own in many cases but because of the number of new MPs.

I had entered the chamber for the first time with Derek Foster.

Derek had been MP for Bishop Auckland since 1979 and would be first Parliamentary Private Secretary to Neil Kinnock and then Chief Whip. He had expected to go into the first Blair Cabinet but this had not transpired and though offered a post as Minister of State had declined. A career of devotion and dedication would thus be brought to a surprising and precipitate end. Since I had known him before becoming an MP, I had followed him into the chamber and would sit next to him on the first bench back from the front bench.

Hardly had I settled when Derek took ill.

He moaned and groaned and rolled around till I thought he must be having a heart attack. My first challenge as an MP would be to take charge of a sick colleague. An innate caution, however, told me to pause, not to shout for a doctor in the House, not to wave a white handkerchief at the Speaker, not to interrupt the debate, which was all friendly stuff since Parliamentary business had yet to kick-off, and not to grasp Michael Foot before me and twist him round so that he might tell me what to do with a sick colleague.

Derek, of course, was not ill at all.

This was his low-moan version of the 'hear, hear, hear!' that radio listeners had heard from the time Parliamentary proceedings had been broadcast but would be lost to

21

television viewers since this particular sound, for the most part, has been extricated like bad static. Others too began to moan 'hear, hear, hear!' and I too began to moan, like those young girls in the Salem witch hunts, grasped not by an indescribable terror but the hysteria of the House.

If this was my first surprise in the Mother of Parliaments another was to follow.

I found another MP had left his chewing gum behind attached to the ledge on the bench before me, though hidden from view; it had been left pretty much as we would leave our chewing gum in the council house, under the mantelpiece, presumably because since this was the only chewing gum we might get for a week or two we could always recover it later.

Perhaps this had been the motive of the errant MP.

Years later, when Opposition spokesman, I would come onto the front-bench to take up the seat vacated by a colleague, who would become a Minister in the Labour government. He would leave behind a small but empty plastic bottle of vodka, which I quietly slipped into my pocket out of harm's way. When the Opposition Chief Whip came to sit beside me I took it out of my pocket and showed the empty bottle to him and told him where I had found it.

'What do you think this was doing here?' I asked.

'I've no idea,' he said.

Parliament as well as God, it seemed, works in mysterious ways.

I did indeed campaign for Roy Hattersley in his leadership Election, visiting constituency Labour Parties who wanted to hear a speaker supporting his cause and I recall one excursion on a Sunday afternoon to a South London constituency, only to find the hall barred, the doors padlocked. No one had been able to explain why this had been so, we had driven slowly around the block, but the hall would not open and we had to conclude there would be no meeting.

It had been an early initiation into the disorganisation of Old Labour.

I had been petrified on the day of my maiden speech. I had prepared this carefully at a friend's home outside London, since we still had nowhere to live, and I had put in the customary note to the Speaker. A former MP, Jim Callaghan, from the Manchester area, had failed to do this in the years when there had been a Wilson government and another Jim Callaghan had been Chancellor of the Exchequer.

He had not been called.

He had gone up to the Speaker, at this time Mr Selwyn Lloyd, and asked why he had yet to make his maiden speech and the Parliament was now several months old. Selwyn had explained that he must put in a note so that his name might be slipped into a list of speakers for a particular debate. This he had done, but on making his maiden speech he had noticed the chamber had begun to fill. This had been pleasing to him, so many MPs wishing to hear him speak, so many in fact that the Prime Minister Harold Wilson also popped in.

Harold had smiled and Jim had understood.

They had all thought the Chancellor of the Exchequer was on his feet making an important statement. The statement was indeed important, important to Jim Callaghan, important to his constituents, and to his consternation the House emptied as quickly as it had filled and was almost empty when he had brought his speech to an end. Jim would serve many years in Parliament and become a friend of mine in the tea room. He had been a great admirer of Bernard Shaw and I had remarked to him how once, in the twenties, Shaw had addressed the Parliamentary Labour Party. I had offered to find him a copy of the speech, but to this day I have not been able to do so.

Years later he would give me a further Parliamentary tip.

'When you speak on the floor of the House,' he said. 'You think all the Tories are listening to you. They look at you attentively. Is this right?'

'It is indeed,' I said proudly.

'They are not listening to you at all,' he said.

'Then what are they doing?'

'They are waiting for you to sit down!'

When next I had spoken on the floor I had indeed noticed so many eager faces on the Conservative side, straining at my every word, half rising to their feet, relaxing again, subsiding almost, pushing their backs into their seats, but watching attentively all the while, pushing forward again if they thought I was reaching what remotely sounded like a peroration, and then when my speech was done leaping to their feet in order to catch the Speaker's eye.

They had indeed been waiting for me to sit down.

On this first day, however, with a full House, I simply did not know how I would be able to rise to my feet, where I would find my voice, if I could recall the words I had so carefully prepared and typed and laid out before me. Winston Churchill and Lloyd George had sat on these benches, they had made glorious speeches before me. There had been Nye Bevan too and in my own time there would be Enoch Powell and Tony Benn and Peter Shore, all giants, like Denis Healey and Michael Foot.

How could I expect to compare with them?

24

I did not need to compare with them, I would not be
called early, the great Parliamentary figures departed, not
to return that evening, and as the House emptied so I began
to relax. I would not be called before half-past six, with only
supporters in the chamber, and those others who wished to
speak after me. Next to me had sat Jack Dormand, MP for
Easington, now Lord Dormand, celebrating not long ago
his eightieth birthday, also an early mentor, one who had
given me a tour of the House of Commons on Budget Day
of all days.

I had learnt my speech by heart but I had also made
notes.

It would be a conventional maiden speech, playing safe,
avoiding controversy, not attacking the government as I had
been invited to do by one MP, not a newcomer to the House,
more senior than I, but praising my predecessor, referring to
his wife Bessie, speaking of my constituency, reminiscing
on my origins, pointing to the gallery where the *Hansard*
reporters sat, reflecting that I might have reached the House
some thirty years earlier, since my ambition had been to be
a *Hansard* reporter.

I had ended with a quote from the socialist William
Morris: '*Socialism is no dream but a cause. Men and
women have died for it, not in ancient time, but in our
time; they lie in prison for it, they suffer all for it, they
even die for it. Believe me,*' William Morris wrote, '*when
such things are suffered for dreams the dreams come true
at last.*'

Socialism was like a flame that would never die.

'Why bring your notes?' Jack Dormand asked. 'You
didn't need them!'

The Speaker of the House, Bernard Weatherill, now Lord
Weatherill, wrote me a note of exceptional warmth: 'That
was an admirable maiden – quite one of the best. I was

so glad to be in the Chair to hear it. Your references to Arthur (a good friend) and also to Dame Bessie were well received, as you could judge. I have no doubt that you will be a worthy successor and I hope to hear you on many other occasions – especially if you continue to speak as you did today both in terms of content and time. Well done!'

Paths of glory may lead but to the grave, the Speaker wrote a similar note to Tony Blair, there would be other notes to other speakers, and though I have kept the note these many years I recall often speaking to a House that had lost interest, where members had begun to talk among themselves, where I have had to struggle to make myself heard over the clatter of members leaving their places for a safer haven in the tea room.

Tony Blair had signed up as a member of the TGWU as I had signed up to the GMB. Gerald Kaufman MP in his time had signed up as a Boilermaker. Tony's chambers represented a number of trade unions and he had been a TGWU delegate to his own constituency party in Hackney. He had typed this into his curriculum vitae for his selection at Sedgefield.

Because he had been sponsored by the TGWU, it might be said he was a trade union MP with a duty to keep his union informed of matters of interest that might arise across the floor of the House. He might send them copies of *Hansard*, speeches that would be interesting, including his own; or there might be the odd copy of an Order Paper where Early Day Motions had been printed. And there would be visits to the trade union office and the trade union representatives.

Tony did none of these things.

'Pop into the Union office in Newcastle,' I said. 'They like to be kept informed. It's the personal touch.'

Tony took my advice and went to see Joe Mills.

26

'I'm glad he came to see you,' I said to Joe when next we met.

'He only stayed twenty minutes.'

He and Cherie would have three children and that might have been the end of the family until a fourth had been announced before Christmas 1997. A friend of mine had come to see me in the House of Commons. I had received an e-mail where the friend had said there would be some interesting news to tell. The interesting news, according to City gossip, was that Cherie Booth was expecting another baby, conceived at Balmoral during a visit to the Queen.

'How can people say such things?' I asked.

I was so dismissive of the news that I did not even tell Margaret till there it was on national television on the nine o'clock news. I had been addressing a meeting on electoral systems in one of the committee rooms of the House on the upper floor and when the meeting was over I had called Margaret to let her know I was on my way back to the flat. She told me that it was official, Cherie Booth was expecting a baby at the age of forty-five. I went back to tell those who had attended the meeting, but I called down the phone to Margaret:

'And it was conceived at Balmoral!'

The baby would come nicely into the world at the Chelsea and Westminster Hospital, with Tony at the birth; he would be called Leo after his father and Tony, who never did like going without his sleep, would take two weeks off Parliament, though one would be in the Recess, so that only a week would be lost, with his red boxes containing Cabinet papers sent up to him in his flat above the shop, as it were, or across to Chequers, the Prime Minister's country house.

Cherie had come out of it well too.

Tony's determination to spend time with his children as

27

they grew up meant he was not often in the tea room and he did not hang around for late-night votes. No career man this. When elected to the Shadow Cabinet he rarely stayed for a full session and this was equally the case when he was elected to the National Executive Committee. Prior to the death of John Smith, Leader of the Party, I had been concerned that this remissness might lose him ground.

'At least get into the tea room more,' I said.

Tony might be euphoric that after only a year in the House he was on the front bench, not yet thirty years old, but he had not found the Labour Party entirely without rough and tumble. In order to win the seat at Sedgefield he had had to defeat the official candidate of the TGWU, that is to say a former Minister Les Huckfield. Les had moved to the left of the Party but with TGWU support not only had he been short-listed at Sedgefield he had reached the final ballot before being defeated by Tony.

'You will always be remembered for your victory at Sedgefield,' Gerald Kaufman told Tony. He might have felt flattered by this till Gerald had added: 'You are the man who kept Les Huckfield out of the House of Commons!'

After the General Election, Tony had accepted an invitation to share a platform at Spennymoor with Dennis Skinner, an MP on the left of the Party. Dennis had been elected to the National Executive Committee in 1978 and had been a regular speaker at Tribune rallies. Tony later felt that his attendance at the meeting had been a set-up by a left-wing faction for as Dennis Skinner spoke Les Huckfield entered the hall, only to be hailed by Dennis as a true socialist.

When I recalled the incident to Dennis Skinner he declared he had not attacked Tony personally; he had never attacked Tony; that Tony had always treated him with courtesy and respect, especially at National Executive

Committee meetings. And at a fund-raising dinner two years after the General Election, making a speech to the high value donors, Tony went out of his way not only to praise Dennis but to tell his audience how much he had valued his advice, especially on those areas where Dennis had felt the 1974–79 Labour government had failed.

But in those early days, at our Regional Conference in Carlisle, now into our second Parliamentary year, he looked from the dining table on the second floor of the hotel where the dinner was being held, looked towards the countryside that rippled away in the evening light towards the Lake District peaks, celebrating again our success, not on getting onto the front bench but on getting to the House of Commons at all.

'A year ago I didn't even have a seat,' Tony repeated.

Looking over the same countryside, seeing the strong light upon the hills, the contours rising, thinking of Neil Kinnock and Roy Hattersley, the one who enjoyed his white wine, the other who enjoyed his beer, though both would intermix, wondering whether I should ask Tony to pass me the salt and pepper or the condiments, and if I asked for condiments would he know what I was talking about, or if I asked for salt and pepper would he think me vulgar. Nothing matters very much, Lord Rosebery once remarked, and very little matters at all.

We were both men of the people.

An Enduring Friendship

My friendship with Tony endured well beyond the 1987 General Election.

In our first year together, we had not only moved onto the front bench but shared a platform at Party Conference at a Society of Labour Lawyers' fringe meeting; we had flown together to Newcastle for a Tyne-Tees television programme, though Tony did not like flying; we had been invited to a quiet dinner by Morgan Grenfell bank who wanted to explain to us the intricacies of investment banking.

I had gone to Oxford for a weekend to attend a seminar on Irish affairs. Tony had been there, too, attending a seminar on a different subject. I had attended the Hackney Constituency Labour Party where he had been a delegate for the TGWU and reflected that it must be a courageous man indeed who would attend such a meeting where those attending had little to do with Labour Party politics but all to do with single issue pressure groups.

Tony had by then left Hackney to live in Islington.

We had canvassed together, too, at a by-election in Greenwich, ferried to the constituency in the back of a van the Labour Party had hired. I had met others at Greenwich who had been ferried in from as far away as Newcastle, but Labour had been so unpopular on doorsteps, even on council estates, that whilst we had a pleasant and homely candidate she was considered too left-wing for the Greenwich constituency.

We had canvassed on a sullen grey day but there had been no support.

'At least we got our name on the attendance sheet,' Tony said.

Margaret and I had met Cherie and Tony at Teesside Airport prior to the 1987 General Election. Prospects were not good for Labour to win this Election; indeed the strategic battle for Neil Kinnock as Leader was to put air, light and water between Labour and the Liberal-Social Democratic Alliance, who had been only half a million votes behind Labour in the Election of 1983. Neil would never win this Election for Labour, there were too many seats to be recovered, but he did ensure that Labour would be the alternative party of government and shortly thereafter the Liberal-Social Democratic Alliance came apart.

But whatever the outcome of the Election, Tony and I would have to make those incremental steps forward. In government, of course, we would both be Ministers since we had been Shadows in the previous Parliament; in Opposition, there would be Shadow Cabinet elections to fight. Either way, there would be a new beginning, though for me it would be a new beginning in an area and on a matter which I could never have foreseen.

That Tony flew into Teesside Airport at all was an indication of his will power and discipline, for not only did he not like flying; he was claustrophobic in air planes. Flying made him genuinely ill. He remarked on this when we had first entered the Commons, probably on that early plane to Newcastle, and yet after our first summer recess I read an interesting article by him in *The Times* of his experiences in Canada.

31

It had been an erudite article.

'But I was over there,' he said.

'I thought you didn't like flying?'

'I don't,' he said. 'But I do it.'

He had also flown to Australia to deliver a lecture.

He would often take a train to the Sedgefield constituency and we would get off together at Darlington Station or return together on the Monday morning. Once he and I read through our constituency mail, only to discover that in the age of the word-processor most of the letters in our folders were the same, although personally addressed.

Another time I told him I thought the Labour policy of unilateral nuclear disarmament was as dead as a dodo, since he had been to Australia and might like the allusion, but since this was not Party policy he gave me another of his quizzical looks and demurred. One of his rare errors of judgement had been to join the Campaign for Nuclear Disarmament Parliamentary branch when he had never been a unilateralist, though he did go on record to say that 'the older generation, accustomed to conventional warfare, has not yet awoken to the real nature of the threat, the "warfare of the end game".'

Later, he would feel that unilateralism was not intrinsic to democratic socialism and allowed his membership of Parliamentary CND to lapse in May 1986.

Tony would receive seventy-one votes for the Shadow Cabinet when he stood after the Election, two places removed from a seat. My own political career would be overtaken by what became known as the Cleveland child abuse crisis. I had returned to Middlesbrough on Friday 19 June 1987 only a week after I had stood in the town hall and heard the returning officer declare the result of the General Election in my constituency.

I had been returned to Westminster with a majority of

32

14,958, an increase of some fifty-four percent from the majority I had gained in 1983, and true to the traditions of the Commons, facing another spell in opposition, I had high-tailed it to London on Monday morning to ensure an office for the new Parliament. This might seem fanciful, but on becoming an MP in 1983 I had been allocated a locker; later I had been allocated a desk in the so-called Cloisters; and it would not be until a year had passed and a sitting Member had died that I had been allocated not a full office but half an office, sharing with another Member.

Even the office allocated to me was not in the Parliament building but in the Norman Shaw North building, named after the architect, a four-minute walk to the floor of the House; but at least it was an office that belonged to me, desk, filing cabinets, sofa and telephone. I had received a number of calls but believed these to be hoax calls, yet they all had the same anguished tone.

They were from parents who declared their children had been taken away.

The calls had continued when I had returned to Middlesbrough, after being sworn in again as MP. I thought they were some kind of fall-out from the General Election. It is not uncommon for practical jokers to call on Election Day with a series of spurious messages to make mischief, to distract or delay a candidate, or simply to have fun, to participate in their own way in a national event.

When I had been candidate at Hexham on Election Day I had been asked to collect a set of tyres from a certain garage at Allendale, the farthest point of the constituency; I had been told my newsagent's bill was outstanding and a writ would be issued against me for non-payment. I had been threatened with a libel suit by a teacher who had appeared on one of our Election photographs, taken at a bus stop. This threw my campaign staff until they too realised they

33

were all a hoax. To my mind, these calls in Middlesbrough
were of the same ilk, the information dubious, and the calls
should be ignored.

Barry Stewart, my head of chambers, had called.

'These are serious calls,' he said.

'What am I supposed to do?' I asked.

'Call in at Middlesbrough General Hospital,' he said.
'Find out for yourself.'

The story as it unfolded was that the children had been
diagnosed as allegedly sexually abused; the implication was
that their fathers were the perpetrators. My first reaction had
been that of others when either they heard or read or saw
such stories on their television screens, that a paedophilic
ring had been at work in Middlesbrough which had been
busted by the diligence of the doctors and social services
and police.

The fathers had been arrested and the children detained
in hospital.

It turned out that a hundred-and-twenty-one children had
been diagnosed, the diagnoses had been made by two
consultant paediatricians working out of Middlesbrough
General Hospital; their diagnoses covered some vaginal but
mostly anal abuse and the discovery of anal abuse had been
based upon a technique known as reflex anal dilatation.

Of the hundred-and-twenty-one children taken into care
ninety-eight would be returned to their parents by the
courts, but these bare statistics disguised the trauma to
the lives of so many families, parents who would see
their children suddenly taken from them, often at night,
children whose childhood would be destroyed, who would
grow up in a twilight zone of unease and uncertainty; and
all of this had been done with a dreaded Place of Safety
Order, an instrument of the state, obtained by a social
worker through a magistrate, which enabled a child to be

taken from his home for at least twenty-eight days without recourse.

Following these events, all within my constituency, long-drawn-out as they became, a report prepared for the Secretary of State for Health and Social Security, debates in Parliament, the setting-up of a public enquiry, evidence to be prepared for that enquiry, each and every case on each and every child to be heard through the courts, a change in the law on how children should be treated both within their families and in relation to the courts, the passage of a Children Act 1989, inquests within Cleveland County Council on how this state of affairs had come about, a review by the Health Authority, more reviews by the Department of Health and Social Security, the reflex anal dilitation test discredited as a sole symptom in the diagnosis of anal abuse, warning booklets put out, the dreaded Place of Safety Order abolished, parents seeking and succeeded in obtaining compensation through the courts, a trust fund to be set up on behalf of the families where donations from the public might be lodged and then distributed, the residue going to the National Society for the Prevention of Cruelty to Children, the personal pain and grief of those children separated from their families, not for days or weeks but months and in one case years, a book to be written so that the outside world might know what could happen in a modern society when bureaucracies conspired and colluded not for the benefit of individuals but to their detriment, and sometimes their destruction.

All this would take five years of my Parliamentary life.

I wrote to Neil Kinnock and resigned my duties from his front bench. I would turn my back on national politics and only when the last case had been heard in court, when the last judgement had been passed in favour of the parents, when compensation awards had been granted amounting to little short of a million pounds, when the new Children Act had been enacted, ensuring that in any proceedings the interests of the child would be paramount, when I had seen the joy of young children meeting their parents again, some to grow up with only the vaguest memory of the events that had swirled around them, that had deprived them of a part of their childhood, when another book had been written, this time a legal book, an annotated version of the Act explaining its workings to practitioners.

Only then would I return to the political scene.

By then the caravanserai had moved on, Gordon Brown had been elected to the Shadow Cabinet at his first attempt, Tony would follow a year later, but I would receive from Bernard Weatherill as Speaker of the Commons a note to say that I had become one of the five or six MPs who by their actions had used their Parliamentary position to change the law of the land. It was not that I had written my name in the history books, become a legend in my own lifetime, as one of my critics wrote, but that I had done my duty by my constituents at the expense of a political career that would never be the same again.

The Daily Mail had been a leading purveyor of the news on the Cleveland child abuse crisis.

Sir David English as editor-in-chief had seen the massive conflict between families and social workers and doctors, the story of the Cleveland child abuse crisis would be headline news for an entire week, the only time in the newspaper's history that the same story would carry a banner headline for so many days at a time. Only a few weeks before his death, Sir David would write to me to say that the *Mail*'s coverage of these events had represented 'a high point' for the newspaper.

I had lost sight of Tony during the crisis, as I would lose sight of many of my colleagues in the House. Indeed, I would hardly know the intake of 1987, but Tony and Cherie had already embarked upon a family of their own, there would be Euan, Kathryn and Nicky, and like many parents they empathised with those traumatised by the events in Cleveland, children spirited away from their homes in the night.

I had written an article in *The Daily Mail*.

Tony had read the article and mentioned it to me when we met.

'A fine article,' he said.

Banal, perhaps, but words gratefully received, since many in the Labour Party had preferred to believe the social workers and the doctors rather than the children, the parents and the courts, a sad misjudgement that had shown a lack of compassion and understanding, the worst aspects of Old Labour supporting organisations and pressure groups, structures rather than individuals, the state knowing better than parents, intervening to their detriment not to their well-being, so that my own standing would be seriously damaged, never to recover.

Though not with Tony Blair or John Smith.

There would be a resolution at Party Conference to support the doctors and social workers that Tony Blair would ensure would be watered down by way of a composite; speakers would rise during the debate to talk about 'nasty things that might happen within families'. There would be attacks upon me by trade union officials representing social workers. I was required to bring a libel action against a Parliamentary colleague. I would make my own speech at conference, not only to those within the audience who were parents but those who were grandparents, for they too suffered when grandchildren were taken away.

Efforts would be made by MPs to the left of the Party to ensure that I did not sit on the Committee stage of the Children Bill. The matter was raised in Shadow Cabinet. John Smith, then Shadow Chancellor of the Exchequer, would have none of it. I was nominated to the Committee and, with David Mellor as Minister of the Crown, together we steered the Bill through all its stages and onto the statute book.

'You should be given an award,' John Redwood MP said.

'What award is that?' I asked.

'Back-bencher of the year.'

An award went instead to Tony Blair.

The Spectator magazine held an annual lunch where various Parliamentary awards were distributed. Tony had been to Tokyo and back and had only just returned to the lobbies of the House when he heard of a financial scandal that had deprived some pensioners of their savings. Many MPs had pensioners so afflicted and accosted Tony in the division lobby, wanting him to address meetings in their constituencies. Tony had been reluctant to do this, but he did take in hand the pensioners' plight and the government had to accept negligence by one of its departments.

They agreed to pay compensation.

Tony had been nominated the award of most prominent front-bencher and when he made his speech at *The Spectator* lunch before Parliamentary colleagues and the Press he read out a letter from one of the grateful pensioners. Tony had long since mastered the gift of understatement and he would read out the letter in his most self-deprecating tone. Commenting on how well he had done, according to articles in the Press, she had written

38

she was pleased 'that at least someone has benefited from the scandal'.

When a book I had written on the Cleveland child abuse crisis, entitled *When Salem Came to the Boro*, was eventually published I had its launch on the terrace of the House of Commons. There would be members of the families caught up in the crisis as well as Parliamentary colleagues and members of the Press who had followed the crisis from its unfolding to its conclusion.

I too had received a letter.

It was from someone who lived at Naphill, near High Wycombe in Buckinghamshire. The signature to the letter did not make it clear whether it had been written by a man or a woman, but began by referring to a television programme which had portrayed parents who had been wrongly accused of abusing their children. 'I cannot believe that in our country administrators are so blind, insensitive and incompetent: above all, allowed to assume guilt before an act is proven and be allowed to mentally bully parents'.

The letter-writer had read an article in a *Sunday Times* colour supplement which had told in depth the story of one of the families caught up in the Cleveland child abuse crisis; it described in detail the trauma of the parents, the allegations of child abuse that had almost destroyed a family, how the courts had found the parents to be innocent, and how the children had been reunited in their family house.

The Sunday Times had been a great supporter of the families during the crisis and had published extracts from my book. The colour supplement editor who had discussed the publication of this article with me said that, on reading it, 'there would not be a dry eye in the house'. It had certainly stirred emotions in Naphill, High Wycombe. The letter writer, however, suggested that I read it and went on:

39

'I am not from the Cleveland area and have no friends or relatives involved but will feel a personal guilt if I don't protest and demand to know what action has been taken against all the people in the various departments who contributed to this incompetence and mind bashing. In private business these people would have been sacked and perhaps sued for professional negligence'.

The letter writer went on to tell me that some of the people who had suffered at the hands of these 'mindless administrators' were from my constituency and would I please write and tell the writer what action I – underlined – had taken to ensure that they had been appropriately disciplined.

The writer added for good measure:

'Nothing, I expect.'

A Peter Mandelson Story

I had first met Peter Mandelson at a dinner party in 1984 when he worked for a Sunday television programme *Weekend World*.

The party had been arranged by Jenni Jaeger, who had been one of the Garden Girls who worked for Prime Minister Jim Callaghan out of Ten Downing Street, so-called because their secretarial offices looked out over the garden. On leaving Downing Street, Jenni had set up a consultancy firm known as GJW with offices in the Clapham Road. One evening she had arranged a dinner party at the offices where I had met Peter Mandelson.

I would not see Peter again till the Brecon and Radnor by-election. He had taken three weeks from his work with *London Weekend Television* to mind the Labour candidate. I had taken the train to mid-Wales with Roy Hattersley and his assistant David Hill; even then it had been a long drive to by-election territory, but when we arrived at headquarters there was Peter Mandelson.

Since I had not seen Peter in over a year I re-introduced myself.

'I know who you are!' he said abruptly.

Our relations had not improved the following year when at Party Conference in Blackpool I had decided to share a platform with a Sinn Fein councillor. I had been Northern

Ireland spokesman and Peter had become the Labour Party's Campaigns and Communications Director. At the time Sinn Fein were in bad odour due to their links with the Irish Republican Army, their spokesmen were banned from radio and television, and whilst I had met with them in Belfast it had not been considered good for the credibility of the Labour Party that I should share a platform with them at Party Conference.

The Tory press too had been critical.

I had been concerned not with Peter Mandelson but from a desire not to let down Neil Kinnock as Leader of the Party. It was explained to Neil that the purpose of my attending the fringe meeting was to assist the call to bring Sinn Fein more into mainstream nationalist politics. At the time, Sinn Fein believed in the ballot paper in one hand and the Armalite rifle in the other; my task had been to persuade them to set aside the Armalite. Terrorism would be attacked more by me at this Party Conference than it had ever been before.

Neil accepted my explanation but not Peter Mandelson.

'You're sharing a platform with terrorists!' he shouted in the press room before the fringe meeting, much to my discomfort.

I had been reminded of this when I attended Peter's first appearance at the Dispatch Box in the House of Commons as Secretary of State for Northern Ireland. Even as a back-bench Member of Parliament, he had called for the removal of the ban on Sinn Fein representatives appearing on radio and television. Now he stood tall at the Box, wearing a dark suit and red tie and white shirt; his face had been a fragile alabaster, without make-up or the touch of a sun-lamp. He stood calmly and made his speech in a clear unemotional voice.

A day or two earlier he had had his photograph taken with the leaders of Sinn Fein, Gerry Adams and Martin

McGuinness, shaking hands, the Good Friday Agreement not only signed but being implemented, reconciliation being sought in Northern Ireland between two divided communities, the one Protestant the other Catholic, the one Unionist the other Nationalist, but Sinn Fein not only seeking to persuade the IRA to renounce violence but also now in the mainstream of Irish nationalism.

All the goals I had sought to achieve myself, as an Opposition spokesman so many years ago.

I had known Peter had been interested in entering Parliament when he had attended a football game at the Victoria Road Ground in Hartlepool only a few days before Christmas. He had been the guest of Tom Burlison, now not only a peer in the Lords but Life President of the football club; Peter is also now President. Tom had been Regional Secretary of the General Municipal and Boilermakers', his Union had sponsored Hartlepool United, and the Union would be a prime backer for Mandelson to take over the Hartlepool seat when the incumbent MP retired.

An apocryphal story had seeped into folklore when Peter had began campaigning for the Hartlepool nomination. It was that he had gone into a fish-and-chip shop and, espying delectable mushy peas, had asked for 'some of that avocado puree'. The story would change, as all apocryphal stories do, from asking for avocado puree to avocado dip to guacamole, but the essence of the story had been the same.

Peter had no real knowledge of the working people of the North-East.

As Peter explained to journalist Megan Tresidder: 'Shall I tell you how it happened? It is a story that was first told in the Chester-le-Street by-election of 1973, about an American journalist going into a fish-and-chip shop. It was then later told about a research assistant for a member of the

Shadow Cabinet working a by-election in the North-West of England. This story has been told time and time again about people coming from abroad, people coming from the South.'

Peter himself would become adept at changing the genesis of the story.

When interviewed by Roy Hattersley for *The Mail on Sunday*, insisting that the story was 'totally untrue', he later photocopied and sent to Roy an article from *The Economist* which reputedly identified the young American researcher who had made the original error back in 1990. By then the story had moved on, from avocado puree to avocado dip and now to guacamole.

This, according to Roy Hattersley, might be defined as 'the once fashionable mixture of crushed avocado, tomatoes, garlic and onions'. The story by now not only had a new name but a new inventor. Neil Kinnock, no longer Leader of the Labour Party, revealed that he had perpetrated the story, introducing the guacomole concept, a view confirmed by Peter Mandelson himself. He told readers of a Sunday newspaper: 'I think a former Leader of the Labour Party owns up to inventing this guacamole story as a joke'.

The point of the story, however, had been entirely missed.

It was not, as *The Scotsman* newspaper claimed, a fact that Peter had been coming out of the Victoria Ground at Hartlepool and stood in line before a fish-and-chip shop and ordered cod and fries and avocado dip or avocado puree or guacamole, a large knot to his Hartlepool United hand-knitted scarf, the scarf wide and deep around his neck to keep out the cold, the tassels tucked into the canvas-blue jacket of his jeans.

It was that, by his own admission, he had never been in a fish-and-chip shop in his life.

~

On becoming the town's MP, Peter would continue to follow the fortunes of Hartlepool United.

He would visit the odd away game, and when Hartlepool played Brentford he would go with Neil Kinnock; he would miss the Hartlepool-Colchester game during the 1997 General Election but follow with great interest and enthusiasm a particularly good Cup run, leaving the House to attend a game in Yorkshire. A photograph of Peter may be found in the archives of the *Hartlepool Mail* of his standing with the lads on the terrace at the Victoria ground. I would surmise, indeed I am certain, that when he went with Tom Burlison to his very first game he had not been on the terraces but in the stands. I had been there before him, forty-three years before him in fact, when I had been a reporter with the *Blaydon Courier* and my local football team had advanced sufficiently to enter the first round of the F.A. Cup.

Blaydon had been drawn against Hartlepool and a bus had been hired to take the team and its officials and the local reporter to Hartlepool for the match, no mean journey in those days, when there had been no motorways, no fly-overs, and dual carriageways had been few and far between. There had been no floodlighting either and though Blaydon were outclassed, Hartlepool winning eight goals to nil, I recall being in the directors' room at the end of the game, enjoying a cup of tea and cake and sandwich, exercising my privilege as a newspaper reporter. I remember the chairman being a tall distinguished man with silver hair, the secretary smaller, more rotund, rouge cheeks, wearing what was known in those days as a box because he had had his bladder removed, bustling into the room with the scores from other games.

45

I would remember, too, the grim coal staiths that stalked out to sea, and my memory of Hartlepool was one of blackness, the blackness of the winter's day, the blackness of the staiths, the blackness of low clouds furling and unfurling, rolling up from the sea, the blackness of the streets. The memory would stay with me till many years and many lives later I would return to Hartlepool as a barrister to seek a matrimonial injunction from a judge who happened to be taking these at the magistrates' court this Friday evening. The blackness had lifted, Hartlepool now a modern town, a happier brighter place than I had known, with McDonald drive-ins and super markets and a modernised football ground.

In one of his many interviews, Peter would respond to questions put to him by a journalist.

Did he now know the difference between guacamole and mushy peas? What chance did he think he had of becoming a Labour Prime Minister? What were his goals for the next ten years? Which Tory MP did he admire most? Did he still believe he was the nicest person he had known and was what he said always the truth as he saw it? The last question had produced the most defining answer. If his house had been burning down and he could rush into the flames and rescue a single object what would that object be?

To which Peter replied:

'My Hartlepool United football scarf!'

Peter had not been asked to specify in which house the scarf might be found, the house he owned in Hartlepool with its three-piece suite he had bought for a hundred-and-twenty pounds, or his grander Georgian house in Notting Hill where there would be a tanned leather sofa by Matthew Hilton, described as *'one of the small band of youngish British designers on whose shoulders the nation's reputation as a creative powerhouse rests'*.

Peter might have friends who called by with the Hoover in Hartlepool, or to mend his shower, but in Notting Hill his house had been entirely refashioned and remodelled by Seth Stein, described as a *'purveyor of classy modernism to the select'*. Indeed, Peter would be so impressed with Stein's work at his house that he would consult him regularly when he wished to buy furniture so that the inner harmony that had been created would be maintained.

In Hartlepool, *par contre*, it would not be quite anti-maccassar, but the house would be furnished with stripped pine and flowery china, 'like a nineteen-seventies Oxford tea room'. He might buy wet fish and Tesco luxury ice cream, perhaps from the new Tesco supermarket in the town, but as he explained when he had sought the Hartlepool seat: 'I was going in search of a home – a place where I could feel emotionally secure and supported; a place I'd be able to put my arms around'.

He would hold summer parties for members of his Constituency Labour Party and invite along leading Labour figures such as Gordon Brown and Mo Mowlam, and of course Tony Blair who would come on by from the neighbouring constituency. Tony would even have his picture taken with Peter, in the days when Peter still had his moustache, before the ends had turned white and he had shaved it off, the picture taken outside the local brewery, Tony wearing a tee-shirt imploring all those who would gaze upon it, that they should:

'Keep the heart in Hartlepool!'

When Tony Blair became Leader of the Labour Party and Peter Mandelson moved onto centre stage, as it were, there were criticisms from within the Parliamentary Labour Party that he was too close to the Leader, he had too much influence, and that influence might not all be to the good. Two senior Labour figures within the Parliamentary Labour Party went to see Tony in his new office.

They criticised Peter and Tony asked what they thought he should do.

'Do you want me to hang him from the nearest lanyard?' he asked.

Both MPs thought that it was not such a bad idea, rather in the manner of Harold Wilson when Prime Minister and being informed that Roy Jenkins, Member of Parliament and Cabinet Minister, now the noble Lord Jenkins, would only agree a particular policy 'over his dead body'. Harold had promptly replied that he might consider this. The two senior MPs might have left Tony satisfied, complaining to him not once but on several occasions, but Peter never was hung by a lanyard or by anything else; and neither senior MP achieved a position in Tony's government.

Peter was simply too important to the project of New Labour.

Aware of such criticism, and aware too that those who did not wish to criticise the leader would criticise Peter instead, I wrote to him to say that he should not receive as a gift any vicuna coats. I based this letter on the case of Sherman Adams, one of the most influential figures in the United States under the Presidency of Dwight D. Eisenhower. He had been Eisenhower's chief of staff in the White House but had accepted a gift of a vicuna coat.

When this became public knowledge, Adams had been forced to resign, though he would live till the age of eight-seven, proving – if proof were needed – that there can be a life after politics. Peter wrote back that he would not indeed be accepting any vicuna coats as a gift, though the gift from Geoffrey Robinson MP of an interest-free loan to help him pay for his Notting Hill house would cost him dear enough.

When Peter had become Secretary of State for Trade and Industry, he had wished to buy new furniture for his office and had called Sir Terence Conran, who owned the Conran Shop in the Fulham Road. Peter would arrive at five-thirty and could the store be kept open for his private shopping session? He had bought a sofa more in the Stein mode than the antimaccassar and his Department had explained that since he had been going on holiday the following day, keeping the store open and the staff back had been a natural thing to do.

Peter would eventually sell his house in Notting Hill at about the time a film of the same name was playing strongly to cinema audiences, as well it might, with Julia Roberts and Hugh Grant playing the leading roles. The film had been shot on location in Notting Hill, to the forefront the markets along Portobello Road. Indeed, the film had been such a success that the owner of the flat where most of it had been shot had grown so tired of enthusiasts having their photograph taken before the doors he had had them removed.

At least Peter, when he left his flat in Notting Hill, had left the doors behind.

Peter had every right to be proud of his Hartlepool United scarf.

Also the Hartlepool marina, built with Teesside Development Corporation money, but wide and deep and facing out to the sea beyond its locks, the wind tugging at the mastheads of the yachts moored by the stone sides, the tugs anchored tightly by the marina walls, the HMS Trincomalee lodged away in a corner, so that only the masts might be seen, a tall ship, a proud ship, the last of the war sailing ships, arrogant really, a true tourist attraction.

Peter had been so proud of the marina that he had suggested it might be a suitable berth for the Royal Yacht Britannia. Shortly after the 1992 General Election, the Queen and Prince Philip had embarked upon a tour of the coastline on the Royal Yacht. This had been by way of a farewell visit for the Yacht, since she was due to be decommissioned, having come into service in 1951. The Yacht would visit the Tyne, sail down to Hartlepool and continue down the East Coast to Great Yarmouth and beyond.

The Queen would step ashore at Hartlepool and pay a visit to Middlesbrough.

I had been asked by the chief executive of Middlesbrough Council whether I should like to be on hand to meet the Queen, not a duty that fell within the remit of a Member of Parliament, since protocol dictated always it would be the Mayor who would receive Her Majesty; but Margaret and I had not wished to miss such an opportunity, and we had been present when the Queen visited the Pallister Park ward in my Middlesbrough constituency. There would be, too, a Command to be in the Queen's presence that evening on the Royal Yacht.

Whilst waiting for the Queen at Pallister Park, a Middlesbrough councillor approached me and asked whether I would indeed be on the Royal Yacht that evening. I replied with some modesty that Margaret and I would be on the Yacht; we had received the Royal Command. The councillor recalled she had sent a cruet set to Her Majesty and Prince Philip for their fortieth wedding anniversary.

'Would you ask her if she received it,' the councillor asked. 'And if she uses it!'

That evening Margaret and I did indeed meet the Queen and Prince Philip. They had been to Hungary on a state visit only a week earlier and Margaret and I were due to leave the Yacht as soon as the Queen and the Prince had retired to fly to Budapest as part of a Parliamentary delegation. We would miss a firework display that would light up the sky around the Yacht before it sailed down the coast to Great Yarmouth. Peter Mandelson had also been on the Yacht and the question of its future had come up.

Would it not be a good idea that the Yacht be decommissioned and settled in the Hartlepool marina? Good idea or not, Peter had taken a first opportunity to raise it on the floor of the House of Commons, breaking one of the first rules, that one is not allowed to mention private conversations with the Queen. Yet Peter had no difficulty in announcing that he had indeed discussed the future of the Royal Yacht with the Queen and she would be perfectly content for it to be laid up in the Hartlepool marina.

The Speaker at this point intervened to say that whilst she knew Peter to be 'a proud man' even he could not refer to private conversations with the Queen. Notwithstanding this word of advice to an essentially new Member of Parliament, Peter went on to tell the House that he had received the permission of the Private Secretary to the Queen to refer to the conversations.

Jeremy Hanley had been the Minister at the Dispatch Box this day.

He had himself a graceful and urbane manner, his father and mother had been Jimmy Hanley and Dinah Sheridan, both famous on both stage and screen. Jeremy's father as a young actor had been adopted by Tommy Handley; not that they had been any relation but it had been too complicated to explain they were no relation. Tommy had been the star of the war-time ITMA programme that, if it had not kept the home fires burning, had cheered up many a household when the war was over. Jeremy had won the Richmond seat with a majority of seventy but had increased this at every General Election until 1997 when the electorate, if not nemesis, had caught up with the Conservative Party.

'If the Queen so instructs,' Jeremy replied. 'I can do no other.'

By then the Speaker had had enough.

'I am in charge of proceedings here,' she declared.

She added for good measure:

'Not the Queen's Private Secretary!'

The Royal Yacht never did end its days at Hartlepool.

It would have fitted nicely alongside the yachts and tugs and sailing boats and HMS Trincomalee, as proud as ever, but sad perhaps not to be on the high seas or even skirting the British coastline It would have been a great attraction to those visitors who might linger on a spring or summer's day, seeking a pint or a meal in the pub set in a corner by the marina opposite the shopping centre, a favourite in the season with some of those football supporters who would call by for a pint before a home game. I had to admire Peter for raising the marina at all. He had been bolder than I discussing with Her Majesty the future of the Royal Yacht.

With all due deference to my well-meaning Middlesbrough councillor, I had not raised the matter of the cruet set.

Peter would always impress me as a man of consummate detail, strong concentration and dedication, and I recall in the corridors of the House of Commons he would listen carefully to every word an interlocutor might say, his eyes not wavering, his gaze steady, the person speaking to him the most important person in the world at this time. He had understood the essence of leadership in the

52

modern television age, that the media was the message, and he would attach himself to personalities within the Labour Party rather than its organisation, its structures, or its policies.

He would build up Neil Kinnock for the 1987 Election and would positively invent both Tony Blair and Gordon Brown, ensuring they were on television or in newspaper articles, using his position as Director of Campaigns and Communications to ensure that this would be so, even though others in the Shadow Cabinet resented this undue attention on two of their number, to the detriment of their own ambitions.

This was especially so when Blair and Brown were allowed to roam not only through the Party's political broadcasts but being anchor men for local and European Parliamentary elections. Peter's judgement in this was absolutely right, Tony Blair and Gordon Brown would become the most significant politicians of their time, much to the benefit of the Labour Party and the governance of the country, but it would cost Peter popularity with his own, and those qualities of detail and dedication would take something from him as a politician.

After the 1992 General Election, upon entering the House of Commons, he would lose the inside track within the Labour Party. His maiden speech had been nondescript, his handling of the House clumsy, intervening on a Parliamentary colleague and neighbour Mo Mowlam no less than ten times during an adjournment debate, which does not entitle interventions unless with the permission of the Speaker. He had been so vitriolic during a debate on the passage of the Maastricht Bill that Peter Hain MP, who would become Minister of State at the Foreign office, asked that he 'restrain the sharpness of his tongue'.

I had run into Peter one day in the long corridor leading to the Speaker's office, a corridor with high wooden ceilings not at all attractive, but with chandeliers that dangle low and brighten the book cases to the left and right. When I had first become an MP I had loved to walk down this long corridor; I had a feeling of 'being there', but each time I look up at the knobbly wood of the ceiling, cracks and all, now I often wonder why.

I expressed concern to Peter that others of the 1992 intake were making progress by way of the whips' office, notably Alan Milburn and Stephen Byers; the whips' office had been a traditional route to the front bench. Peter appeared to be languishing, a former Director of Campaigns and Communications cut down to size; but I had welcomed his support in the campaign to abolish Cleveland County Council that had given the country the child abuse crisis.

It had been over this that he had fallen out, temporarily at least, with Mo Mowlam.

'You must have a game plan,' I said.

'I always have a game plan,' he said.

After the 1992 Election, during a short Parliamentary recess, Margaret and Malcolm and I had flown to Sicily for a few days' holiday, and also because I was writing a novel about the origins of the mafia, or cosa nostra. I had mentioned to Peter our visit, though not the purpose. We had arrived at Taomina and would spend an evening around Mount Vesuvius, a volcano never at peace with itself, its flames and cinder and sparks lifting high into the air, the lava seeping out of the skin of the mountain down well-worn paths to the plain beneath.

On the day of our arrival, Judge Falcone had been

assassinated at Palermo airport. The Judge had been assiduously pursuing the mafiosi and had paid with his life. There had been headlines throughout the world and back home family and friends had worried about us, especially those who had known the purpose of our visit, making a wrong assumption from an association of ideas, even though we had not landed anywhere near Palermo.

I had seen Peter Mandelson upon our return when Parliament reassembled.

'I was really concerned about you,' he said.

Who said he had no heart?

When he had resigned from his post as Secretary of State for Trade and Industry, he had found himself in a political no-man's land because of the interest-free loan he had taken from Geoffrey Robinson MP; the amount of the loan had been £375,000, more than the odd vicuna coat. Peter had neither declared the loan in the Members' register of interests nor to his Permanent Secretary when becoming a Cabinet Minister, nor to the building society when taking out a mortgage, not to his friend the Prime Minister. The loan had been to top up the mortgage to finance the purchase of his Notting Hill home.

The building society declared he had done nothing wrong, the Standards Committee of the House of Commons made little headway, the Conservative opposition blasted their blunderbusses to the sky but to no avail; yet in the climate of the times Peter had been required to resign and return to those dolorous back benches. Geoffrey Robinson too had resigned from the government.

The Amalgamated Electricians' and Engineers' Union had financed for Peter a trip to South Africa to advise the African National Congress and upon his return I ran into him one Saturday morning at Durham County Hall. He had been there to address a meeting of Labour Party organisers.

I had been there to address the AEEU regionally.

'Why not come and say a few words?' I asked.

'Do you think it's a good idea?'

A politician, I reflected, who does not like to make speeches.

'They'd love to hear from you,' I said.

After all, they had just financed his trip to South Africa. And so it turned out.

I had heard that he had been depressed at losing so important a post in government. This would have been natural, given all the years he had worked for it, achieving what must be the ultimate goal of most MPs who arrive at the Commons, not with a marshall's baton in their knapsack but the hope of a Cabinet appointment in their breasts. His rise had been dramatic following the death of John Smith, he had regained the inside track, he had organised an Election victory, he had moved effortlessly and seamlessly into government, only to find himself on the outside again two days before Christmas.

'I heard you're depressed,' I said.

'I'm not that depressed,' he said. 'Considering all that I've gone through.'

'You'll be back,' I said.

Somebody up there truly loved him.

In the early days when we had become MPs together, Tony Blair and I would attend a TGWU dinner in Stockton for one of their retiring officers. It must have been a big event for not only were Tony and Cherie there but Cherie's father was also there. Tony Booth had been known as a television actor in a series called *Till Death Do Us Part*; he had been visiting Tony and Cherie at Trimdon, but he would recall this evening years later when Tony became Leader of the Opposition and I met him when the result of the leadership election had been announced.

The TGWU would also arrange a political meeting one Saturday morning at Stockton after the 1987 General Election and after Peter Mandelson's appointment as Prospective Parliament Candidate. This had taken place almost a year after his first appearance at the Victoria football ground. Tony had also been invited and would arrive late because he had a meeting of his General Committee of the Labour Party that morning.

I had been down to speak last, I cannot now recall the subject, certainly I recall I had not been particularly briefed, but it hardly mattered since I would sweep up on the comments of the other speakers. Peter Mandelson had been due to open the debate but the chairman reversed the order, I was called upon to speak first, and fumbled my way somewhat self-consciously through opening remarks.

Tony did indeed arrive but I cannot now recall his contribution. Except when the meeting was over and I left by the back of the hall to the car park I found Tony and Peter in deep discussion, the matter so confidential both of them paused and stopped talking when I arrived. We said our farewells in the politest of fashions, but I knew then that my friendship with Tony would never be the same again.

The torch had passed to a new generation.

A Lump to the Throat

As my mother would have said, it brought a lump to throat.

We had gathered in an auditorium at the Institute of Education in Central London to hear the announcement that Tony Blair had been elected Leader of the Labour Party. He had beaten both John Prescott and Margaret Beckett, though John had been elected Deputy Leader. The curious and the cognoscenti were there, party organisers and Members of Parliament, those already in the Lords and those who wished to join them, those who had titles and those who would like them, members of the press, reporters and sketch writers and diarists, camp followers all, the good, the bad and the ugly.

There was even Roy Hattersley and Gordon Brown.

Roy would come to sit by me in the auditorium and we would rise and applaud together when the announcement had been made. Following John Smith's funeral, Roy had called Tony on the phone and urged him to stand for the leadership. 'But Gordon has wanted it so much,' Tony replied. 'Much more than I ever have.'

'I wanted it too,' Roy said. 'So did Herbert Morrison and Denis Healey. Many others have wanted to be Leader of the Labour Party. Gordon will have to join a long and distinguished line.'

Prior to his election to the Shadow Cabinet in 1988, I had run into Tony in the committee corridor after a meeting of the Parliamentary Labour Party. 'Not only will you get on,' I predicted. 'You'll be half-way up the list.'

'That's worth a pint,' Tony said.

I had not drunk beer since leaving England for France in 1960 and would not take Tony up on his offer, not even in the Labour Club at Trimdon, but after the 1992 General Election I noticed that his position had begun to slip in the Shadow Cabinet elections. He was not, as he should have been, among the top three or four but actually sixth or seventh, hardly a position that reflected either his ability or his potential. It seemed there had been a deliberate withdrawal of support from those who wished to favour other candidates.

I asked him to meet me at the Atrium in Four Millbank for a coffee.

'You must be seen around more,' I said, my refrain to him over many years. 'In the tea room and the like. You should be doing as well in the Shadow Cabinet elections as Gordon Brown.'

'I don't care who ends where in the Shadow Cabinet elections,' Tony said. 'As long as we win the next Election. Gordon's friendship with me is unbreakable. It doesn't matter if he gets more votes than me.'

Even before the 1992 General Election support for Gordon Brown as a future Leader of the Party had been running so high that Nick Brown MP, Gordon's most prominent campaigner, had been asked to get the message around the Parliamentary Labour Party that Gordon would not be a candidate for the leadership should Labour be defeated.

He would not stand against John Smith.

When Neil Kinnock did step down John Smith had been

the inevitable choice of the Party, both with MPs, trade unionists and constituency parties. But who should be his deputy? John had actually canvassed the name of Gordon Brown, but the view prevailed that the Party would not accept both a Leader and Deputy who were Scottish, though my wife Margaret disagreed.

'There's no reason why Gordon Brown cannot be Deputy Leader,' she said.

I had not seen Tony Blair during the General Election campaign of 1992 other than on the platform at the famous Sheffield rally held by the Party a week before polling day. The rally had been to ensure there would be no flagging in the last week before the Election. In reality, by bringing thousands of workers from the streets to the rally, valuable campaigning time had been lost, and Neil Kinnock had forgotten his own recipe for success.

'If you like jugged hare,' he would say, quoting from Mrs Beeton's cookery book. 'You must first catch the hare!'

Although not a regular attender at Welsh night, a party held for Welsh MPs in the Jubilee Room off Westminster Hall, I had popped into the last Welsh Night before the 1992 General Election. Neil had been strumming his guitar and singing his Welsh songs till his throat had gone dry and his voice hoarse. He had not particularly minded there would be a Prime Minister's Question Time the following day when he would need to put questions to John Major.

A vote had been called at ten o'clock and opinion polls to be published in the morning gave Labour a lead. I told Neil this when I met him in the Members' Lobby after the vote. He had been hurrying back to Welsh night, to his guitar, his songs from the valleys, taking him back down a vista of years. He hardly paused for breath. With the knowledge that soon he might be Prime Minister, he had every right to be happy.

'Enjoy yourself,' I said. 'You deserve it.'

And so he did.

On the night of the Sheffield rally Neil had revealed this more relaxed side of his nature, the Neil that loved life and had the desire to express this love, the tension easing from him, enjoying his audience as the audience had enjoyed his jokes. The impression had been given that Labour had already won the election and were celebrating.

The rally had over-run into the BBC nine o'clock news, so that the more evangelical side of the proceedings had been shown to the viewing public, giving the impression of a triumphalist Party. For those on the floor it was indeed a revivalist rally, but for Tory voters reluctant to vote they decided after all they wished to keep Neil Kinnock out of Downing Street, and rather than stay at home on Election Day they would turn out to give John Major the largest popular vote in Conservative Party history.

Watching the proceedings again on video, with the benefit of hindsight, I noted the reaction of members of the Shadow Cabinet standing with Neil on the platform. They might have been enjoying the moment, the mood of relaxation, creating as they thought an assured image with the British people. Only one hovered at the back of the platform looking uneasy, out of place, uncertain whether this was indeed an appropriate platform, an appropriate occasion.

That member had been Tony Blair.

I had called Tony at his flat in Islington.

'You have to stand for Deputy Leader,' I said.

'It's all sewn up,' Tony said. 'John Smith has asked Margaret Beckett. There'll be an announcement shortly. But I want you to know. I *really* wanted it.'

When Leader of the Opposition, Tony would appear on the Des O'Conner television show and would be asked about the Spice Girls and their number one hit, what they want, what they want, what they really wanted. He had been invited to compare them with Margaret Thatcher. Tony had referred to the jewellery the Girls wore and where particular items had been embedded on their persons.

'Can you imagine Margaret Thatcher wearing her jewellery like that?'

'And I suppose,' Des O' Conner said. 'The Spice Girls would say what I want, what I want, what I *really really* want!'

Tony had wanted to be Deputy Leader just as in the song by the Spice Girls.

With a fresh leadership election upon us, I had met Tony in the members' lobby.

'Don't let anyone push you out of the race,' I said.

'I'll give you lists of MPs to contact.'

I had heard from lobby correspondents that Tony was hesitating; Roy Hattersley's conversation with Tony had confirmed this; but the ambition was too strong, the desire too great, the certain knowledge that if time and chance happeneth to us all this was the time and this the opportunity. I might urge him not to give way, not to pause, to take the tide at the flood, to avoid the shallows and miseries as Shakespeare had written, for those who missed the tide.

But it would be Gordon Brown's act of self-immolation that would leave the way open for Tony.

John Smith had reappointed me to the front bench as spokesman for trade and industry under Robin Cook. I had known John since he had been campaign manager for Roy Hattersley in the 1983 leadership contest. He had paid me the courtesy of visiting my constituency not once but twice when he had been Shadow Secretary of State for Trade and Industry, though I disliked reminding him of his second visit.

62

He had received a speeding ticket on his way home.

I had later urged him to stand for the National Executive Committee of the Party to strengthen his political base. John would not be tempted and wrote to say that his decision was irrevocable. I would use the same word in a letter to Roy Hattersley when I told him I did not wash to stay on the front bench because of my involvement with the Cleveland child abuse crisis. As with John Smith, the word put an end to any attempt at dissuasion, but Roy did say with some prophecy that I should not resign.

'It'll be harder to get back than you think.'

I had had lunch with John Smith prior to the 1992 Election.

It had been a quiet Friday in the House and he had dropped into the members' dining room where I had been dining alone. I had lost touch with John, as I had with many colleagues, though he had given me full support on my stance on the Cleveland child abuse crisis. He had been short and testy this day, disgruntled because he was in London rather than in his Edinburgh constituency, his diary filled with too many engagements he thought others should handle. John had been Queen's Counsel, a Scottish advocate, a man with a famously ordinary name but who in the words of his biographer, Andy McSmith, '*though he did not send pulses racing, had an exceptional intelligence, sharp wits and a ruthless grasp of reality*'.

He disliked writing.

I suggested I should write articles for him to use in the forthcoming General Election.

'How about articles on the national minimum wage?' he asked.

I would write a series of articles for John and send them to his office, but I have no idea whether he used them or whether he even saw them. With Parliament dissolved, the

General Election upon us, I returned to my constituency. After the Election, as Roy Hattersley had predicted, my return to the front bench had not been easy. My route back would be to stand for the Shadow Cabinet elections, a route now quite unknown to the 1997 intake of Labour MPs.

My friend George Robertson MP suggested that I not stand at all, I would be humiliated, but such was my determination to play a full part with the Labour Party, starting again as it were after an Election defeat, that I would write personal letters to all those whom I felt would support me.

I would write these letters some from an Edinburgh hotel where I had been staying during a conference of the British-Irish Inter-Parliamentary Body which I had helped to set up to promote understanding and cooperation between MPs from the United Kingdom and the Republic of Ireland. Some I would write from my London office over a weekend and others from my home in Middlesbrough. An excess of zeal, you might say, but if I did not get onto the Shadow Cabinet I would get some sixty votes, a reasonable enough total, and I had laid down a sufficiently strong marker to be considered by John Smith.

I called Tony Blair at Trimdon and asked that he help me get a post in one of the economic teams. He would be appointed Shadow Home Secretary, a post that suited him, and where he would make a strong impression, reversing what had been a perception that Labour placed more emphasis on the well-being of the criminal than on justice for the victim.

'You'll find Gordon's team pretty well full,' he said.

Gordon had been appointed Shadow Chancellor of the Exchequer.

I had gone to see Gordon in his office in Parliament Street and he explained that he had chosen his team on a regional basis, that he needed a place for his campaign manager Nick Brown, who also came from the North-East. I called Robin Cook, who asked that I speak to John Smith directly. 'Though not today,' he said. 'It's his birthday.'

I did not feel sufficiently close now to John to call him on the phone, on his birthday or any other day, but I would run into him coming out of the strangers' dining room.

'Could I have a few words with you?'

'I've not got a lot of time,' he said.

I did not have any particular hopes of going on John's front bench after such a brusque exchange.

'He has other things on his mind,' Alan Keen said.

Alan had entered the House in 1992.

He had been a scout for Middlesbrough Football Club for seventeen years. I spoke with our chief whip, Derek Foster.

'It was very hard,' he said. 'Don't ask me why – but it was.'

John Smith had called me at my flat in Dolphin Square.

'I'd love to go on your front bench, John.'

'Speak to Robin Cook,' he said.

Robin had wanted to stand in the leadership election and I had canvassed members of the Parliamentary Labour Party to ascertain the level of his support. An opinion poll gave Robin's support at three per cent and if he could not win the election why should he stand at all? His Party base was secure, he had headed the poll for the National Executive Committee and the Shadow Cabinet in the last elections before John Smith's death. Why put his prestige and power at risk when he was certain of a major portfolio in a future Labour government?

Robin withdrew in sufficient time to allow me to become one of Tony's sponsors for the leadership.

~

Tony Blair and Gordon Brown had shared an office together when they had first entered Parliament but they had been attracted each to the intellect of the other, defining policies, probing weaknesses within the Labour philosophy, seeking not problems but solutions, dining regularly with each other either at an Indian restaurant in Horseferry Road, where they could go through paperwork undisturbed, or sometimes in the members' dining room of the House.

After the 1987 Election, I had entered the dining room to find Tony and Gordon sitting alone, working together on a document, scrutinising it carefully. I sat next to them because that is the custom in the Members' dining room, sitting with your colleagues, provided they are of the same Party. I joked how lucky they were to have youth on their side.

'A steadily diminishing asset,' Gordon had said.

They worked through their document as assiduously as they worked through their meal, with full concentration, heads over the paper. When it came to dessert a fine, glowing apple or sponge pudding arrived for Tony, wreathed in thick steaming custard. Tony always had a hearty appetite, he would enjoy his breakfast kippers on the morning train on a Friday when returning to his constituency, and now he looked with anticipation and enthusiasm upon the deep rich pudding.

Just as he picked up the spoon, Gordon found something wrong in the document.

'It has to be changed!' he said.

Tony's spoon hovered over the pudding with its exciting wreaths of steam and warmth.

'Where are they?' Gordon asked.

'In the Shadow Cabinet room,' Tony said.

'You must tell them at once! You must phone them now!'

I never did find out who they were, nor the content of the document, but as a decision was made, looking beyond the table to the Thames and the South Bank of the river, I reflected on the French Dramatist, Pierre Corneille, born in Rouen 1606, son of a lawyer, soon to be a lawyer himself, destined for the Bar as Tony Blair had been destined, pleading even in courts of law before a passion for the stage had driven him into the theatre.

Why had I thought of Corneille?

Because he had written a number of plays, histories or tragi-comedies, with the theme of conflict between love and duty. He would create the classic theatre. He would substitute the drama of intrigue for the drama of characters. His heroes would be human in their affections but determined upon glory, passionately attached to the highest motives, triumphing over numerous obstacles to achieve their destiny.

They put their sense of duty above their devotion to love.

Now Tony Blair had to choose between love and duty, the duty he bore for Gordon Brown and the document before him and the meeting in the Shadow Cabinet, and the love he had for this steaming pudding, heavy as a mountain, steaming like a volcano, rich with life, eager to be taken, to be ravished, devoured as no pudding before or since, seductive in its warmth and undoubtedly passionate in its consummation.

Tony chose duty.

He set aside his spoon and napkin and left the table and trundled to a telephone by the side of the desk where the cashier took the MPs' money or signed bills for our lunch. The pudding cooled, disappointed, its ardour diminished, the heat going from it, the steam lingering but fretful, the volcano extinguishing, the mountain deflating, the pudding all sodden and viscous and now uneatable as the simmer and glow left it.

Such are the sacrifices of politics.

I would recall the saga of the pudding when the Labour Party came to decide upon a successor to John Smith. Would it be Gordon Brown or Tony Blair? Both had the ability, the high aspiration, both held in high esteem within the Party, so high that the former Leader of the Labour Party, Neil Kinnock, would never have been able to choose between the two.

Gordon, too, had chosen duty.

He had stood aside for his friend and written his acceptance speech at the Institute of Education.

At the Institute, sharing in this moment of history, had been Tony's father-in-law, Tony Booth, who would not only recall the dinner we had all had together at Stockton so many years ago, but who had been the main speaker at the dinner. It had been Joe Mills, Regional Secretary of the Transport & General Workers' Union, who had hosted our dinner at Carlisle. Joe had presented an award to a local TGWU official and since at the time the Labour Party had been beset by division, he recalled how he had spoken to a lady who had joined the Party fifty years ago.

'Which faction of the Party had you joined?' he asked.

'There was only one Labour Party in them days,' she had replied.

There was only one Labour Party now as Tony accepted the leadership.

Tony Booth's father had barred the door to him once he had left the family home for the stage. He had been an extremely distant relative of another actor called Booth, who had shot Abraham Lincoln at the theatre. He lived with Pat Phoenix, better known as Elsie Tanner in Coronation Street, whom he would marry a few days before she died.

Together they had canvassed for Tony when he had first stood in a by-election at Beaconsfield.

They would canvass again at Sedgefield in the 1983 General Election, spending two weeks on the sandstoned doorsteps of miners and their families, more recognisable in the pit villages than the candidate himself or his wife. Tony had not long been an MP when Pat fell seriously ill, and though Tony had constantly been asked to give interviews only once had I seen him on television when he had been door-stepped after visiting her in hospital.

He had not sought publicity at any cost.

Just as Tony Booth had recalled to me our dinner at Stockton, so I recalled Tony's first broadcast on Radio Tees. Tony had never been one who liked to rise early, he was not at his best on the morning train to his constituency, and when he received an early call from the local radio presenter and asked to say what the weather was like for voice level, Tony replied:

'I dunno. I'll have a look out the window!'

Now the man I had first met in the office of Tom Burlison when he had been looking for a seat in the North-East; who had lunched with me in the old court house in Middlesbrough when we had been barristers together; the man who had come into the House with me in 1983, who had told Jim Callaghan that we 'hunted' together; who would celebrate with me and our wives our arrival on the front bench; who would gaze with me over dinner to the hills beyond the streets of Carlisle in wonderment that we were MPs at all; who had been a friend and colleague all these years.

Tony Blair was now leader of the Labour Party.

As my mother would have said, it did indeed bring a lump to the throat.

Tony Really Loves Me

'You know,' I said to Margaret. 'Tony Blair really loves me.'

He had called me in my flat in Dolphin Square and offered me a post in his shadow government.

'Will you take defence?' he asked.

'Will it be Minister of State level?'

'That can be arranged,' he said.

'Of course I'll take it, Tony.'

'What did you really want anyway?'

'I really wanted to stay where I am.'

'I'll call you back,' he said.

He called me back a few minutes later.

'Stay where you are,' he said.

I would be one of the few on the front bench who would be given the post he wanted.

I had spent the last three years as Trade and Industry spokesman under Robin Cook and had dealt with City of London matters. As a young man, I had spent four years in the City, first as a typist and then as a shorthand-typist. I cannot put my hand on my heart and say I had ever been a secretary. I had worked as a temporary for the Lawsen Employment Agency working from a second floor office near the Moorgate Underground, with steep narrow staircase and dark windows that rarely caught the sun. I had indeed been a rarity, a male typist in the City.

Mrs Garcke, who owned and ran the Agency, never let me down.

She found me a job week in week out, as a typist when I had little shorthand, later as a shorthand-typist when my speed had sufficiently picked up after taking my classes at Pitman's College in Southampton Row. Each Friday I would climb those stairs to see Mrs Garcke, with no money to get me through the following week, and each Friday she would give me another assignment with another firm for the Monday.

I had settled in Tufnell Park and answered an advertisement for a job in the civil service and had gone for an interview in Holborn Square. I had been offered entry into the civil service at three pounds a week and since my board and lodgings came to two pounds I would have a pound a week on which to live. The woman who did the interview was kind and matronly; she pointed out that the great advantage of such entry would be that I would have a job for life with a pension at the end of it.

I had been eighteen years old.

With the thought of the pension receding, I had worked for a few weeks as an office boy for Swift's of Chicago, a meat-packing firm on the south bank of the river near Borough Underground. The manager of the mailing department gave me a gray coat and my task had been to tie parcels and change towels in the men's rooms on the various floors of their building. These might have been easy tasks for anyone but me; I had been hopeless with my fingers, I had never succeeded at woodwork at school; I could not tie a knot nor remove the towels. They would jam in the machine and would need to be cut free.

The boss I recall had a difficult job with directors who

did not like him very much. 'The mail must get through!' he would shout, as if driving the pony express; and I recall one particular director of the firm finding himself in Glasgow and calling to complain that the mail indeed had not got through. He had dark hair and a moustache and now and again would disappear, wearing a bowler hat, so that those in the packing department with me thought he had gone off to attend a shareholders' meeting somewhere in the City.

I would keep my writing hand by describing the boss as *'tall but not too tall, thin but not too thin, rather wiry and active. His hands are hard, his fingers active and nimble with constant use. He walks quickly, eagerly, his body trying to pace his restless energy. To live he must be active; he drives, he urges, he cajoles; he asks nothing of his staff that he does not first demand of himself.'*

I cannot now recall his name but at least he lives on in my mind and through these pages.

On my arrival in London, I had also gone to an employment exchange in Islington to sign on and to describe my skills. As a former newspaper reporter, they were few and far between, my shorthand was rudimentary; it might have got me through court cases at Blaydon Magistrates held at Gateshead, but I had no dictation speed. My typing too had been sluggish, tentative, though sufficient to get me through a day in a typing pool.

'We'll find you a job,' the employment officer said.

That at least had been hopeful.

'But don't go to any of these employment agencies,' he said. 'They give you some money but take a lot more from the employers.'

I had never heard of an employment agency but took the Underground into the City and alighted at Moorgate station. I found the Lawsen Employment Agency next door. And since I had not signed on the dole no dole was received either then or since. For four years I would work for Mrs Garcke, in insurance and banking and shipping and stock-broking; I would even work for solicitors handling the libel work of the then *Sunday Pictorial* that would become the *Sunday Mirror*.

I would be in the City at the time of the Bank Rate Enquiry in 1957 when the bank rate had shot up two percent, from five to seven; there had been allegations of a leak, gilt-edged stock had been sold, causing a collapse of the stock market. Perhaps inside information had been passed that the Conservative Chancellor of the Exchequer, Peter Thorneycroft, was about to make an announcement of the so-called swingeing rise.

Lord Kindersley had sat at the Court of the Bank of England who advised the Chancellor on rate rises. He was also on the board of a City merchant bank. Had he been the source of the leak? The concept of Chinese walls between departments or within law firms or merchant banks had not been known in those days, but there had been a City concept of my word is my bond, a gentleman's honour, that went with the bowler hat and rolled umbrella, and Lord Kindersley had denied that he had passed information from the Court to the merchant bank or that they had profited by selling gilts.

Labour had then been in opposition, its Shadow Chancellor had been Harold Wilson, and he had made some incautious statements on the floor of the House of Commons, raising allegations of the leak. He had spoken under the cloak of Parliamentary privilege and had been dared to make the same comments outside the House so that he could be sued. Harold, of course, had not been so foolish, but the Enquiry had taken place and no evidence of a leak had been discovered.

Lord Kindersley had been cleared but the allegations killed him.

~

One evening, as Shadow Trade and Industry spokesman, I had gone into the City to make an after-dinner speech and found myself sitting next to Lord Kindersley's son. I remarked that I recalled the details of the Bank Rate Enquiry as if they were yesterday and he recounted that though his father had been cleared of any allegation that he had passed on the Bank of England's secrets, nevertheless his health had been so affected he had not lived long afterward.

In those days, after my work in the City before I had settled into the routine of taking shorthand lessons at Pitman's College, I would walk down to Parliament, a thin mist across the Thames, the face of Big Ben staring back through the mist. I had come down to the House on such a night when the bank rate leak allegations had been at their height and seen Jim Griffiths in the Central Lobby, either talking to another MP or a constituent or member of the public or newspaper reporter. Jim had been one of the great stalwarts of the Labour Party. He had come into the House in 1945 and I recall interviewing him for the *Blaydon Courier* when he had visited the area to launch a by-election.

William Whiteley, former chief whip in a Labour government had died, and Jim had given the date of the by-election when leaving the miners' hall halfway up Blaydon Bank. The writ had not been issued from the floor of the House, this was a bit of a scoop, but it had been neither here nor there in the grand scope of things, and neither I nor my newspaper had been able to make anything of it.

Now I heard Jim's voice booming across the Central Lobby.

'Not yet!' he called.

He had been indicating to his interlocutor that nothing much had yet come out of the bank rate allegations.

Mrs Garcke had placed me at Lloyd's and I had been working there when the new building had been opened by the Queen Mother. There is another new building now, resembling the Pompidou Centre in Paris, all tubes and metal and outside lifts; but this had been a pristine building of scrubbed stone, stolid as Lloyd's itself, or stolid as Lloyd's had once been, the building curving into Leadenhall Street down towards the market.

A beautiful painting had been made of this scintillating evening, when royalty had come into the City, men in their tails, women wearing their tiaras, the Queen Mother resplendent, the Lutine Bell somewhere in view, with no sign of the temporary typist who would take messages between the underwriting boxes, sometimes being asked to take a policy around for signature, otherwise ensconced before a Remington typewriter, bashing at the keys to create a staccato fire upon the paper, copies and carbons and all.

It had not been easy in those first months, working for the Lawsen Employment Agency, being sent to a different job every week, the only man in the typing pool, not the odd man out, the only man out, speaking with a broad Geordie accent, unaccustomed to the softer Southern tones, timid and bashful, keeping one's own counsel, but listening to the cattish conversation of the other typists.

When my shorthand speed had sufficiently improved Mrs Garcke had sent me forth, not as a typist but as a shorthand-typist. She had sent me to work for an Indian carpet dealer who had his own warehouse. I had been called upon for a week to replace his secretary who had

75

been on holiday. The dealer had spent many years in India and had a brownish glow to his complexion. He had also been testy and ill-tempered, he spoke too quickly for my inchoate shorthand skills, I badly transcribed his letters, and in his frustration he refused to pay Mrs Garcke's bill.

Mrs Garcke and I persevered, however, and I would spend some eighteen months working for an insurance broking firm called Bevington, Vaisey and Foster, now merged with other broking firms, working my way through all of their departments except the finance department, standing in for secretaries either on holiday or ill. A severe Asian 'flu had swept through London and this had sent more than half the shorthand-typists to bed. I had suffered a permanent cold as a child, but the Asian 'flu would pass me by and I worked throughout the epidemic.

I would keep a writer's notebook at this time, setting my thoughts and descriptions to paper in my partitioned room in Tufnell Park, writing on a small table afflicted by woodworm, or in an Italian eatery at Archway. The ending of the war might be twelve to thirteen years behind us, but London had stayed flattened, the cranes had hardly swung into action, the rebuilding to begin; the Barbican had been rubble and weeds and broken walls stretching far beyond the Moorgate Underground Station.

The Tower of London and Tower Bridge and St Paul's Cathedral had remained intact, but as I wrote: *'There are great holes in the earth and the sides of adjacent buildings look as if they had been sliced clear, standing out grotesquely. You can see the original foundations, you can see old bits of paper which had fallen into niches in the mortar, and here and there, brown and battered, utensils left since the bombs had been dropped'.*

I would write of construction work along the south bank of the river where the warehouses rose from the Thames, sheer faces of blackened brick, but half a mile away on the north bank, near St Paul's, *'several new buildings have been erected, very tall and slender, of white plaster which on a bright day pains your eyes'*.

I would write of one crane swinging viciously, arcing and dipping and dropping suddenly, a miscalculation, smashing into the side of a lorry, iron grappling hooks swinging heavily before suddenly being lifted upward and out of difficulty. I wrote that no-one paid any attention, no-one inspected for damage. The stevedores continued their work and so, too, did the wharf-keepers and labourers.

In those days, too, rather in the manner of Charles Dickens who would write about the river, and perhaps under his influence, I would go down to The Upper Pool of London and describe not only the leaden sky, the drizzle fine as mist though not as blanketing, the mud pools caused by the rain and the rubble caused by labour gangs reconstructing blitzed warehouses. I would describe the narrow alleys congested with transport lorries and vans, even a horse and cart, describing the cranes working on the dockside in an age before containers, lifting their loads from the holds of the ships to the dockyard.

When Tony Blair became Leader of the Opposition, he would mould his own front bench.

Robin Cook would move from Trade and Industry to Foreign Affairs, a move he had originally resisted because he had done so well in his Shadow portfolio. He had to reconcile himself, however, to a future as Foreign Secretary which, come to think of it, would be no bad future. I had indicated that though I had enjoyed working with him I had preferred to shadow the City rather than go with him to foreign affairs.

'I've made a strong recommendation to Tony that you stay in your present job,' he said. Gordon Brown would become Shadow Chancellor of the Exchequer and told me that he wanted me to stay where I was within the Trade and Industry team. Jack Cunningham would take over the team and also say that he had made a recommendation to Tony that I maintain my present Shadow portfolio.

Tony came on the phone and asked that I take defence.

Allowing me to stay with the City brief I was able to retread those steps of forty years ago, not among the rubble and overgrown bomb sites, not by the river with its docks and cranes and ships and wharves, but among those tall sky-scrapers of glass and concrete, its bankers and accountants and lawyers and stockbrokers, young upwardly mobile, all of whom I had made my own for so many years.

And who now I would make New Labour's too.

That is why I said to Margaret:

'You know, Tony Blair really loves me!'

'I love you too,' she said.

Tony Loves the Miners

'I love the miners,' Tony said.

Of course he loved the miners.

He represented what had once been a mining constituency and had been brought up in Durham by the cathedral where a service was held each year on Gala Day. I cannot recall that he had been with me at the very first Gala after we had become MPs together in 1983, but certainly I recall his presence after the General Election in 1987.

He had appeared on the platform facing out from the old racecourse and I recall that he had been asked by one platform speaker to ensure that a future Labour government would ban the import of coal. He had been Shadow Treasury minister but now held a Shadow portfolio on Trade and Industry. He wore a casual jacket this day with leather patches to the elbows, but if he heard the exhortation he gave no hint that it would become future Labour Party policy.

Ten years would pass before Labour had the opportunity of putting any policy on the statute book and by then there were no pits left in the Durham coalfield, no coal left to be won, the pits had all gone the way of the Fishburn coke works, and any pledge that might have been given had become as redundant as the miners themselves. Still there would be the Gala and the procession to the Cathedral.

In the run-up to the 1997 General Election, I had taken a train with Tony to Newcastle.

As Leader of the Opposition, he would visit his constituency once a month and his agent, John Burton, would arrange for him a series of engagements, including radio and press and television interviews. He had agreed to speak this day at the University of Northumbria and give out diplomas, and I explained to him that I had been invited too because I had once been a governor at the University.

'I didn't know you had been a governor there,' he said.

'I'll write a short story,' I said. 'I'll call it *Remembrance of Things Past*.'

'What does that mean?' he asked curiously.

'It means you did know but you've forgotten. Anyway, the miners would love you to come to their Gala as Leader of the Opposition.'

In 1983 I had not only attended the Gala but marched behind the banner of Chopwell colliery.

My own pit village was not two miles from Chopwell, less if you went along the railway line, and on the night I had left grammar school my father had suggested we go to Chopwell where he worked and where a new banner would be unfurled by Arthur Horner. I had already decided to be a writer, a newspaper reporter no less, and to keep a diary of my voyage through life, its shallows and its miseries, and there seemed no better place to begin than on a football field at Chopwell where the banner would be unfurled.

We had waited with other men outside the Chopwell hotel till Arthur Horner arrived.

Arthur had been secretary of the National Union of Mineworkers and would be speaking at the Durham Miners' Gala the following day. We had stood on the corner of the hotel, some of the men hunkering down in the time-honoured fashion of pitmen, and had moved onto the football field behind the hotel where a platform had been built in the centre circle. A newspaper reporter and photographer had arrived and pushed their way to the front.

The reporter stood before me in the crowd, shorter than I, and wearing a gabardine raincoat; he had too a haircut known as a DA, standing for duck's anatomy for the refined but duck's arse for the rest of us, his black hair sleek and oiled and neat around his neck. He would be no more than three or four years older than I, but he had achieved what I had wanted to achieve, he had become a newspaper reporter, his name was Jack Amos, and in the none too distant future he would be my news editor on the *Blaydon Courier* and *Consett Guardian*.

Later still he would visit me in the House of Commons.'I remember your first newspaper report,' he said. 'Miles and miles of smiles at Chopwell!'

Jack's pencil had poised to take down the pearls that would drift on the wind from Arthur Horner's mouth, but just as Arthur began to speak a storm drove from the peaks of the Pennines, racing down the Derwent valley, sweeping across the football field, raindrops large and heavy upon Jack's notebook. The men stood in their cloth caps and faced the storm, rain lashing into their faces, but none flinched, not a head turned, not a muscle moved, not an eye squinted as the drops ran like tears down their cheeks.

All wanted to hear what Arthur had to say.

'In the old days,' he said with his Welsh lilt. 'At the time of the General Strike in 1926, there were two Little Moscows. The one here at Chopwell. The other at Mardy in the Little Rhondda.'

He recalled The South Wales News had declared Mardy to be under the heel of a knot of '*sullen, arrogant hobble-dehoys*', and then *Daily Express*, now *The Express*, declared that visitors to Mardy would go in fear of their lives.

81

According to *The Express*, the hobbledehoys exacted money from trades people, insulted the vicar and interrogated strangers, before running them out of the village.

Arthur had been a small man, compact and stocky, with a rugged skin and silver hair and glasses. He had been vice-chairman of the miners' lodge at Mardy, a member of the National Executive Committee of the Communist Party when the Communist Party had been the hope of thousands in pit villages and mining valleys; and had been both a boy preacher and male boxer. He had seen the inside of a prison for refusing to join the Army when there had been conscription in the 1914–18 war, and whilst sentenced to two years had been released early because he had gone on hunger strike.

Arthur had been a real hobbledehoy.

He had been elected checkweighman at Mardy, the only way he could get a job at the pit, checking on behalf of the men each tub of coal they had won in the days of piece rates. He had stopped the pits in both Rhondda valleys when the coal owners had sought to sack him for 'failing to confine himself to his duties at the weighing machine', that is to say he had continued his agitation among the men.

He would spend another month in prison.

He would be fined for leading a march to feed hungry schoolchildren, would be charged with unlawful assembly and incitement to riot for seeking to help tenants evicted from their colliery houses by the coal owners; he would be given fifteen months hard labour. Finally, he would become miners' agent at another pit and begin his rise to become Secretary of the National Union of Mineworkers.

Now he had made a pilgrimage from one Little Moscow to another.

In the same General Strike Chopwell had been described by *The Newcastle Chronicle* as '*a spectre of a miniature*

Russia', then firmly in the hands of the proletariat, or the Communist Party. Chopwell had been '*seething with sedition, economic sabotage and Communist Sunday schools*'. The chairman of the County Police Court had dealt with at least fifty breaches of emergency regulations at Chopwell during the General Strike.

The national newspapers had taken up the cry.

'*Precocious Lenins dwell in Marx Avenue*,' declared the *Morning Post*, forerunner of today's *Daily Telegraph*. Chopwell had changed two of its street names to Lenin Terrace and Marx Avenue. '*The village is known far and wide as the reddest village in England. Chopwell had become a Communist paradise whose overbearing rulers tyrannised the rest of the inhabitants. A village of suspicion, of whispering neighbours and of fear.*'

But not of hobbledehoys.

Those who lived through the General Strike saw things differently. They were going to share in a great cooperative movement, the village would be as a city set upon a hill that could not be hidden, like a candle under a bushel; a new Jerusalem would banish poverty, destitution, crime, all the by-products of capitalism. Socialism would be builded not for their time but for all time.

Chopwell might be Little Moscow, but one day it would be '*the Moscow of the Workers' Empire*'.

The General Strike had long passed by the time of my birth, but its tide had not ebbed, the sands of bitterness and bile had stayed damp, and when I began my working life in Chopwell colliery office the senior clerk would name all those who had been black-legs, that is those who had worked through the Strike; those who had run traps in and

83

out of the village, those who had carried supplies, those officials who had sought to maintain the pit on behalf of the hated coal owners.

He might have said too, though he did not, those who had manned the colliery office.

As a child I had been regaled with stories of those who had gone to jail, the proceedings in Gateshead courts, how one uncle had thrown a stone at a policeman but that his brother had been arrested and charged. He had been sentenced to three months in prison for a crime he did not commit, our family had all been in the magistrates' court, but not a word had been spoken, he had not shopped his brother, he would serve his sentence and return to the village if not a hero at least to a grateful family.

He had maintained their honour.

I would revive the Little Moscow tag when I worked in the colliery office and did lineage for local newspapers. Communism still flared in the village, like embers upon a fire; the lodge secretary at the colliery had been a Communist and in a local election stood against the lodge chairman who had been Labour. A strike was threatened at one time, when I had left the office and worked full-time for the *Blaydon Courier*, and though it was averted the manager was sent to look after another pit in the No.6 Area of the National Coal Board. The lodge secretary would also receive a New Year's greetings card from Moscow and an invitation to attend a reception at the Russian Embassy in London.

All of which ended on the front pages of the newspapers.

When the Chopwell banner had been unfurled by Arthur Horner, raindrops to his spectacles, it depicted those Communist stalwarts Karl Marx and Vladimir Illych Lenin as well as Kier Hardie, the first leader of the Labour Party. The

84

banner bore too the crest of the Labour Party as well as the
Red Star of the Communist Party and had been inscribed
with the hammer and sickle, those emblems of the worker
and peasant. The first Chopwell banner had been torn at
the time of the General Strike and another commissioned
in 1935.

The portraits had been oil-painted on silk, the silk
stretched on wooden frames; the silk had been coated with
India rubber, improving quality and durability, explaining
why the banner was always so fresh as it floated above the
crowds on Gala Day. The old banner would be given to
Russians from the Donbas coalfield, not on the night the
new banner had been unfurled but the following day at the
colliery institute.

The old banner would be hung in the Hall of Trade
Unions in Moscow, '*a fitting resting place for the relic
of the militant British miners who earned for their village
the name of Little Moscow*,' as John Gorman recorded
in his book *Banner Bright*. I had come cross the book
whilst moving from one Parliamentary office to another
and, idly looking through it in the hope of catching sight
of the Chopwell banner, I had come across a photograph
that had been taken the night the new banner had been
unfurled, taken by the photographer who had pushed past
me towards the platform.

There would be the Communist lodge secretary and the
Labour lodge chairman, and there would be a young Bob
Woof, then lodge treasurer, completing the triumvirate of
powerful union men within the colliery, not yet become
Member of Parliament; but all of them looking at the
banner, showing their satisfaction, their pride, their sense
of history that would carry them and the banner through
many a Gala Day.

The lodge secretary would become a strong Labour man,

he and I would carry the colliery banner in 1983, the Communist embers in Chopwell would die, but it did not surprise me when the Conservative government under Margaret Thatcher introduced the so-called poll tax fewer people in Chopwell paid this than any other village in the country. As Communism died so too did the pit, though the two are not connected, and on my last visit to the Gala I would call by the village, I would leave my car at the top of the hill overlooking the football ground where the banner had been unfurled, I would talk to the man in his garden who lived in a house that had once been a colliery office.

'How long have you lived here?' I asked.

'Twenty-five years!' he said.

The Mardy pit would close too, but Arthur Horner would have been proud that after the year-long pit strike that ended 5 March 1985 the Mardy miners would be the last to go back in the Rhondda Valley. They would return at half-past six in the morning, the ground hard beneath their feet, the frost freezing their breath, their banner held firm and aloft, the motto 'Peace – Forward to Socialism' vague in the early mist.

I learnt too in 1983, as I marched with those pit lads who had worked at Chopwell, that a colliery banner is no easy thing to carry. There are leather straps, brass buckles and pole caps; eight men form a team to carry the banner, two to each pole and one on each guide rope and tapes. The banner would sway and swirl as we wended our way towards the County Hotel and the famous balcony where year in and year out Labour leaders had stood, on this occasion Neil Kinnock with his wife Glenys.

Truth to tell, Neil was not yet Leader of the Labour Party, but he saw me under the banner and smiled and waved and pointed me out to Glenys, a new boy in the House; and I waved back as the banner swirled again and we marched on

towards the famous cricket field, once a racecourse, where
the Gala would be held and the speeches made: speeches
that would not be much different from the one that Arthur
Horner had made after he had unfurled our banner on the
football field.

The Gala almost died when the pits closed, but a man
whose memories of past Galas had been as sharp as my
own had come forward as a benefactor to ensure that the
Gala would continue, the march through the narrow cobbled
streets of the town, the banners furling and unfurling, men
and women and children threading across the narrow bridge
towards the County Hotel, the crowd gathering again on the
old racecourse, the MPs and other trade union representatives gathering on the platform, the speakers, left-wing as
ever, Old Labour you might say, but their voices carrying
over the heads of the crowds to the past.

There is talk, too, of recovering the old Chopwell banner
from the Hall of Trade Unions in Moscow. Communism
has passed there too, the banner is redundant, a relic of
long-gone miners' solidarity; it should be brought back
to the village; funds will be raised, to buy the banner
if necessary, to ship it back to the old coalfield, so that
it might be hoisted with the new above the heads of the
crowds at the next Durham Miners' Gala.

The words on the banner read: *'We take up the task
eternal, the burden and the lesson. Pioneers Oh pioneers!'*
The pioneers had indeed done their work, they had taken up
their task, they had carried the burden and learnt the lesson.
Labour had lived through the General Strike and the miners'
strike of 1984–85, the miners might no longer be with us,
their pits closed, Old Labour had defined itself into New,
but none of this was far from my thoughts as I took the
train to Newcastle this day with Tony Blair.

We had gone to the University together where Tony had

donned his robe and mortar board and prepared his speech. He had a slight cold and I sat behind him and offered him a glass of water should he need it. I made sure the photographers did not take any odd picture of him with his mortar board lopsided, or catch him out in any other curious poses, and the photographs that appeared in the next day's newspapers were pleasant and attractive.

I shielded him from reporters and television interviews, since he was not keen to be door-stepped, and when he had handed out the diplomas and returned for coffee and removed his robes and mortarboard I ushered him from the University into his car where his agent John Burton would take him on time for another engagement in his constituency.

'Thank you for looking after me,' he said.

'Don't forget the miners,' I said.

He would not make the Gala this year, but he would visit Durham Cathedral and open a precinct for miners in the presence of the Bishop. The service in the Cathedral after the Gala is one of the most moving for the old miners and their families, the singing of the hymns reaching up to the ancient rafters, the deep strains of the duty band, the candles flickering in the darkened recesses, history moving past the Bishop in procession down the aisle to fill the alcoves, the banners lined along the Cathedral walls.

'I love the miners,' Tony said.

'I love them too,' I said.

A Bust for Nye

Tony and I came into the hallway off the Central Lobby but from different directions.

He had come down the long corridor past the library, with books or lockers on either side, with the high ceiling and chandeliers, no natural light here, all the way from the Office of Leader of the Opposition, not taking the office of John Smith, moving down from a first floor suite to the old office of Neil Kinnock, walking tall and straight and determined along the passageway skirting the Chamber till he had reached the library corridor and the cold marble of the hallway, with its own tower-like ceiling.

I had travelled down that morning from the North-East and, arriving in the members' cloakroom, had left my coat by the red tape for my imaginary sword, walking up the narrow winding steps that would lead me to the Members' Lobby, and from there across the spacious area of the Central Lobby, with its images of the four saints George and David and Patrick and Andrew, past the paintings of ancient times, through the heavy doors to the same cold marble hallway where a few of our colleagues had gathered this quiet and lonely Monday morning.

We were to unveil a bust of Nye Bevan.

There had been a subscription to pay for the bust and Michael Foot, former Leader of the Labour Party and greatest living Bevanite, still having an office in the *Tribune* newspaper, home of the Bevanites for so long, would unveil the bust at the bottom of the marble steps. The bust would be of bronze, showing Bevan full of face, his quiff across his forehead, the eyebrows thick and bushy. The Editor of *Tribune*, Mark Seddon, had also been there as had Lord Bruce of Donnington, who as Donald Bruce had signed the first Bevanite tract after the war called *Keep Left*.

Nye Bevan had been my early political hero for many reasons.

He had come from a South Wales mining town called Tredegar, and as a young man he had crossed over to Mardy to celebrate the release from prison of Arthur Horner. He had anthracite blue to the cuts in his skin. He worked nine years in the pit and would not forget even in his sixtieth year how once his foot had stuck in a rail as a full set had approached. The speed of the set, hauled by steel ropes through the darkness, down narrow ways, glistening with damp and carbide traces, through sumps where water had gathered, would be a reminder that death too worked the pit.

He had entered Parliament in 1929 and if he had not followed in the footsteps of Lloyd George he had used the same silvery Welsh tongue to make his speeches, made the more unique by a stammer. No-one had quite known the origins of the stammer, because he had imitated an uncle, because of an innate shyness, or because he had been brought up in a cramped house with brothers and sisters, some of whom had died in childhood.

He had been in the first post-war Labour government and had created the National Health Service, pushing a battered pram filled with his private papers when he had left office. He had been a strong supporter of pit nationalisation and in the war had called for a Second Front to help the Russians.

All this had created an echo in my own pit village.

'I'm a Bevanite mesel',' Mrs Shields said.

I had taken over the Sunday paper round aged fifteen and my interest in Labour politics must have been sufficiently known, for Mrs Shields raised this with me as I settled my newspaper bag on her back step and sought from the bag the paper she had ordered. There had been a kindly light to her eyes as she had taken her copy of *Reynold's News*. She had been a party member and indeed there had been a regular little ward party on my housing estate whose influence within the Labour Party would range wider than one might expect, for it would be the Labour Party who chose the governors of schools and even their heads and deputy heads.

I never did discover the first name of Mrs Shields but often I would write of her long garden with the greenhouse at the bottom, the thick leeks with their white stems and heavy tilting green leaves. Her sons had allotments too where pigs would be nurtured and fed and finally slaughtered and hung upside down so that the blood could run from them into pails standing on the concrete base by the greenhouse.

Bevan had fallen out with the Chancellor of the Exchequer, Hugh Gaitskell, over the introduction of prescription charges and a cost for spectacles under what should have been a free National Health Service. The service had certainly transformed health care in our village. Where the doctor's surgery had been empty, by appointment only, now it was filled as every complaint was brought before our local doctor for investigation and treatment, even though investigation and treatment rarely passed the small window on the opposite side of which the good doctor would sit.

A prescription for a cough bottle would normally follow.

When Bevan had walked out of government, pushing his battered pram, he had sparked an internecine war which in the end would not be resolved until Tony Blair became Leader of the Labour Party. Bevan had formed a left-wing newspaper called *Tribune*; he had created a Tribunite faction in the House of Commons, composed of left-wing MPs of his own ilk; but he himself had seen the dangers to Labour by the creation of such a group. He would urge its disbandment.

'To perpetuate the group now is to perpetuate schism,' he would say.

The group had survived, first as Bevanites and then as Tribunites.

High Gaitskell, who would one day rise to become Leader of the Labour Party, had sought a more enlightened pragmatic socialism, seeking to curb costs in the health service, a Labour government unable to deliver a free service at the point of delivery to be paid for within the scope of taxation. This conundrum has yet to be settled. The clash between Bevanites and Gaitskellites would rumble throughout the fifties and I recall following a month-long national newspaper strike in 1955, when it had been brought to an end, the front page of *The Express* had shown a jousting knight-like Bevan and Gaitskell with the headline:

'They're at it again!'

I had never quite been a Gaitskellite.

I thought Hugh Gaitskell had made an historically incorrect decision when he had turned the face of the Labour Party away from the European Economic Community in 1962, again an issue which only came to be resolved within the Party when Tony Blair became leader. Perhaps too the Bevan phrase that Gaitskell had been '*a desiccated calculating machine*' had been too close to the truth for comfort. I was a bit surprised when, on entering the Commons, David Winnick, MP for Walsall, North, took me aside and declared:

'You're a Gaitskellite!'

Certainly I had moved to the right of the Party from my days in the pit village. I had been a founder member of the right-wing Solidarity group which had been set up on the defection of Labour Members to the new Social Democratic Party. Certainly the views of Roy Hattersley and myself were identical and he had been a leading member of Solidarity. I would never join the Tribune Group of MPs in Parliament and indeed, upon my own election, became secretary of the Solidarity Group.

'At least I heard Nye Bevan speak,' I said.

Upon leaving school, after six weeks trying to get a job in newspapers, I had gone into the Chopwell colliery office, where I had also written lineage for the local press. I wrote up weddings and funerals for the *Blaydon Courier* at two-pence a line; Women's Institutes would send me their programmes; and I would play my last game of competitive football for a junior team and begin instead reporting football matches on Saturday afternoon.

My first hard newspaper story had come from a conversation I had overheard on a bus. A man from the village recounted how his father had died in the night and he had found him in the morning; he had been to the doctor to report his death. *Man Dies in Sleep* had been the thrilling headline the *Newcastle Journal* gave to the few lines of my very first story, using it as filler, much to the surprise but quiet pleasure of the man on the bus.

Another story had been the closure of the colliery canteen, only this time a full-time reporter from the *Sunday Sun* called Bert Horsfall, who covered the Tyne Valley, had been told not only to check it out but build it up. The closure apparently warranted a few more paragraphs than had the story of *Man Dies in Sleep*. Bert, not unnaturally, drove his own car that was still novel for us in the village, and he had visited my home to talk to me.

I had been at the colliery office when he called, but my mother told him how when the Queen Mother had visited Newcastle all police had been pulled off the delivery of wages to colliery offices this particular Friday, and colliery clerks, linesmen and surveyors had been asked to come in especially early to ensure any robbery attempts at the office might be thwarted. Without police protection it would be an ideal time for such robberies to take place.

I had seen a possible story in this and wanted to be on hand for the robbery. There had of course been no robbery, though an unidentified car had followed the wages van along the rickety road from the main road to the colliery office and I had followed its progress, pencil in hand, hovering over a shorthand note-book so that I might record the robbery as it took place. The van pulled up to the office and the car behind moved on over the bumps and runnels towards the officials' houses higher up the hill.

'Did you see that car?' I had said to one of the surveyors, who had come to the office armed with an iron bar. 'Were you worried when you saw it?'

The surveyor had waved the bar in the air.

'I wasn't worried,' he said. 'But I had my eye on it.'

'My word,' Bert Horsfall had said, when my mother recounted to him the tale. 'That's the spirit!'

Such was my enthusiasm for newspaper reporting, and my determination to get a full-time job, that I had taken up shorthand classes in the evening at Blaydon Grammar School near Swalwell. One evening, on coming out of the class, a fire engine had hurtled by, bells clanging, firemen holding onto the sides as they did in those days and I had literally chased the fire-engine, running as I had run as a

94

child, fearing a crocodile snapping at my backside, running so hard that I had been able to catch the fire engine as it pulled up before a terrace house, smoking billowing from a fire in the front room.

'You got here quick!' the fireman said.

My father had been more pragmatic.

'What would've happened had it been gannin' to Hexham?' he asked.

'Probably run all the way there too,' I said.

I did lineage for *Coal Magazine*, a publication of the National Coal Board, attending the opening of pithead baths, travelling by bus on Saturday morning to where the baths would be opened, always in the Durham coal-field, listening to a speech by the chairman of the local National Coal Board or by Sam Watson, Secretary of the Durham National Union of Mineworkers. There would be brass-band competitions and gymkhanas and colliery sports-days and the like, so that I created a regular market niche for myself.

I had gone as a *Coal Magazine* reporter to Newcastle City Hall to listen to Nye Bevan.

I had been ushered to the press desk at the front of the hall, but there would be no great newspaper interest in the speech; it would take place Saturday afternoon and the only other reporter there came from the *Northern Echo*. The hall had been filled with Labour faithful and Bevan had referred to the splits in the Party that he himself had foreseen. He had made a joke of them. 'They say in the Tory Party there is peace,' he said. 'So there is in the graveyard. If we are alive we are bound to be active.'

These are the only lines I recall, but Bevan would travel

to Manchester Belle Vue to make the same speech to the same faithful, only on a Sunday afternoon; *The Manchester Guardian* would pick up his words and report them the next day, reinforcing my own memory. I doubt if my copy had been used by *Coal Magazine*, but after the speech I had hovered on the stairs leading from the City Hall.

Nye Bevan had come past me, no more than a yard from my elbow, allowing himself to be led, hesitant and shy, submissive, the great and the good of the Party taking him downstairs to a car that would drive him to Newcastle Central Station to catch his train to Manchester. Perhaps I should have sought a few words, pushed my face into his, notebook ready, but I was there from the pit village, he was one of our own, and he passed me by on the stairs.

My brush with greatness had come and gone.

At about the same time, one of my aunts had taken me to the City Hall to hear Harry Pollit, leader of the Communist Party. Her husband had been a Communist, he read the *Daily Worker* each day, she had begun reading it and in some curious way it had turned her into a zealot. She would recite its propaganda, what British troops had been doing to women in Korea; she loved Willie Hamilton MP who had been anti-monarchist but who had actually defeated the Communist Willie Gallacher in Fifeshire; she would defend Harry Pollit who had been roughed up when he had visited the crew of HMS Amethyst which had fled down the Yantgtze river under a barrage of artillery fire from Chinese communist batteries; but there had been lighter moments too when she had described how she had been asked to carry the banner at a Communist march. She had felt it a great honour until she learned that the egg-throwers concentrated their fire on the banner carriers.

'Joe Stalin's turned her head,' my father would say.

I would attend, too, a Conservative party rally at the City

Hall during the 1964 General Election campaign and commit my first overt political act. I heckled Lord Hailsham, a leader of the Conservative Party. My cousin Geoffrey had managed to get two late tickets from the Conservative Party Office in Jesmond and we would sit in the back of the Hall and respectfully heckle Lord Hailsham, who had then reverted to his untitled name of Quentin Hogg.

Twenty-five years later the entire Hailsham family would become friends of one sort or another, Lord Hailsham would come down from the Lords to dine in the Commons, and though I would chat with him I would not remind him of how I had heckled him at an Election meeting in Newcastle, not that he would remember; Douglas Hogg who would follow his father not only into politics but into the Bar would become a Cabinet Minister and a Queen's Counsel and when last I saw him in the Members' Lobby he carried a red bag so huge that I remarked it was the largest red diplomatic box I had ever seen.

'It's filled with briefs!' he had said.

He had returned to the Bar after the Tory election defeat in 1997.

His wife Sarah would share many an economic platform with me when I was front-bench Opposition spokesman for Trade and Industry and also write an alternative column for the *Financial Mail on Sunday*. Her father had been Lord Boyd-Carpenter and on my first visit to the House of Commons he had been a Minister of the Crown speaking from the Dispatch Box. My little joke to her had been:

'I knew your father before you did!'

My early claim to fame as heckler at a Tory Party meeting would give me and my cousin a line in the *Newcastle Evening Chronicle*. When Lord Hailsham had congratulated the government for having signed a Nuclear Test-Ban Treaty I had shouted: 'You and the Russians!'

Heckling had been unheard of at the time and there had been some curiosity from the audience, a Conservative official had moved in, but had smiled and told me to 'keep it clean'.

I had, however, been rebuked by my father.

'What good d'ye think that did?' he asked.

There had been another meeting at the City Hall in 1979, when I had been candidate for Labour's nomination to fight the European seat of Northumbria, and Jim Callaghan as Prime Minister had come to address a Local Government Conference. There had been great hostility from those unions representing the low-paid, banners and jeers awaiting the Prime Minister as he had entered the Hall.

The weather had been poor, drifting snow cutting off villages, electricity lines down, low-paid workers on strike so that some dead had not been buried, causing great offence to the nation. During the 'flu epidemic in the first winter of the new millennium so many old people had died burials had been deferred for up to three weeks, without comment in the newspapers, but the fact that low-paid cemetery workers refused to carry out their duties and left the dead unburied gave the newspapers the headlines from which the Labour government would not recover:

'Winter of discontent!' they cried.

When I became Member of Parliament in 1983, the Parliamentary Labour Party had split itself into three: the hard-left Campaign Group under the tutelage of Tony Benn, formerly Cabinet Minister and candidate for the Deputy Leadership of the Party; the left-wing Tribune Group, flowing from the days of Nye Bevan with Michael Foot and then Neil Kinnock as its leader; and the right-wing Solidarity Group, heirs to Hugh Gaitskell, under the effective leadership of Roy Hattersley.

I had become Secretary of the Group and would organise a slate for Shadow Cabinet Elections.

With genuine governmental power not even a distant mirage, ambitions and Parliamentary careers had to be laid through the Shadow Cabinet. I would ensure that from a slate of fifteen there would be at least ten elected. One year one of our members – John Gilbert MP, who became Lord Gilbert, Minister of State for Defence until his retirement – had been on a Parliamentary trip to Lisbon, but had not left a proxy to enable another Solidarity member to vote for the slate in his place.

I called his wife at home, who gave me the telephone number of his hotel. I called John at the hotel. It was important, I said, that he telex his proxy to the Chief Whip. This was in the age before the facsimile machine, let alone the mobile telephone or e-mail. 'There's no telex in the hotel,' John had said.

'Then you must go out into the night and find a hotel with a telex,' I said.

Such was Solidarity discipline that John did as he was requested and telexed the proxy to the post office at the House of Commons. It arrived after ten o'clock at night, I picked it up and sought the Chief Whip in the press bar. The Chief Whip had been Michael Cocks, now Lord Cocks, and he had been able to cast John's vote in accordance with the slate, ensuring that Solidarity achieved its ten members to the Shadow Cabinet.

The last on the elected list had been Donald Dewar.

He had made it by one vote, the vote cast from a strange hotel in Lisbon, found on a darkened night, via a telex machine, but Donald would build on this success to become a future First Minister for Scotland as well as Labour Chief

Whip in his own right when Tony Blair became Leader of the Opposition. I had recalled to him a conversation some four years previously when he had said that never in his wildest dreams did he imagine himself as Chief Whip. Indeed, prior to his appointment, he had never served an hour in the whips' office.

He had called me in to see him.

'Do you know there's still money in the Solidarity account?' he asked.

Solidarity had been wound up after the 1987 General Election, its leadership considering its job done, the Labour Party saved from an ultra-left takeover and the shock waves receded from the creation of the Social Democratic Party. The Tribune Group would be flooded by a mass of newly-elected Labour MPs and would lose its effectiveness, and only the Campaign Group would continue as a coherent and cohesive force.

'There's not enough money to pay for the bust of Nye Bevan,' Donald said. 'The subscriptions have not been sufficient.'

The bust would show Nye as a robust young politician, the bronze reflecting what might have been dark hair and brows, a face full of strength and conviction; not the silver-haired weary man he had become through years of commitment to the Labour Party. Subscriptions had been called for, but his name had faded, and modern Tribunites had not been sufficiently forthcoming to pay for the bust.

'Would you mind,' Donald asked. 'If we used your Solidarity money?'

'Not at all,' I said.

'There's a delicious irony,' Alan Howarth said. 'The heirs to Hugh Gaitskell paying for Nye Bevan's bust!'

Alan, at the turn into the new millennium, would celebrate twenty-five years working in the Parliamentary Labour

100

Party offices. One of his many tasks would be to write the obituaries of past MPs that would be read out at the meetings of the Parliamentary Labour Party. He would prepare these meticulously and be given particular praise for his obituary of Willie Hamilton, read out in the presence of Tony Blair.

Alan had been a friend of John Smith and together they had climbed the Munroe mountains in Scotland after John's first heart attack; he would tell me at the Bournemouth Party Conference 1999 how he had walked the entire length of the Pyrenees; and Tony Blair would recall at this particular February meeting that Alan had helped him draft his first ever speech in politics. With the Nye Bevan bust completed, Alan had stroked his white beard and reflected on the ironies of politics.

It was not that I had entirely shunned my Bevanite origins that lay deep in the pit village. I would write articles for *Tribune*, I would be a subscriber and attend their fund-raising dinners. This created mirth in the breast of John Smith when he had been Leader of the Labour Party. John had been a prominent Solidarity member who had benefited from our slate, but upon becoming Leader of the Party he and I had attended a Tribune fund-raising dinner, and I recall having coffee with him after a meal when he had arrived at Harrogate to speak to the Confederation of British Industry.

I mentioned I had an article in that week's *Tribune*.

'Writing for *Tribune*!' he said.

Now Solidarity was paying for Nye Bevan's bust.

Tony Blair had not been much into Labour's tribal politics and had not joined either Tribune or Solidarity upon becoming an MP; there never would have been a possibility of joining the Campaign Group. His view had been that he had no intention of working in any formal organisation of MPs and did not see any value in these. He would join Tribune after two years in Parliament upon the prompting of the then Chief Whip Derek Foster; Gordon Brown had joined Tribune immediately he had become Member of Parliament, and both would benefit of the Tribune slate when they put their names forward for the Shadow Cabinet after the 1987 Election.

When John Prescott had announced he would stand against Roy Hattersley for the Deputy Leadership of the Labour Party in 1988, Gordon Brown and Tony Blair had walked along the Shadow Cabinet corridor to Roy's office to offer him their support. They had also offered to campaign for him. Roy, as former leader of Solidarity, had been impressed and pleased.

'It's nice to have the support of Tribunites,' he had said.

'We're not talking about us,' one of them replied. 'We're talking about real Tribunites!'

Now Tony and I stood at opposite sides of the small crowd who had come to listen to Michael Foot as he prepared to unveil Nye's bust. I had last seen Nye Bevan in the flesh when I had attended a rally for nuclear disarmament held in Trafalgar Square in 1957. I had not been there as an enthusiast of nuclear disarmament, rather to see Nye Bevan standing on the plinth, now rotund, now wearing a beret, heavily muffled, yet his Welsh lilts floating across the Square from the microphones, speaking as he had spoken of old, before the war, against unemployment, with banners waving, in those days even a banner bearing the portrait of Joe Stalin held high behind him.

When he had fallen ill and left hospital after an operation he had made a comment that I often use, as possibly do others. He had agreed to be interviewed by the press on condition that politics would not be mentioned and the interview had ranged widely on what he might or should be reading. '*Newspapers, of course,*' he said. '*I read avidly. It is my one form of continuous fiction.*' Many of the newspapers had not liked this and had taken it as confirmation that he was back to rude health.

On the day after his death – 6 July 1960 – I had been travelling from London to Newcastle by train to begin yet another journey through life, not a political journey, not even a writer's journey, but to marry and settle, my future wife meeting me at Newcastle Central Station. The pit village seemed a long way off now, as did the meeting in the City Hall, but to my astonishment the newspapers I had read on the journey north had nothing but praise for Nye Bevan, for his life and his work.

In his time he had not only been decried and vilified; he had been considered a threat to the British constitution. He had once called Conservatives 'lower than vermin', an attack which he regretted and from which he would never recover; he was reputedly '*eaten away by ambition and class hatred*'; but on his death he became '*a brilliant orator, a true democrat, a loved British character*'. Or as Walter Terry would write in *The Daily Mail*, '*the roistering, excitable crusader who more than once split the party had become the great unifying force.*'

Nye would be taken back to Tredegar, to his pit village, his cremation service would be held within the confines of his family, a memorial service would be held, and the ashes would be scattered, as Michael Foot would write, '*high on the mountain above the Duffryn valley underneath the mountain ash and where the bluebells grew; that was the wild place which, from his youth, he had loved most of all*'.

Nye had been told he might recover from his operation in the Royal Free Hospital, but Michael would reflect that if the cause of cancer from which Nye Bevan had died could be discovered, '*it would be found to be inextricably connected with mental distress and frustration. It seems almost certain that the political agonies he had endured contributed to his physical destruction*'.

In other words, the Labour Party killed Nye Bevan.

When he had himself become Leader, Michael Foot had taken Tony Blair under his wing. He had canvassed for him when Tony had fought and lost a no-hope by-election in Beaconsfield; he would later remark of Tony's ascent that anyone who had joined the Labour Party when he had been Leader could hardly have been acting out of ambition; and he would call upon Tony's skills as a barrister when Labour had been confronted with the entrysm of the Militant Tendency. Tony himself would recall a conversation after the 1983 General Election between himself, Michael and Jim Mortimer who had been Labour's National Secretary at the time.

'If the Election had lasted a day or two longer,' Jim had said. 'We would have won!'

'Jim,' Tony had replied. 'If the Election had lasted a day or two longer we would have been wiped out!'

Perhaps all these things passed through Michael Foot's mind as he unveiled the bust to Nye Bevan.

Perhaps he thought of his early Bevanite work, *Keep Left*, that he had signed with Donald Bruce, of his two-volume life of Nye Bevan, how Nye had kept alive the democratic socialist creed, how he had sought to explain the national mourning: '*It had not been confined to his political friends or his own Party; it burst all banks and frontiers. It was maybe a sense of national guilt, a belief that he had been cheated of his own destiny, that some part of his greatness had been thrown away*'. Or perhaps Michael had been thinking of another of Nye's phrases, as true today as the day he had said it:

'*It's no use*,' he had said. '*Waving banners at a by-gone age.*'

I looked up and found Tony Blair glancing my way.

I smiled at him. And he smiled at me.

And perhaps the bust smiled at us both.

Journey's End for Tony

Tony had played Captain Stanhope in *Journey's End*.

He had played the part in a house play at Fettes College in Edinburgh. According to the school review, he played Captain Stanhope with *'febrile intensity, wiring himself into his ever more circumscribed troglodyte world, speculating moodily'*. His house tutor had said that he had been brilliant and with his height and diction, in Army uniform, he would have made a splendid Captain Stanhope.

I had seen *Journey's End* at the Whitehall Theatre, on a spring evening, returning from Belfast when I had been Labour's front-bench Northern Ireland spokesman. I would enjoy my stint on Northern Ireland and recall my first visit to Belfast when the local people talked to me of King Billie: I had thought in my simplicity that they were referring to a local bookie. When I visited Dublin I would be shown where there had been an attack on the local post office, where a shot had been fired across one of the bridges over the Liffey, and when I had professed to having missed this in the newspapers, and enquired when this had happened, I had been told:

'Nineteen fifteen!'

I had been in the post a year when I heard there were to be front-bench changes. John Smith had been Shadow Secretary of State for Trade and Industry and Geoffrey

Robinson MP had wished to leave his front-bench team to pursue his outside interests. Geoffrey had been nervous for some while that these interests were crowding out his Parliamentary performance and as Secretary to the Solidarity Group I had interceded with John on Geoffrey's behalf.

'I'm not chasing him,' John had said.

Nevertheless Geoffrey would retire to the back benches and make way for Gordon Brown, a significant move at the time, sending Gordon on his way, but creating a bond of gratitude between Gordon and Geoffrey that would live on into the years of a New Labour government. I had heard of these changes and asked John Smith whether he felt it wise that I should stay with the Northern Ireland portfolio.

'If there are changes,' I said. 'I want to be part of them.'

'There are lots of brownie points staying in Northern Ireland,' John had said. 'As a barrister, you'll know all about making bricks without straw.'

'We'll get you out of there soon enough,' Roy Hattersley promised on my appointment, but I would stay with Northern Ireland until the General Election 1987. The redeeming feature of my shadow years had been in persuading the Labour Party to accept the Anglo-Irish Agreement, thus ensuring broad all-Party support across the floor of the House.

The Agreement had never been accepted by Unionist politicians, since it provided for cross-border consultation with the government of the Republic of Ireland. It is a measure how far we have come in so few years that until the signing of this Agreement there had been no contact at all north and south of the Irish border, no politician from the north ever visited the south and none from the south the north.

This Agreement would lead to the possibility of a Good

Friday Agreement entitling full devolution for Northern Ireland, encompassing the aspirations of both the Nationalist community, who essentially wish for a United Ireland, and the Unionist community who wish to stay within the United Kingdom. However, it had changed the nature of the governance of Northern Ireland; it had created a condominium arrangement, a fact which I had pointed out on the floor of the House and at Stormont in Belfast when I had visited the Assembly.

I had flown from Newcastle Airport rather than from Heathrow and for reasons of security would always fly into Belfast under an assumed name. The name that had been designated me this trip had been Blair. This had confused the security officers at Newcastle Airport who looking at me, looking at my passport, looking at my ticket, with its assumed name, asked:

'Why are you masquerading as Tony Blair?'

On one trip to Belfast I had decided to combine this with a train journey to Dublin.

I enjoy train journeys and in those days particularly enjoyed the hearty breakfast available, certainly on the train from King's Cross to Darlington, so popular with travellers that you had to book a seat prior to departure. I had sought to book my seat on the Belfast to Dublin train, I had especially asked that the seat be in the restaurant car, but no bookings had been possible, and so I had arrived early at the station to ensure my seat.

Even when I had bought my ticket I had been apprehensive that the restaurant car would be fully booked.

'You're sure I don't need a reservation?' I asked.

'Absolutely certain,' said the ticket agent.

'How can you be so certain?' I asked.

'Because you're the only one on the train!'

As it made its way slowly through IRA country, with IRA

slogans on the walls of the houses, recalling that the train had often been derailed or hi-jacked, I could understand now the reluctance of passengers to travel south in its comfort. I had to wait till the chef and the staff had their own breakfast before I was served mine, but as I stared out at the images of camouflaged men carrying Armalites I did the best I could to enjoy my Ulster fry.

The ratification of the Anglo-Irish Agreement would turn out to be a high point in my Parliamentary career, though I had not seen this at the time. I had been called upon to wind-up the debate to a full House of Commons, speaking for half an hour, holding the attention of the House so that MPs did not talk among themselves, the House so crowded that front-benchers like Tony Blair had not been able to find a seat and had stood by the Speaker's chair. The high point had been that never again would I wind-up a debate on the floor of the House.

'Ten marks out of ten!' Neil Kinnock had said when I sat down.

I had stopped off to see *Journey's End* not because Tony had played Captain Stanhope but because I had first heard the play on the wireless as a child. There would be no television in our pit village until the fifties, the wireless would be a great source of family entertainment, and late on a dark night I would listen to the *Man in Black* with Valentine Dyall, the voice and story so scary I would race up the stairs to bed and hide my head under the clothes.

There were comedy programmes such as *Take It From Here* on a Tuesday night at seven-thirty, the programmes lasting no more than half an hour, the comedians Dick Bentley and Jimmy Edwards and Joy Nichols, a favourite with my sister. There had been *Dick Barton Special Agent* every night at a quarter-to-seven, with Jock and Snowy, and I recall one particular evening they were hauling themselves over the Himalayas on a yak, with snow and wind so realistic I could almost feel them in my sitting room with the fire to my back.

'They're not in the Himalayas at all,' my sister said.

'Why eye they are!'

'They're in a studio. One man blows the wind and another beats a drum. They're all standing around a microphone!'

Such are childhood illusions destroyed, but such was the hold of Dick Barton that when we played football around our ring, not with a ball but a piece of coal, the window would have to be open and the sound turned up so that I could both play my game of football and listen to the episode at one and the same time. There was a severe childhood crisis when *Dick Barton Special Agent* – played by Duncan Carse – was replaced by *The Archers*, which plays to this day, though quarter of an hour later.

There would be boxing matches commentated by Raymond Glendenning, who would also commentate the F.A. Cup Final, calling one player in one Final: 'What an arse!' We learned later this was the Southern way of pronouncing ass, but it struck me as daring and exciting coming as it did over the air waves. There would be Bruce Woodcock, heavyweight champion, and I recall his fight with Gus Lesnevich at Haringey Arena when I was only eight years old: the exact date 17 September 1946, as I would learn from Woodcock's obituary.

Bruce would of course retire but in 1963 he would tell a story which has stayed with me all my life. He had wanted to buy a Jaguar car but he had thought the car too expensive. He had heard like the rest of us of the assassination of

John Fitzgerald Kennedy, understood the shortness of life, the inevitability of death, and had walked into the nearest Jaguar dealership to buy his car. He had no longer wished to store up his riches where dust or moth might consume.

I would listen, too, to *Saturday Night Theatre*.

There would be Bernard Shaw's *Devil's Disciple*; a play about the American song writer, Stephen Foster, who had written such notables as *The Old Folks at Home* and *My Kentucky Home*; he had written too *Beautiful Dreamer* and *Jeannie with the Light Brown Hair*. His talents had been lost to a sea of alcohol and an early death, but his songs would enjoy a revival almost a hundred years later when their copyright expired.

There would be *On the Spot* by Edgar Wallace, a play around a villain based on the life of the Chicago gangster Al Capone, where a detective seeks to nail the villain but cannot find the evidence. The villain in the play has an Oriental girlfriend, devoted, loyal, subservient, but the detective tells her that she will know her affair with the villain is over when he finds another girl and asks back the jewellery he has given her 'so that it can be cleaned'. When this happens she commits suicide. She leaves a suicide note but the detective tears it up and he gets the villain for murder.

The only crime he did not commit.

Gladys Cooper would be one of the regular stars of *Saturday Night Theatre*, though I cannot now recall the parts she played; but one play I do recall is *Journey's End*, set in a dug-out in the British trenches before St Quentin. The play is set in March 1918, only a few months before the end of the war. It had been written by R. C. Sherriff, who had joined the Army at the outbreak of the war and served as a Captain in the East Surrey Regiment.

Sherriff escaped both the war and the Spanish 'flu, as

it came to be called, that swept the world and killed twenty million people; it killed more American soldiers in France than the war itself. The play would be produced in 1929. Bernard Shaw had recommended that it be put on stage, though he felt that *Journey's End* was more a documentary than a drama: '*The war had produced several such documentaries*,' he wrote. '*They required a good descriptive reporter, with a knack of dialogue, with accounts of catastrophes and sketches of trench life that were useful as correctives to the romantic conception of war.*'

Captain Stanhope, the hero of the play, had first been played by Laurence Olivier. The wireless version had left a strong impression upon my childish imagination, but all that I would recall would be one particular scene where Captain Stanhope comes to the dug-out for the first time to find his fellow officers in a high state of mirth and revelry, raucous and inebriated.

'How can this be?' he asked.

He is taken aside and told the awful truth.

'Because we're all going to die!'

The life expectancy of an officer in the trenches would be no more than six months and that of a private no more than three. My father had been called up in his eighteenth year, just as the war was ending, at about the same time as the setting of *Journey's End*; he would tell me of his war-time experience, how he had gone with other lads from the village; how some had wearied of the mud in the French camp and volunteered for the Front; how he and his best friend from the village had counselled caution and remained behind; and that when the war had ended he had marched from France into Belgium as the Germans retreated.

My father would describe the march and the vineyards the Germans had cleverly booby-trapped and he would describe, too, the voyage home across the English Channel. A band of Highlanders had been discontented with the food; they had attacked the galley and bound up the cooks. They had barricaded themselves in and refused to move. They had threatened to cut the throats of the cooks if anyone tried to enter.

'It was more scary than the war,' my father recalled.

During the last two days of the voyage the rest of the boat had lived on tinned meat and raw vegetables the rebels condescended to throw out; but having survived the war fighting the enemy they preferred this to hazarding their lives fighting their own. The mutineers were much chastened by the time they reached port, but they were still holding out when the ship unloaded, and it was not till the last bottle of beer had been drunk, the last tin thrown out of the porthole, that eventually they gave themselves up.

'What had happened to them?'

'Whee can tell,' my father replied.

I have a photograph of my father, taken at the end of the war, which hangs upon my office wall in my home in Middlesbrough, a large photograph more like a sepia portrait, taken in his eighteenth year, his dark hair neatly-partened but thin, a fore-runner of his baldness, his face handsome, settled, reflecting his quiet nature, the uniform tightly-buttoned, the buttons large and polished, a button to the top of each pocket.

Fortunately for me, born so many years later, there had been no *Journey's End* in Flanders fields.

Winston Churchill had come to see *Journey's End* when it had first been produced.

He had been Chancellor of the Exchequer, but he had

also served for a while in the war as a Colonel and would recall how on visiting the trenches a shell had exploded no more than fifty yards away. He would have been familiar with the officers' dug-out as it appeared in Sherriff's play. He caused a letter to be written to the theatre from Treasury chambers making a number of points.

Why had the sergeant-major thought it odd that a character in the play, when wounded, should be brought to the Company's dug-out? Why had Captain Stanhope asked for this character immediately afterward? Had it been his intention to send him down the line again? I mentioned to Churchill's grand-son, Nicholas Soames MP, then a Minister of the Crown, how impressed I had been that Churchill would take time off to cause such a letter to be written. Perhaps it showed that politicians in those days were interested in other things than politics, or that they had more time to spare.

Or perhaps that Churchill had more intellectual curiosity than the others.

There had also been *All Quiet on the Western Front*, a film from the book by Erich Maria Remarque; I had seen this too as a child in our village picture house. Remarque, who would marry the American film actress Paulette Goddard, had served in the First World War on the German side. I would read his book later, but the film had made a strong impression, telling the story of a class of teenage schoolboys excited and enthralled at the thought of war, manically encouraged by their teacher who would incite them to sign up to fight for the Fatherland.

The boys all signed with great enthusiasm and the entire class would be killed save one, who would be the hero of the film. He would return to his village on leave, or to recover from a wound; he would find the master still inciting his new pupils, using the same manic rhetoric, the same misconceived patriotism. He would return to the Front to be killed on the final day of fighting, leaning over a parapet because he had seen a fragile butterfly that had rested upon a sandbag. The collection of butterflies had been his hobby, he had a book filled with them, their fragile wings neatly pasted into the pages; but as he leans forward to catch the butterfly, his fingers outstretched, a shot rings out and he is killed by a sniper's bullet.

The report to the High Command that day was that it had been 'All Quiet on the Western Front'.

Tony Blair had not only played in *Journey's End* when at Fettes; he had formed his own acting group and they had presented two of the plays of Harold Pinter, the *Dumb Waiter* and *Trouble at the Works*. He had also played Drinkwater in Shaw's *Brassbound Conversion*, a play I would see years later at Her Majesty's Theatre with Ingrid Bergman playing Lady Cicely. Tony had even played Marc Antony in *Julius Ceasar* and the school magazine would say that '*as the instrument of Ceasar's revenge, Blair emerged as a somewhat youthful Antony, but nevertheless a very promising actor who should prove indispensable for school productions in the next few years*'.

In 1980 I had visited the United States during the Presidential election.

I had wanted Jimmy Carter to be returned to office, but he had been defeated by Ronnie Reagan. Reagan had made some fifty films, most of them in black and white, many of them passing across our screen in the village picture house where I had gone three times a week; they were called B-movies and Reagan would be the object of much sarcasm that he had once been an actor before taking charge of the Actor's Guild and then becoming Governor of California from 1967 through 1974.

A friend of mine remarked during the election that

in a television age it would only be a matter of time before an actor became President of the United States. The actor had consummate political skills, struck a chord with the American people, and his acting skills had been subordinated to his politics rather than the other way round. My friend had meant this as a joke, but I had been reminded of this when Tony Blair as Prime Minister read the lesson from Corinthians at the funeral service of Diana, Princess of Wales in Westminster Abbey.

Tony had stood as he would in the Commons, using his full height, his shoulders back, his voice soft and modulated, every word audible, his diction perfect, addressing not the congregation but the nation, not afraid, not diffident, changing the word 'charity' in Corinthians to 'love', reaching out with solemnity and dignity to those who might see him but where he could not see them.

Neither the Archbishop of Canterbury nor the singer Elton John would achieve the same perfection. The Archbishop had a word or two out of order from his prepared text and Elton John choked as he sang the last verse of his song, *Candle in the Wind*, the words having been changed at the last moment for the occasion, yet so poignant that in the mind's eye there were indeed the flames of candles shivering in the wind.

Only Tony had been word perfect.

Captain Stanhope had paid off for him in the end.

A Walk Down Whickham Bank

'What will you do,' Margaret asked. 'If you don't get into the government?'

'I'll go for a walk,' I said. 'Down Whickham Bank.'

On the day after the 1997 General Election, Tony Blair had made his way to Buckingham Palace from his home in Islington. New Labour had won with a landslide. All the world loves a winner and they loved Tony Blair as the car made its way slowly through cheering crowds, through the Palace gates, through the porticos into the Palace itself, up the red-carpeted staircase, wide as a river, to meet the Queen herself.

A new Prime Minister is required to kiss the hands of the Monarch, though it has been known for at least one Prime Minister to overlook this, no doubt in the excitement of the moment, causing in this instance the King to write that if they had not kissed hands perhaps they could take it that they had. There is no record whether the Queen asked Tony to kiss her hands, whether the hands had been gloved, or whether she had dispensed with the formality. Her first Prime Minister had been Winston Churchill and in the none too distant future she would celebrate fifty years on the throne.

When Tony had returned to Downing Street, or rather when he set foot in Ten Downing Street for only the second

117

time in his political life, such had been the parsimony of invitations from his Conservative predecessors, there would be more crowds, not spontaneous crowds, specially-organised crowds, Labour Party workers and their children, but unashamed in their Union Jack hats and waving their Union Jack flags, no Hammers or Sickles here, no red flags flying as they had done in the hymn to the Labour Party from its birth, a modern party for a modern age, a young party for a young people.

And a young Prime Minister for a young nation.

Tony would make his more important appointments early, including Margaret Beckett as President of the Board of Trade, though the title would soon be changed to Secretary of State for Trade and Industry. I had been in her front-bench team for two years now, since she had taken over from Jack Cunningham. The question had often been asked of me whether those shadows in opposition would come into the sunlight in government, taking on the portfolios they had been shadowing, and though this had been the general idea it was not always likely to happen.

I called a friend in Tony Blair's private office.

'Probably you'll be doing what you're doing now,' he said.

That meant I would be Minister of State for Trade with responsibility for City matters, such as accountancy and corporate governance, two jobs in one, which I did not expect. I did expect to be Minister of State for Trade. I had held this particular brief for five years, I had written tomes on the European single market and the World Trade Organisation. I had put forward innovative ideas for an Export Forum. I had made speeches up and down the land. I had made speeches in Paris and New York.

I had persuaded the City that New Labour was a safe bet.

118

I had made a note to myself: '*I have no doubt at all that I shall be appointed Trade Minister tomorrow. But since I am not controlling events but being controlled by them – a situation to which I am not really accustomed – and should I be wrong – I shall stay a Member of Parliament and a writer.*'

My call to the friend in Tony's office had been interrupted by another phone ringing in the house and I had called him back. I gave him every opportunity to indicate that this was his view, not necessarily the view of the new Prime Minister, that there was many a slip between cup and lip, changes might be made, I should not build up my hopes, but he said none of these things.

I broke the news to Margaret and Malcolm.

There had been joy to their faces, that their husband and father would be Minister of the Crown, the absolute delight that shone back at me, from their eyes and from their smiles, all this had made the sharing of the knowledge worthwhile. Margaret and I had been together now for the whole of my political career, some twenty-one years; Malcolm, aged fifteen, had not known his father other than as a Member of Parliament who would spend three and four days every week at Westminster, away from the family home.

They had shared the highs and lows of my political career, *les rayons et les ombres* as Victor Hugo would entitle a book of his poems, but now too they would share in my political success. Never mind that to be a Minister of the Crown meant that I would work harder, be more tired, be at home less, travel abroad more, attend more conferences, see little of either of them, that I might become nothing more than a voice on the telephone.

'Don't tell anyone else,' Margaret said cautiously.

On Saturday morning a senior civil servant called from the Department of Trade and Industry to say that my files

119

were ready in the Department, they had all been prepared in accordance with my policies, the civil servants were standing by, even though this was a holiday weekend, and they would be pleased to come to the Department if I felt I needed them. They would even be prepared to come in on the Bank Holiday Monday.

'Have you heard from the Permanent Secretary?' he asked.

'Not yet,' I said.

'Have you heard from anybody?'

'I have an indication.'

There would be no need, I said, to come in over the weekend; we had worked hard enough and long enough to know where we stood on policy, it was all in the documents anyway; but I wondered out loud with Margaret whether I should indeed drive down to London, to be in the Department on Sunday, to hit the ground running as it were.

This would be my first and last Ministerial decision.

In the week before the Election, Margaret Beckett had authorised me to give interviews on what our policies would be when we formed a government, and there had been more calls this Saturday morning from Sunday newspapers. In responding to these, I reflected my wife's caution and whilst giving a steer to some of the stories advised that I had not heard from the Prime Minister, and they should not use my name. It had been a sunny Saturday morning, the front door had stood open, flowers were out in the garden; a constituent from down the street had come in, sitting in our living room, enjoying the moment when I had taken the call from the civil servant, anticipation like pollen in the air.

Margaret Beckett called at lunchtime.

'Should I call you Madam President,' I asked. 'Or should I call you Margaret?'

120

'Call me Margaret,' she said.

She explained that she had seen Tony at Ten Downing Street and that he had said he wished to reduce the number in the Trade and Industry team. She had pointed out that the team was well established, it had the confidence of business and the City, and that to change it would be unwise. She said that the point had been 'well taken' and she was calling to let me know the position. She had also called other members of the team. We had a pleasant enough chat, she had been thoughtful in calling, but when I put down the phone I knew that my chances of being a Minister had decreased.

I also knew Tony.

The point might be 'well taken', but he would already have made up his mind, the Ministerial lists would have been prepared before the General Election; he would not be changing his mind now, not with a majority of one hundred-and-seventy behind him; he was a young man who knew what he wanted; and though we might have been friends from before he had found for himself a seat, this not only would count for little but should not count for anything at all.

'I'm entirely in his hands,' I said.

'Where is Whickham Bank anyway?' Margaret asked.

On leaving the grammar school, I had written to the *Newcastle Evening Chronicle* seeking a job as junior reporter. It was known that the *Chronicle* took on two juniors a year. In my fifteenth year, I had gone to school camp at Killin in Scotland and decided I would lie awake all night until I knew what I wanted to do with my life. Fireman? Postman? Civil servant? What career did I want?

Within a few seconds of settling on my palliasse, I decided I wanted to be a writer and fell asleep immediately.

I felt I was too young to write novels, though I had already written a series of short stories; I had written my very first short story at the age of eight, an account of a fictitious football match. But if I was too young to write novels I would begin as a newspaper reporter. I felt I would not be ready to write my first novel till I was around twenty years old. This turned out to be about right.

I had raised my future career tentatively with my mother.

'I want to be a newspaper reporter,' I said.

'That's not for the likes of us,' my mother had replied. 'We're pit folk.'

She had also said that she and my father had kept me for sixteen years and it would be time that I kept them. I had not demurred. This was the philosophy of the pit village. I did not hold it against her. Years later, when I was written up by *The Daily Mail*, the first part of my views had been imparted but not the second, causing a family rift with my brother and sister, who felt I had demeaned the memory of our dead mother.

The fact is, however, I did leave school at sixteen, even though I had no job to go to, returning after the school holidays, from habit really, but no-one urging me to stay on to sit my A-levels or go to university. I had at least been given an interview with the *Evening Chronicle*, meeting Arthur Wilson, their News Editor. I had made sufficient impression to be short-listed and had returned to the *Chronicle* offices in Kemsley House, as their building had then been known, wondering how best I might enhance my chances.

I was neatly turned out, with flannels and dark blue blazer, white handkerchief to my top pocket, my fair hair brushed back and parted, but I knew this might not be enough; I might need something extra. I had gone into the School Furnishing bookshop and bought myself a paperback which I had pushed into my pocket. I had wanted to show Arthur Wilson that I had a hunger for knowledge, a thirst to get on, that my education would continue even though I had left school.

'Oh!' had been his succinct response.

I had not felt that I was likely to get the job and, not hearing further from the *Chronicle*, I had called Arthur Wilson from the telephone box at the opposite end of the village from my home, the box standing across from the Cooperative Store and next to the newsagent's. You had to put pennies in the box in those days; there was an A and B button, the one to release the pennies, the other to get your pennies back if the call did not go through. Nor did you dial directly but passed through an operator.

'You didn't get the job, you know,' Arthur Wilson said.

'I didn't think so,' I said. 'Not havin' heard, like.'

'I hear the *Shields Gazette* are looking for juniors.'

South Shields was a long way from my pit village, a bus into Newcastle, across the city and another bus to South Shields; the journey could not be done daily and if I were to apply for the job and get it I would have to leave home. Could I make such a sacrifice at sixteen? My mother and sister had been doing the washing when I had returned home and told them that I might need to move to Shields. My mother had refused outright to countenance the idea; I had gone for a walk around our local fell to think things through and had returned home, resolved that I would indeed write to the *Shields Gazette*.

My mother's attitude had changed by the time I returned, my sister had put in a good word for me, and I wrote to the newspaper. On this occasion, however, I did not even get an interview. I was not returning to school, I was not going to be a newspaper reporter. What was I going to do? I am not aware that I had any plan or strategy, but my Aunt Jane burst into our living room to say that Frankie Backhouse, formerly of my grammar school, now colliery clerk at Chopwell, would be leaving to do his National Service and they were looking for a replacement. National Service consisted of an obligatory two years in Her Majesty's armed forces.

Without hesitation, I went to the second call box in the village, the one closest to my home, opposite another Cooperative Store in Hookergate Lane, by the bus stop, and called the colliery office. They asked me to write to Area Six of the National Coal Board. By then I knew that I had five O-levels to my credit – English Literature, English Language, History, Geography and Scripture – and soon I was called for a medical. This had been a perfunctory examination of a sixteen-year-old with nothing wrong with him, and in a few weeks I was taking the two-mile bus ride to Chopwell to work in the colliery office.

Little Moscow and me would become as one.

I would work nine months in the office, formative months that would stay with me for years to come. It would complete my life in the pit village, not only the son of a pitman, born into a mining family, but would add the experience, not of working underground, but working on bank, no anthracite blue to the cuts in my skin, but looking down from the colliery office to the headstock, the screens, the maintenance sheds, the hoppers, wagons loading for the journey down railway lines shiny with use, the clang of the steel gates as men descended or rose from the earth.

There would be the daily tonnages book to keep, the sick notes to receive and log, concessionary coal books to mark; there would be queries from the men on their wages, knocking as they did on the wooden panels of a closed box window to the office, sometimes waiting patiently if I were on the phone, even though they stood black and weary from the pit. There would be time sheets to prepare. We worked five and a half days, the office would be full Saturday morning with officials and deputies and overmen as well as clerks and surveyors and linesmen, many of them standing with their backs to the large fire that always burned in the grate, warming the backs to their legs on chill winter days.

There would be records of those entitled to a colliery house, or the swap of a house, and there was also the sad duty, when a man was killed in the pit, to visit his home and have his wife sign over papers dealing with insurance and the like. There had been only one fatality in my time in the office, but the widow – of the same name as myself – had not been able to read or write, and had signed the papers with a cross. There would be consultative meetings not to attend but to write up, though the colliery clerk Jimmy Robinson would do these whilst I solidly practised the touch-typing I was also learning at Blaydon grammar school evening classes.

I would either return to my own village at lunch-time, catching the bus there and back, or bring sandwiches, having them on the sloping desk with the fire to the front of me, or by the typewriter as I not only practised my typing but wrote a short story. The story had something to do with the building of pylons from the new power station at Stella, near Blaydon; there had been violence in the work camps, and when one of the surveyors came in and read the description of a particularly gruesome fight he was so tickled by the lurid language he wanted me to bring it next door and read it to the other surveyors and linesmen who were his colleagues.

125

I knew the work had no merit and declined.

Besides, their giggles would have been too much to bear.

I would not make a successful junior clerk, my mind was always elsewhere, on the next story I wanted to write, on the next piece of news to file to the newspapers. My copy would one day end on the front page of the *Newcastle Journal* when a snow storm had cut off the village, buses could not get through, burst pipes had flooded sitting rooms, a flood had cascaded into the dining room of the chief surveyor, and I had walked home through the snow, the wind so harsh and biting it would give me ear-ache in my right ear.

I would do my lineage not only for the *Blaydon Courier* and *Coal Magazine* but also for the *Kemsley Press*, that is the *Evening Chronicle*, the *Newcastle Journal* and the *Sunday Sun*. My football reports of a Saturday would go to the *Evening Chronicle* as well as the *Blaydon Courier*. Newspaper stories would include the derailment of the colliery coal wagons on their way to the staiths in the valley, the opening of a centre for St John's Ambulance, the sad story of a woman who would lose her son when an RAF Shackleton crashed into the sea and he had been a crew member.

I would meet Bert Horsfall.

Bert would be a tall stocky man with sandy hair and moustache. He would do lineage himself, that is he would work for the *Evening Chronicle* but sell the same story to the national newspapers. He would leave the Tyne Valley in 1963 to live in Arenal, Majorca, owning a club called the *Ali Baba*, and years later I would see a story under his by-line on the front page of the *Sunday Express*, a true name from the past. The story dealt with the happenings of the crew of an American aircraft carrier which had apparently docked at a Spanish port.

126

Bert would be known for his colourful stories, and though I would meet him briefly again in the seventies, when he had asked me to market some novels he had written, but which he did not wish to publish himself, I would not see him before his sudden death in Newcastle where he had returned to live in his mother's house. In fact, he had returned on his sixty-fifth birthday to claim a bus pass. He had been swimming in the local baths and had died before he could see in the millennium.

There would be Jimmy Dumighan.

Jimmy had been general and sports reporter to the *Blaydon Courier* when I had begun my lineage and I had asked to meet him. We had agreed to meet at a social club off the Highfield football ground, not two miles from my home, and I can see him now with his dark wavy hair, his brown scarf and his kid gloves, looking very much the part, though he was only eighteen. He made not a note of the match yet reported it accurately from memory in the next week's edition of the *Courier*.

When Jimmy went to do his National Service, I went to Consett to see the Editor of the *Blaydon Courier*. A business man, Ramsden Williams, had owned the *Consett Guardian* as well as the *Blaydon Courier*, both newspapers long defunct, but both had been published at Consett. The Editor had been an old man who had spent his entire life in newspapers, and local newspapers at that, and he had offered me the job at something above four pounds a week. I had been paid two pounds seventeen shillings and fivepence in the colliery office.

I had been nervous about handing in my notice.

So nervous, in fact, that I did not dare mention it to the colliery clerk Jimmy Robinson, and only after returning home for lunch, getting the bus back again to Chopwell, did I summon the courage to tell Jimmy that I was leaving.

I blurted it out, sitting on my high chair with my hands on the sloping top of the desk. He asked that I write my notice for the colliery manager and I did, noting that it was my seventeenth birthday.

'Where've ye been fixed up?' Jimmy asked.

'The *Blaydon Courier*,' I said.

'Ye're deein' the reet thing,' he said. 'There's nowt here.'

Nor had my departure from the colliery office pleased my father.

He had worked in all the pits in the area, now he had worked at Chopwell Colliery and it was an honour, a pride and joy, to have his son in the colliery office rather than with him down the pit. Perhaps he thought that it was a job for life, but the pits would close, and the office too, Jimmy Robinson had been right and there would be no security looking from the wide windows towards the Derwent Valley and upward to the Consett Iron Works, with its iodine cloud hanging heavy over the houses stapling towards the Valley floor.

Even at the *Blaydon Courier* I had continued my lineage for the *Kemsley Press*. The *Courier* had been a weekly newspaper that came out on a Friday, I would work out of the Blaydon office overlooking the engineering works a target for German bombers during the war, with the Tyne flowing beyond, leaden in the dull light. The office would be small, only a single room, no facilities that I can recall, the window smeared with dust and grime, no-one to clean it. In later years, thinking of the grime, I regretted that I had not brought my mother down to clean the window for me, but it would stay that way till I left.

My lineage had been my undoing.

It had been common if dubious practice for weekly newspaper reporters to lift stories from their own newspapers and file them with national or regional newspapers. On what must have been my first week on the *Blaydon Courier* a story appeared on its front page, written by a second reporter – there had been two of us in the office at the time – about a cripple girl, a picture of the girl running alongside the copy.

I cannot now recall the precise nature of the story, but I casually re-wrote the copy and sent it to the *Newcastle Journal*. The news editor had been excited by it; it had been more than run-of-the-mill. He had sent to Blaydon a reporter and a photographer and the cripple girl had sweetly said how nice it was to see them, since her story had already appeared on the front page of the last edition of the *Blaydon Courier*.

The Journal banned me from filing any further copy.

It had been a summer's night and I had been to Whickham, sitting as it does above Newcastle, to attend a Council meeting, since Whickham was in our circulation area. I had no car and travelled everywhere by bus. I had arrived late. A junior reporter from the *Chronicle* had covered the proceedings, not that they ever took long, for the minutes of the meeting were all prepared, this was a Labour-controlled Council, the stories would be in the minutes, in decisions already taken, and with a few nods of the head the meeting would be over and we would all be back in the sunlight.

'Did I miss anything?' I asked.

'Just lift it from the *Chronicle*,' the junior reporter replied.

I had another story that night for *The Journal* which I would file from the telephone box at the top of Whickham Bank, but when I was put through to the copy-taker he told me they had instructions not to take any further copy from me. He could give no reason. Later I would find out through the second reporter at the *Blaydon Courier* that *The Journal*

had been irked when they discovered the story I had filed
had already appeared on our very own front page.

The fact that *The Journal* would take no further copy
devastated me.

At seventeen-years-old, I had managed to get myself a
job on a newspaper within a year of trying, no mean
achievement when there were no television or radio outlets,
only the local newspapers. I had a full-time job on the
Courier and could still file my newspaper reports to the
Chronicle on a Saturday and any immediate news stories
to the *Kemsley* newspapers. I could still write for *Coal
Magazine*.

And I could follow in the steps of Bert Horsfall and file
worthy copy for the nationals.

I walked down Whickham Bank from the telephone box
to Swalwell, where I would take the bus home. My sense
of devastation would not dissipate. My life had come apart.
I had collected in my bedroom at home a sill-full of pennies
to use when phoning my copy from the local telephone box;
some of the pennies had been more than thirty years old, the
copper black, the pennies lying among dead flies on the sill.
I had walked in the sunshine of a summer's evening to my
local cricket ground, set among woods, where youngsters
were playing as I had played.

My sense of failure was profound.

Soon my shock began to dissipate, my over-reaction
subsided, I still worked for the *Blaydon Courier*, I still
had a future ahead of me, and I reasoned if *The Journal*
had banned my copy this might not be the case either for
the *Evening Chronicle* or the *Sunday Sun*, though they were
in the same group. Perhaps I could still report my football
games. And so it turned out. Except one Saturday I came
across a copytaker brought in from *The Journal*.

'We're not supposed to take your copy,' he said.

'That's *The Journal*,' I said. 'Not the *Chronicle*.'

'Hang on,' he said.

I had waited not patiently but nervously.

'All right,' he had said.

Even *The Journal* would relent.

An eighty-two year old woman had been attacked in her 'lonely' cottage above my village, the cottage standing by the road leading to the bridge over the railway line and the fell. Actually, she had been raped of a Saturday night, but it had been deemed too delicate to announce this fact, and 'attacked' had been sufficient. Given its immediacy, I had phoned the story to *The Journal* and the news editor had asked if I might provide a photograph of the woman. I knew her relatives in the village, came up with a photograph and took it personally into the offices in Newcastle and into the hands of the news editor.

'How've ye done?' he asked.

The photograph appeared on the front page the following morning.

My life had begun again.

Forty-three years later, Margaret and Malcolm and I waited for the phone to ring in our Middlesbrough home.

It rang many times that weekend, from journalists who wanted to know if I had been informed of my portfolio, from friends and family, from others whom I had met in foreign ministries, some of whom called from abroad, one call from Washington, but there was no call from colleagues and none from Downing Street. I had called Roy Hattersley in his Derbyshire home, Roy no longer in the Commons, now a noble Lord, a strong supporter of Blair but not part of any inner circle.

'You know I can't do anything for you,' he said.

'I'm calling for comfort,' I said.

We left Malcolm in charge of the phone and Margaret and I drove to Saltburn, taking with us our mobile, parking above the cliffs, watching the tide go out, a solemn expanse of water stretching tightly towards the horizon, the sea leaving its imprint damp upon the sand and in pools around the rocks, the cliffs flecked a mournful grey in the sunlight.

Other appointments would be made from Downing Street, the Cabinet was completed by Sunday evening, and still without word I had telephoned at home the civil servant who had been so helpful in calling me and indicating that my files were ready. He had given me his phone number in case I needed to contact him over the weekend. What had gone wrong? Had anything gone wrong? I certainly had needed to contact him.

'Not all the appointments have yet been made,' he said. 'By the way, you should think of having a PUS.'

'What's a PUS?' I asked.

'Parliamentary Under-Secretary.'

More appointments were made on Monday and still there came no call from Downing Street.

On Monday evening, when the telephone did ring, it had been my friend and colleague Nick Brown, who had been appointed Government Chief Whip. I had known Nick for twenty years, since his appointment as legal officer to the General and Municipal Workers' Union. He had been my campaign manager when I had sought the European nomination for Northumbria. He had come onto Newcastle City Council with me after the 1979 General Election. He and I had entered the House together in 1983 and he had followed me onto the front bench as Shadow Attorney General.

132

He announced with the utmost regret and genuine sadness that I was not in the government.

He could offer no explanation. I replied that it was obvious I was not in the government since all the appointments had by now been made. He explained the Prime Minister had not rung personally because it would simply have lifted my expectations, only to see them shattered; this had been the case with other unfortunate colleagues; but as a friend of long-standing he would write to me in his own hand. Nick assured me with the government's large majority and the patronage at his disposal I would enjoy being on the government benches, I would enjoy being in Parliament, I would enjoy our great victory and the achievements to come.

'What will you do now?' he asked.

'I'm going for a walk,' I said. 'Down Whickham Bank.'

Book Two

A John Major Story

I told John Major I thought Len Hutton had been the greatest English batsman.

'David Gower would run him close,' John replied.

'Had he the concentration?' I asked.

'He had the stroke play.'

Before the General Election, John had stopped by the smoking room for a chat and drink with colleagues. He had entered the smoking room from the members' dining room and probably he would call by the tea room before a ten o'clock vote. Prime Ministers would often stop by the dining rooms and bars to see their Parliamentary supporters, especially if they had run into difficulties, and this was one of John's trawls.

The smoking room is not as renowned as it used to be among MPs.

Nye Bevan would hold forth from a corner seat overlooking the Thames and when I first became an MP Michael Foot would do the same. He would be no longer Leader of the Opposition but would have many a good story to tell, and sitting with him not at his feet but in the deep horse-hair sofas, aware that Nye Bevan had sat here too, one had a sense of participating in a continuation of Labour history. And of course, when we had placed the bust of Nye Bevan at the bottom of the staircase, it had been Michael Foot who had unveiled it.

Margaret Thatcher would not come into the smoking room; she might have tea in the Tory part of the tea room; and sometimes she would have dinner in the members' dining room. I remember her marching in one evening when it had been full. I had bumped into her on the way out. 'I adore Welsh rarebit,' she declared with startling boldness, handbag at the ready, before again marching past, her Parliamentary Private Secretary trailing behind like ice from a comet's tail.

I cannot recall the particular difficulty that had driven John Major into the ranks of his Parliamentary colleagues, but Jimmy Wray happened to be in the smoking room and when he saw the Prime Minister he asked if he would sign for him a bottle of House of Commons whisky. Jimmy was a Glaswegian MP and explained that the signed bottle would bring a hundred pounds for charity in a raffle at his Scottish club.

'Of course, Jimmy,' the Prime Minister said.

Jimmy went off to find a bottle of whisky and John Major and I chatted about cricket.

It would hardly be appropriate for an Opposition MP to ask the Prime Minister his analysis of the latest political difficulty, how complicated and arduous it must be to govern without a majority, not to have the support of the Tory press, and now to be confronted with Tony Blair as Leader of the Opposition. Far more diplomatic to talk of the sport that he loved and would always love.

He had in his time been an excellent cricketer, winning the *Evening Standard*'s Best Young Cricketer of the Year award for bowling figures of seven-for-nine in a schoolboy match; but his knee had never recovered from an injury sustained in a road accident when twenty in Nigeria. He had spent a year in hospital and had not been able to play cricket again. He had followed the game closely and recounted the story how he had been offered his first Ministerial post on the day England had regained the Ashes from Australia in 1985.

Even as Prime Minister he liked to be told the scores.

'Fortunately,' he said. 'My private secretary was keen on the game and passed them to me.'

He would play in Harare at a Commonwealth conference, scoring five runs, and sometimes when television caught him at the nets, you could tell from the elegant stroke play he would have played the game well. He understood its intricacies and its artistry. Even as Prime Minister he had been offered a role as guest presenter for BBC's *Test Match Special* and there had been talk, should he be a success, of asking him to be a regular guest for radio long-wave coverage.

My own cricketing career could hardly match the promise of that of John Major, though my batting average at the grammar school one summer had been forty-eight. I had been brought up on the batting of Len Hutton and saddened when I learned that, because I had been born in Durham, I could not play for Yorkshire. I had seen Hutton play at Lords' in a *Gentleman v. Players* game, when my father and mother had taken me to London in 1951 for the Festival of Britain.

Hutton scored thirty-three immaculate runs, but Denis Compton scored a hundred-and-fifty. My father would sit through the whole the day's play, from eleven-thirty till six-thirty, but could not persuade me to leave. He had no time for cricket and it showed great devotion as a father that he should allow me to sit through what for him were so many boring hours.

'Do you want to go home now?' he would ask.

'No!' I would shout.

In my childhood, the greatest cricketing influence on me

had not been Len Hutton but Rob Higson, who appeared each summer in the *Rover* comic, one season as a batsman – *It's Runs That Count*; another as a bowler – *It's Wickets That Count*. He would not appear as a fielder but I do recall some great batsman being caught at square-leg because when he came in to bat, take his mark at the crease and look around the field, Rob happened to be fastening his boot-lace behind the square-leg umpire. The batsman had not noticed Rob and lobbed an easy ball to square-leg where Rob caught him out.

We would take our summer holidays at Whitley Bay, staying in a boarding house not far from the sea front. The owner of this boarding house had been a professional cricketer and showed me his bat. It was a proper cricket bat, three springs down the handle, the face dark with linseed oil and cracked from stroke play; I had been so fascinated my father had bought me the bat, just as a year earlier at Cullercoats he had bought me my first football.

My brother would make me another bat, more practical, strapped by steel thread, with no spring or bounce, painted yellow here and there; and with this flashing bat I would score many a run on our field, playing with a composite rubber ball, the ball soaring for a lofty six into the nettles. It was always a painful experience seeking the ball from the nettles, but some of the bigger lads, playing with us on Saturday morning when they were not down the pit, using my first-class cricketer's bat bought in Whitley Bay, would hoist our rubber ball over the allotment greenhouses into my own garden some fifty yards away.

I can remember my first game on a real cricket pitch, playing for the village second-eleven, coming in one from last, as befits a thirteen-year-old, with no white flannels, only a white shirt and jumper and brown trousers tucked into the pads. I remember the first defensive stroke I played;

it came straight out of Len Hutton, my bat straight, my head over the ball; and I can see now the ball onto the bat.

If I had been opening bat for my grammar school I had also been opening bowler.

I had played for the village junior team and had opened the bowling against Colin Milburn; he had been no more than thirteen, small, tubby, rose-coloured cheeks, brown hair and eyes, but with the eye of a hawk and the stealth of a mountain lion; he took every ball I bowled and hauled it around the ground as if playing with a pelota bat, a round basket on the end. He would score seventy in no time and would be out caught on the boundary.

He had left to play for Warwickshire and would earn his first England cap in 1965.

By then I had learned to drive and bought a new car and I had run out of petrol driving down the old A1. It simply had not occurred to me to keep my eye on the petrol gauge whilst listening on the car radio as Milburn sought to score his first hundred. He had been easily run out in the first innings, for a duck I believe, but went on to score a century in his second.

In my teenage years I had been so mad about cricket that, when I became a sports reporter for my local newspaper, I took off one Saturday afternoon to play for my village team when supposedly covering a sports day. I incurred the displeasure of Jack Amos, the news editor of the *Consett Guardian*, who had come by the stadium to see how I was getting on; only to be told by a friendly journalist on another paper that I had made arrangements to lift my copy from him.

And when at school, with two games to play, one in the morning for the school team, another in the afternoon for the village, I found on this particular Saturday I could only fit in one game. I opted to play for the village rather than the

141

school. I should have told the sports teacher of my dilemma; we might have resolved it together. Instead I reported sick and went to play for my village team. I did exceptionally well, taking six wickets against a handful of runs, and was written up in the local Sunday newspaper.

My sports teacher read the report and dropped me from the team.

'Lack of commitment,' he said.

I got my own back on the sports teacher, though not intentionally, when I wrote up cricket matches for the *Blaydon Courier*. His own village team had been having a bad season; he was secretary of the club and did not like a jocular piece I had written which said that his team took to the bottom of the league '*as a duck takes to water*.' He invited me to his home and gave me a ticking off; he had been right to do so and I never denigrated his team again.

After my eighteenth year I would never don another pair of pads or bowl another ball, but in 1957 I would spend a day at the Test Match at the Oval where England played the West Indies. Apart from the career of Colin Milburn, this would be the last real interest I would take in the game for twenty years. Ramadan and Valentine played for the West Indies and David Sheppard had the highest score for England.

He scored a hundred-and-forty-odd that day.

David went into the Church and became Bishop of Liverpool. I would meet him at the General Synod at York shortly before his retirement. 'The last time I saw you,' I said. 'You were opening the batting for England against the West Indies in 1956.'

'It was 1957,' he said. 'The Aussies were here in 1956.'

142

'And you didn't open the batting,' I said. 'Richardson did. He scored a hundred too that day.'

'There were bags of runs,' David said.

David could recall not only the number of Test matches he had played but the scores he had made. He told me how he had begun his cricketing career at Cambridge University and then how he had played for Sussex. He had played twenty-two times for England and had been recalled twice. He should have been captain for the tour of Australia but the selectors had decided upon Hutton. He had gone on to an even more distinguished career in the Church, rising from Bishop Suffragan of Woolwich to Bishop of Liverpool, where he had been for the last twenty years.

I would see Colin Milburn again in London.

His career had come to an end when he had been involved as a passenger in a car crash and lost an eye. The career could never be rebuilt. It had been tragic. He had tried changing his stance, batting with his left hand, but it had not been a success. He had commentated the game for *Radio Four*, with his blunt Geordie accent, but it had been a sad man I would meet at the Sportsman's Club in Tottenham Court Road, where he came for a drink with Freddie Truman and Godfrey Evans, both great English cricketers. He would return to his native north from Warwickshire, but his life would degenerate and his great talent would die with him at the age of forty-eight.

'What happened to Jimmy?' the Prime Minister said.

Jimmy finally came back with his bottle of House of Commons whisky.

Jimmy had been educated in the Gorbals. He had been a goods vehicle driver as well as a member of Stratchlyde Regional Council. He had been involved with St Enoch's drugs centre and Scottish ex-boxers and Gorbals United; he had been Scottish President of an institution for the blind.

He also spoke with a strong Glaswegian accent and when I had been Deputy Chairman of the Inter-Parliamentary Union I persuaded my colleagues to let Jimmy come to Copenhagen to attend an international conference.

'He cannot string two words together,' I was told.

But when Jimmy did attend the conference and spoke on behalf of the British delegation every word had been crystal clear. The ruggedness had gone, the eloquence had been resonant, and his speech well applauded by the delegates. Jimmy would remarry and hold a celebration service in the Crypt within the Palace of Westminster. Afterwards he and his bride would entertain over a hundred guests on the terrace of the House of Lords.

Jimmy would also choose the most beautiful day of the year for his wedding; the sun beat down upon the red canvass awnings of the terrace, the champagne sparkled in the sunshine; the stone balustrades running towards the Commons threw back their heat in a grudging defiance. Later I would see Jimmy and his wife and new-born baby often in the corridors of the Commons while Jimmy awaited a late-night vote.

Now he beamed as the Prime Minister signed his bottle of whisky.

Some weeks later John Major was in difficulty again and came into the members' dining room with John Ward MP, his Parliamentary Private Secretary. I was having dinner in the Labour part of the room with Jimmy Wray and suggested, since the Prime Minister had signed his bottle of whisky, Jimmy might like to send him down a bottle of vintage wine. This he did and the wine was duly delivered to John Major and his party with Jimmy's compliments.

The Prime Minister showed his appreciation by standing and raising his glass.

'To Jimmy Wray,' he said.
'To Len Hutton,' I said.
'To David Gower,' the Prime Minister called back.

A Name Writ in Water

On the day John Major dissolved Parliament and called a General Election for 1 May 1997, Malcolm and I walked from Westminster up Whitehall to Trafalgar Square.

It had been a spring day, the sun warm to the air, the light bright upon the clean stone of Whitehall, reflecting from the roofs of the black taxis and the dull windows of the red London buses as they strained their way to the Square. In the Square the water of the fountains sprayed translucent in the light, the white bubbles at the inner edges contrasting with the green of the outer.

Years ago, when I walked in the evening around Trafalgar Square, standing with my arms folded upon the white balustrade, the National Gallery behind me, I would survey not only the dark of Nelson's Column, for it had not always been white, the fountains with their spray, the tourists sitting on the edge of the fountains, but beyond Whitehall to the tower of Big Ben to see if the light were on above its face.

The light would always shine so long as the Commons were sitting.

In my early days in London I would visit the Commons, following the light as if beckoned down Whitehall to the Parliament buildings. In the evening there would be no queue for the public gallery and I recall a debate one evening where a Minister of the Crown and his Shadow

146

had been having a regular to-do, much to the amusement of the gallery, since the House had been empty at the time.

The Speaker himself had been in the chair, not one of his deputies, and I recall his hands hanging across his knees, the fingers long and white; he wore his black garb, his buckled shoes, his flowing wig. Both Minister and Shadow appealed for his intervention, to protect one from the other, and both sat down to await the Speaker's verdict.

It had been handed down as a Judgement of Solomon.

'Perhaps the protagonists should fight it out among themselves,' he said.

There had been a particular advantage in visiting the House of Commons in the evening to listen to a debate. The Sergeant at Arms' office would offer you not only a ticket to the public gallery but a voucher that would entitle you to go to the Strangers' Cafeteria for a meal when you had walked down the carpeted stairs from the gallery. The food had been cheap and wholesome and pleasant and I had been surprised when, thirty years later, making it back to the Cafeteria, to find that nothing had changed, the small latticed windows overlooking the terrace, the shiny stone frames to the windows, the dust to the ledges, hopefully not the same dust as thirty years earlier.

In all, I would work a little over a year for the *Blaydon Courier* and *Consett Guardian*.

Just as I had gained my job in the colliery office because the junior clerk had left for his National Service, just as Jimmy Dumighan would leave the *Courier* for the same reason, leaving a vacancy for me, so I too would need to do my National Service as the days, weeks and months slipped towards my eighteenth birthday. I had not given thought to whether I should serve in the Army or Air Force, if choice there was, but I knew this would soon be upon me.

I had worked only a few months out of the Blaydon

147

office when a car had stopped on the opposite side of the road – a Morris Minor – and a tall man, far taller than myself, got out and strode across to the office. He was Jon Lander, new managing editor of both the *Blaydon Courier* and the *Consett Guardian*. Jon had been with *The Daily Mail*; had married the daughter of the proprietor of the *Guardian* and the *Courier*; and he had been invited to manage both newspapers. Later Jon would leave to enter television and would work as lobby correspondent in the House of Commons for the *News at Ten*.

He suggested that I leave the Blaydon office where I worked on my own and move to the Consett office. It was no great distance to Consett from my pit village, two bus journeys in fact, a long winding road up the hill leading to the iron works that enveloped the town, not only in its cloud of fumes and dust, but in its work ethic, since most of the men were employed by the Consett Iron Company.

Years later, I would go back to the town for a demonstration led by Labour MPs Dennis Skinner and Bob Cryer opposing the closure of the works; there would be a twenty-six mile march from Consett to Jarrow that would leave me with weak knees for a year. I would make a speech to the local Rotary Club, climbing from the valley floor where the weather had been fine into the low cloud that now covered the town like the dust and fumes of old.

But in those teen-age days I had found a town facing inwards upon itself, not outwards towards the Pennines, ignoring the moors harsh and flat, the blue line of the horizon, the roads like silver strands seeking their way to the west coast. Blaydon had been on the river, facing the sea and the city, the attitudes were different, strange though it may seem, but in an age of bus rather than car, the sea and the city were a long way from Consett and few people ventured so far.

Nor were my newspaper duties inspiring.

I found myself standing outside churches and graveyards getting the names of mourners when a fine upstanding man of the parish had died and was being buried. The government had decided to go for a form of National Lottery through premium bonds, commonplace enough now, but disturbing to the elders of Consett who had sent a missive as important as a telegram to the Prime Minister, raising their objections.

There would be a rail strike during my days at Consett and I would visit the cabin where the workers grouped together over a stove. A future Tory government had the cure for railway strikes in this part of the world; they closed the railways. There was an Orange Club too where I might slip in with my fellow reporters for a lunch-time drink and I would also attend weekly sittings of the magistrates' court.

One day I was able to report to the national newspapers a story of a row in a cinema because, as I recall, a nut from a chocolate bar had gone down the wrong way when being eaten by a woman in the back row; she had made some spluttering protestation, causing a row that led to a fight that ended in the magistrates' court. Perhaps she had been bound over to keep the peace, perhaps not, but nothing so exciting had yet happened at Consett.

The story had played well with readers of the *Daily Sketch*.

I would leave the *Consett Guardian* to free-lance shortly before I was due to be called up for National Service, but I would leave behind two good friends in journalism: Jack Amos, whom I had first seen if not met when he had covered the unfurling of the Chopwell Colliery banner; and Nora Cook, now Nora Warner, a junior like myself, with whom I would share the reporters' office. There was a peculiar facet to the office in that a stream ran between our desks, not a sewer to be sure, but a stream nonetheless.

'Where do you think it's going?' I would ask.

'Where do you think it's been?' Nora replied.

We would never know as we typed our copy for the *Guardian*.

Nora would stay in touch and when I left the *Guardian* and moved beyond the North-East to London she would write to me there. She would be offered a job with the *Shields Gazette*, if not following in my footsteps, for I never did receive such an offer, at least following in the direction I had wanted to travel. What should she do? I replied it was entirely up to her, no-one could make the decision for her, since the benefits would be hers, and the downside too, if there was to be a downside; but I suppose I penned the letter in such a way that she really felt she had no alternative but to take up the offer and advance her career through journalism that would take her to the *Young Reporter of the Year* award and Editor of the *Girl Guides'* newspaper.

Thirty-one years later she would be in touch again when she saw my name in *The Sun* newspaper and wondered if I was the young reporter who had shared an office which had a stream, if not a river, running through it; and since I replied that I was she and I and Jack Amos and Jon Lander and Jim Dumighan would begin to meet up once a year for lunch at the House of Commons, swapping stories, keeping up to date with families, reminiscing, each one remembering something entirely forgotten by the other.

I recall one year photocopying some of Nora's earlier letters to me and returning them to her.

The stream that had run between our desks would become a flood of remembrance, rather like the poem of D.H. Lawrence, except that we did not weep like children for the past, but rather drew pleasure in the success of each and every one of us in our various domains. Jim Dumighan had ended as senior producer with BBC Pebble Mill; he had invited me to Birmingham for lunch one day before his retirement and I would meet Ivy his wife, whom I had last known as a Blaydon telephonist; Jack Amos had worked for the *Evening Chronicle*, he would get my copy into the newspaper when I became Prospective Parliamentary Candidate for Hexham; and he would become secretary too to the Clubs' Institute and Union Durham Area. Jon Lander had ended with *News at Ten* and trained their young reporters before retiring to write a book about his village.

I had not entirely failed in journalism since I wrote for *Associated Newspapers*.

As a free-lance I would continue writing for the *Blaydon Courier* a sports column under the sobriquet *Traveller*. I would work out of my little room at the back of our council house, typing my stories on the typewriter I had bought with my lineage fees one Whit Monday in Newcastle. The shop in the Bigg Market, owned by a namesake, had been specially opened for me, and I would leave with a portable typewriter that eventually I would bring with me to London, a Remington with green keys that I would laboriously plod when I had settled the typewriter first on our kitchen table.

'I can write faster than that,' my father would say.

Nevertheless, he had come with me to Newcastle to buy the typewriter and set me on my way. He would light too a fire for me in the grate of my room when the days grew cold, but I would be so absorbed with my writing that I would let the fire go out. He would return to see how the fire was getting on and would be annoyed that I had let it go out. He lit it again and again he left me, but again I was so absorbed in my writing that it went out.

He was much angered when he came to my room a second time.

'I'll light it one more time,' he said.

I kept one eye on my story and one on the fire.

I had typed the following words from Anton Chekhov and placed them on my bedroom wall: *'They talked without ceasing, talked hotly and genuinely; all three were excited, carried away. To listen to them, it would seem they had the future, fame, money in their hands. And it never occurred to any of them that time was passing, that every day life was nearing its close, that they had lived at other people's expense a great deal and nothing yet was accomplished; that they were all bound by the inexorable law by which, of a hundred promising beginners, only two or three rise to any position and all the others draw blanks in the lottery, perish playing the part of flesh for the cannon.'*

I was one of those beginners, determined to be a writer, and a writer of fiction once I had made my way out of newspapers, conscious not that time was passing, for I had all the time in the world, but that success might elude me. In those early months before National Service, reflecting upon the journey ahead, I would write in my diary – 14 July 1956: *'Perhaps it will not be as spectacular and strewn with incidents as the journey Stanley undertook to find Dr Livingstone; nor will it match the excitement of Mr Malone in his voyage into The Lost World. Nevertheless, it is a journey and its results and consequences have not yet been unveiled before me.'*

Nor have they some forty years later.

I would take the bus into Newcastle and haul old newspaper volumes out of the City Library. I would look for odd

152

newspaper stories that could be converted into titillating pieces for the weekend magazines. I would write a story on the origins of beer for the *Sunday Dispatch*. I would write stories for the *World's Strangest Stories* series in the London *Evening News*; I recall one on the Boston Tea Party, but of the stories I would write only one would be accepted, for which I received a handsome and stunning fee of eight guineas.

I remember reading the letter of acceptance so quickly that I had not understood it.

My stories for *Weekend Mail* were accepted and published under such resounding headlines as *Sweetheart Bit Off Lover's Nose* or *Killer of Three Continents*. However, I suffered the dread of all free-lance writers, the rejection slip, and even when a story had been accepted it would take some time before it was published let alone before I received payment. My diary tells me that in August 1956 I was one pound five shillings down and awaiting a cheque from the *Daily Express* that would '*level off this deficit*'.

However, the cheques that came from *Weekend Mail*, owned by *Associated Newspapers*, came in exactly the same form as they do today, when I have contributions accepted by *The Mail on Sunday*, *The Daily Mail* or the *Financial Mail*. But if I did well with the *Weekend Mail* I would do less well with its competitor *Reveille* and I would get only one particular story placed, about the Russian equivalent to Elvis Presley, which I wrote following a trip to Moscow a year later.

I had been thankful when the day came for me to attend my National Service medical at Newcastle General Hospital. My free-lancing had not entirely been a success. I would cover football games on Saturday for the *Sunday Dispatch*, the *Daily Express* paid me two guineas for three stories, I would do a series on the Olympic Games to be held later in the year; I would write a weekly piece for the *Evening Chronicle* sports edition dealing with a pit team in each pit village; but there might be a limit to such stories as *Hypnotised into Harem, Russian Wife had Sixty-Nine Children, King Fell in Love with Witch*, though you might say I was a fore-runner to the American supermarket tabloids.

However, it was all getting too much for me, so much so, as my diary records, '*that I decided to throw in the sponge and withdraw from the battle. The responsibility of finding my own wages week after week, the despair and sickness which it leaves, the lack of all future hope, the discontent, it is all driving me much too far.*' I was astonished to find, when re-reading my diaries, that such was my anxiety I had actually gone to the Army Recruiting Office and asked to be taken off to National Service early.

In those days I had not understood that the lag between writing and acceptance and publication and payment fell within the category of cash-flow, that the problem could be covered by bank overdraft, and perhaps if I had I would still be in the back room of my council house, not with a typewriter or word processor but a laptop computer. Instead, with the sensitivity of the incipient artist, I would write in my diary: '*The days are long. They grow cold, the skies are grey and disparaging. So too is my future. Night falls quickly, a curtain of darkness on the light. I hope that a similar curtain will fall on this free-lance career shortly.*'

When I arrived for my medical, I was required to sit in a waiting room with other future recruits into Her Majesty's Armed Forces. They were, of course, not from my pit village; one came from as far away as Sunderland. Three of us began talking among ourselves, congenial in each other's company, impatient of the wait. Spontaneously we decided

154

to leave the waiting room and treat ourselves to a drink in the local pub.

A newspaper reporter lived in those days out of the pub, though I had started so early that it would be forbidden for publicans to serve me alcohol, I had been under age, and I was offered free lemonade instead. Later I moved not to beer but to lager, half a pint at a time, and in the pleasant company of strangers, talking of sexual experiences I had yet to encounter, the time passed sufficiently quickly and happily that we almost forgot to return to the hospital for our medical.

When I did return I was not so much flushed with alcohol but cheerful and merry and cheeky with it. There were a number of specialist doctors in the room and we were required to be examined by each and every one of them. I had suffered a severe acne in my teens, on my face rather than my chest; I had too a weak bronchial chest and had suffered severely the previous winter; and I had a painful conjunctivitis that left the lids of my eyes sore and tender, the eyes themselves bloodshot. I pointed out each ailment to each and every one of the doctors and when I was handed their final report I discovered that my health only warranted a Class Three.

'What's that mean? I asked.

'It means you won't be called up.'

The government were already easing out of National Service and reducing the intake to Class One. Class Two and Three would only be called up in a state of emergency. I left the hospital bemused. I should have been elated but I was not. What would I do now? My free-lance days were over but what beckoned in their place? I had expected to join the Army or the Air Force. Now both were barred. It was not that I had one foot in the grave; I knew there was nothing wrong with my health, but my parents were none

155

too happy that I had been classed as nothing more than a seven-stone weakling, to use a phrase from a Charles Atlas advertisement.

They wanted to know what I would do next.

'I'll go to London,' I said. 'I'll get into Fleet Street.'

I had spent my first two nights at the YMCA off Tottenham Court Road before finding a place to live in Wood Green.

The YMCA had been a ruinous five guineas a night, no doubt to encourage young men to move on, and I had found a kindly couple who having seen their only son leave home to marry, had put his room out to rent, offering bed and breakfast. They had been getting on in years and I recall how I had enjoyed listening of their experiences during the war, and what they had thought of Winston Churchill.

'He cheered us up,' they said.

My mother had bought me a pair of new shoes in order to confront the London streets and they were harder on my feet than the stones of Fleet Street. I had taken the night train to London from Newcastle Central Station, telling myself as the train clicked over the tracks that '*the past is dead, the future is tomorrow*' and though it might have been an overnight train it was not a sleeper and I sat hunched and sprawled in a corner seat, with the shutter down, listening to the clickety-click till we reached London.

I befriended a Scots boy on the train who was looking to sign up for the Merchant Navy. He felt he might find a ship in the Port of London. He and I took an Underground to Piccadilly and we had stepped out by Eros with the November sky crystal, the crystal giving way to a pale dawn, a single solitary star subsumed into the greyness.

We had walked to Leicester Square and from Leicester

Square to Trafalgar Square to the Strand and onto Fleet Street, home of the national newspapers, the *Daily Express* and *The Daily Telegraph*, the bust of Edgar Wallace, himself a reporter turned crime writer, set in a wall at the corner end of Fleet Street facing towards the Old Bailey and St Paul's.

I would meet the Editor of the *Weekend Mail*, I had arrived in London during the Olympic Games in Melbourne. Christopher Brasher had won an Olympic gold medal and, still the newspaper reporter, I had looked up his mother's address in the telephone book and called from a kiosk at the bottom of Aldwych. She had been very cheerful, as you might expect, her son having won a gold medal, but I do not know what I did with the story, probably nothing, since she ended the interview by saying:

'The *Press Association* have called already!'

If they had given out the story to the national and provincial press there would be nothing that I could do.

I had promised that first day in London to meet up with my new-found Scots friend outside the Odeon Cinema in Leicester Square where a film had been showing called *The Battle of the River Plate*. Although by now my feet hurt terribly, I hobbled into Leicester Square at the appointed time, but there was no Scots friend, perhaps he had already found a vessel. If I had known his name I have long since forgotten it, but I went to see the film and would see it three times before my first stay in London was over.

Wood Green had been a long way out, an Underground ride followed by a bus, but before making the journey I would return to Trafalgar Square, sitting upon the rim of the fountain on the east side of the Square facing Parliament. They had already put up the eighty-feet high Norwegian Christmas tree and it stood in the Square, twinkling red and yellow and green.

157

I would write in my diary how a fog had shrouded the tree and enveloped Nelson's Column, '*the Column standing aloof yet majestic with lions strewn about its feet, as impressive as the marble column; sea-wraiths throwing chalk-white jets high into the air from the fountain, lines of green bubbles swirling in pools beneath*'. I would also write of '*a white artesian mist lifting up to the lingering fog*'.

Whatever that had meant.

I remember too the Christmas lights of Regent Street, hopeful in the mist, resisting the drizzle, but in the Square there had been children carolling around the tree, their voices blending and carrying their carols towards Charing Cross. I would write in my diary of a young man sitting on the edge of a fountain dribbling a finger in the green water with perceptible intent.

'What are you doing?' he is asked.

'Writing my name,' he replies.

'In water?'

The young man had been looking for peace and contentment, for happiness, sitting by the fountain listening to the Christmas service in the Square, a fog thick around him, as thick as the depression he had felt, a young man with talent and ability and a future, but overwhelmed with uncertainty, doubt and lassitude. The young man had put on his gloves and walked from the Square towards St-Martin's-in-the-Fields. I had been that young man, I had indeed written my name in water, reflecting my despair, that I had no job, no future that could be discerned through the fog around Nelson's Column, no-one in Fleet Street interested in my talents. But if written on impulse, it was not original. John Keats had placed the words on his tombstone:

Here lies one whose name was writ in water.

My own despair on coming to London to seek a job in

Fleet Street and not finding one cannot mirror the despair of a young poet so brilliant, so sensitive, so evocative that his works live on to this day, yet who had died aged twenty-six, ceasing upon the midnight with no pain, as he had written in *Ode to a Nightingale.* He had died of consumption, a cast had been taken of his hands and feet, and when his body was opened his lungs were found to be completely eaten away.

There also appears on Keats' tombstone a lyre and the same lyre is reproduced on the front of the house in Rome where he had died. The house stands off the Piazza di Spagna, I visit it each time I am in Rome, though I remember the nearby Spanish Steps more for the drug dealers who move in and out among the crowds than I do the home of John Keats. He had come to Rome in the hope that the heat would help his consumption. He had worked as a dresser at Guy's Hospital, he had left the Hospital to be a poet; but his knowledge of his own internal anatomy had enabled him to judge the consequences of his deteriorating condition. *'Lift me up, for I am dying,'* he had said. *'I shall die easy. Thank God it has come.'*

In the constituency of Tony Blair, you will find park benches with quotations from Keats' poems inscribed upon them, apparently to deter vandals and litter louts. Keats' collected works come to some four hundred and sixty pages of small print, his ballad *La Belle Dame Sans Merci* and his three odes – *To a Nightingale*, *On A Grecian Urn*, and *On Melancholy* – are true masterpieces.

It can hardly be said that he had writ his name in water.

This day, so many years later, with Parliament dissolved, I was no longer an MP. I was again out of work. Malcolm and I could relax and stroll around Leicester Square to see

what might be on at the cinema, we could walk around
Piccadily with Eros at its centre, wandering in a circle till
we found ourselves again in Trafalgar Square, watching the
traffic and seeing the light make rainbows from the fountain
sprays as the white water rose and fell back upon itself.

I remembered the Christmas tree and the carols and the
lights and the fog of those far-off days. In my diary piece
the young man pulling on his gloves and walking across
the road had not made it to St-Martin's-in-the-Fields. He
had instead been run over by a car and his troubles had
ended rather in the manner of John Keats. In real life I had
continued my walk into the future.

I pointed to the fountain on the east of the Square.

'Forty years ago,' I said to my fifteen-year-old son
somewhat grandly. 'I wrote my name in water.'

'Do you think it's still there?' he asked.

160

An Easter Story

The House had prorogued for Easter and would dissolve for the General Election.

I had been to my Parliamentary office in Millbank to collect my papers, read and answer constituency mail, pick up telephone messages, and tidy my desk before the Serjeant at Arms locked my office and banned me from the premises. Upon dissolution, signed by Order-in-Council, there would be no such thing as a Member of Parliament because there would be no Parliament, or at least no Commons, though the government would continue oblivious of this fact.

And if there were no Member of Parliament there could be no office, no car parking, no cafeterias or restaurants or bars, no library facilities, no souvenir shops, no terrace. The MP would become again an ordinary citizen of the realm, deprived too of his Parliamentary salary and allowances, his travel vouchers, his secretaries and assistants.

'I may never be back,' I told my assistant.

'In that case I'll be out of a job,' he said.

'I'll be out of a job too,' I said.

There were those Members of Parliament who would never be back because either they would take retirement upon dissolution or because the electorate would cause retirement for them. They would be beaten at the polls. The new Parliament would be a changed institution, with at least

161

a hundred new members, depending upon the number of retirements and the swing of the electoral pendulum towards one party against another.

There would be a staff exodus, a scrabbling for new posts between secretaries and assistants, where Parliament was also for them a way of life; a new beginning with the Election over, a new office, perhaps a changed environment, moving from one Parliamentary building to another; and a new boss where their former boss had taken voluntary or obligatory retirement.

All this had dawned on my own assistant.

'Wish me luck, at least,' I said.

'Better wish *me* luck,' he said.

At the end of the Parliamentary week, I would normally take the fast five o'clock train from King's Cross to Darlington and on to my Middlesbrough constituency. I would arrive at the station early and have a cup of tea and a shortbread in the lounge, but this Maundy Thursday – as if in sympathy with the mournfulness of Holy Week – the tea was too stewed and sour and I decided to leave the lounge and take the four-thirty slower train through Newark.

I had not been to Newark in fifty-one years and as the train pulled into the North Gate Station, of a sudden as Somerset Maugham would often write, I decided to get off and wander around the town. The nights were drawing out, the sky cast a pallid blue, the clouds were high and white and clean, no dark rims here, the river reflecting dull in the cold, its currents catching the fronds of the willows, a slight wind scuffing the chilly brown surface waters.

There was the castle where King John of Magna Carta fame had died, its battlements dark, bedraggled, gaunt you might say, yet proud too of its history, besieged three times in the Civil War, pounded, obliterated but still standing, overlooking the town to remind it of ancient glories; that if shopping precincts, circular roads and throughways might be modern and sophisticated, they were not enough compared to the splendour that had been Newark and the fame that belonged to John.

I had come looking for hot-cross buns.

The precincts were filled with bakers' shops and confectioners' and self-service cafeterias and super-markets, all selling hot-cross buns, some selling six for ninety-nine pence with fruit added, some with icing in the cross, some with the buns linked where the baker had not severed the dough; but all of them fresh, the aroma of yeast, fruit, spice and candied peel mingling and rising in a Christian warmth.

I had tasted my first hot-cross bun in Newark fifty-one years ago.

I had been seven-years-old when a bus trip to London had been organised from our housing estate and I would travel with my mother and father to visit my Uncle Bill and Aunt Flo at Leavesden in Hertfordshire. The bus had set off around nine o'clock at night on a twelve-hour journey, passing down the old A1 through every town centre: Chester-le-Street, Durham, Darlington, Doncaster, Newark, Grantham, Peterborough, pausing at Barnet where we might alight.

There had been a comic incident at Chester-le-Street where the bus had stopped to pick up additional passengers, friends of a family already on the bus. They were not at the bus stop. The family had gone to look for them, the friends had then showed up, and we had to wait till the family returned. It had been a long night for a seven-year-old, curled into his mother, the lights dimmed in the bus, but through the windows the street lighting had reflected yellow from the damp streets as the bus heaved its way through all the town centres.

The bus had arrived at Newark about dawn.

The passengers relieved themselves in public toilets and made their way to the baker's shop.

'What's them?' I asked my mother.

'Hot-cross buns,' she said.

'What's hot-cross buns?'

I had never seen a hot-cross bun in all the war years.

'Buy him one to shut his face,' said a kindly passenger.

I would recall my first Easter eggs wrapped in old wallpaper and hard-boiled in a saucepan over the fire, the paper coming away in the bubbling water, but not before the patterns had stained the shells. One Easter Sunday an uncle would bring me a very special chocolate egg with the Lord's Prayer engraved a delicate white upon it, the egg so rare, so precious, that it would not be broken let alone eaten, the dark chocolate and cream lettering mouldering on the top of our high chest of drawers in the living room.

I would roll my Easter eggs down the grass bank by the all-purpose grocer's shop and once when my mother had sent me to buy tea cakes I had rolled them too, the cakes sliding down the grass on their sides till they curved into the burn at the bottom of the bank, sometimes lost to the reeds, sometimes sinking into the white froth of the burn. The burn ran from the colliery, flecked with coal dust and dark fragments of coal, so that when I recovered the tea cakes I recall their edges blue as the anthracite scars to my father's hands.

The hot-cross buns were not unlike the tea cakes.

They were small and round and warm and in the early morning filled the window and the shelves in the baker's shop. The cross imprinted upon them had indeed been the mark of Christ and lay across their brown sugary surface white as light, etched deep as history. I cannot recall their taste but the dough was heavier than it is today, there were currents to the dough and they pleased my sweet tooth.

I recall Barnet being very swank, very posh to those eyes that knew only the honey stone of colliery houses, a colliery wheel and headstock, or the quieter red brick of a council house. The buses were green-painted, pretty much as they are today, with high steaming engines, the aisles narrow, the seats tall and steel-rimmed as we made our way from Barnet beyond the elegant private houses and green swards all the way to Leavesden.

My Uncle Bill and Aunt Flo lived close to an aerodrome with their three children: Margaret, Sylvia and Irene. My cousin Sylvia would write a poem about Leavesden that she would send me in later life. She would recall the blacksmith's shed with its irons and bellows; she would recall the cobbler tapping nails into leather shoes, the village school with its two small classes and playground. There would be the post office, with its penny sweets and fizzy pop and small neat cottages with blazing coal fires, gas lamps flickering in the night, for there would be no electricity in these cottages. Sylvia would recall a russet brick chapel, the cottage where she lived surrounded by fields and woods; there would be dripping with the toast at tea time, and there would be but a single cold tap and toilet at the bottom of the yard.

We had gone one day to London from Watford Junction and I recall seeing the twin towers of Wembley Stadium, feeling privileged to be so close to the home of football, yet the stadium shabby and in need of fresh paint, as if it too had suffered in the war. We had alighted at Baker Street, home of Sherlock Homes, Madam Tussaud's waxworks museum nearby, but in particular I recall walking through Green Park towards Buckingham Palace.

My cousin Margaret had wanted to pay a visit, as it were,

and we had formed a ring around her and she had hunkered down, a child of eight no less, and when we had walked off an old man with a stick had come by and my hot-tempered Uncle Bill had sworn that he would be passing to see what we had been doing. But the old man had kept walking, into time and history, like the rest of us.

I had walked hand in hand with my cousin Margaret, a year older than myself. She had come to live with us during the war when the Germans began to doodlebug London. The three sisters had been separated into different households within my uncle's family, Margaret to live with us, Sylvia with another aunt, and Irene with a third.

Margaret would be six years old at the time and I would be five.

She and I would be put to bed early, but I recall the light through the thin yellow curtains, for we had double summer time then, there was no going to sleep with the dark, and Margaret and I would make up stories for each other. My sister had been nine when I was born, beyond my childhood reach, and Margaret became the surrogate sister on long summer nights, with no war for us, only the joy of school and playing and running and fighting, as she would remind me years later.

When the doodlebug scare passed Margaret and her sisters would return to Leavesden, but when my Aunt Flo fell ill with tuberculosis and had a lung removed they would return to our village, staying for eighteen months whilst she recovered. Only this time the family arrangements would be different. Margaret would stay with another aunt, Sylvia would stay with my family, and Irene would go to her uncle and aunt in Newcastle.

It has always seemed to me looking back that life is filled with adult disregard for the feelings of children. I was reminded of this in the Cleveland child abuse crisis. They

166

are treated as objects incapable of genuine emotion, their feelings rarely taken into consideration. I was not asked my views whether I wanted Sylvia to stay with me rather than Margaret, which company I would have preferred; nor were the sisters consulted, though Margaret would recall that she had pleaded with her aunt in Newcastle to take Irene because she felt she would be better looked after.

The two sisters would thus be separated.

For Sylvia these would be the happiest days of her childhood, playing in the tussocky fields around our village, playing too in the woods, the air fresh and untainted, with only a single smoke stack from the brick flats, making friends at school, feeling free and unfettered. In later life she would be comfortable with her memories, crying when she returned to Leavesden, having so settled in the village, now leaving it all behind.

She and her family would become great friends of mine, they would come to my first book-signing in Newcastle so many years later; they would visit me in the House of Commons and I would follow their trials and tribulations, as they were, through life. When Margaret Beckett, as an Opposition spokesperson, had visited a residential home where she had been warden, Sylvia would speak of her past in the pit village and my own origins.

But as a child I had resented the switch and thrown a terrible tantrum in our living room.

Truth to tell, Margaret had only moved two streets, and I would see her at school and in the evenings, but there would be no more story-telling or white light through yellow curtains. She had been tall and blonde and bright and would pass her eleven-plus brought in by the 1944 Education Act. She would wear a black coat that never did leave her back in all the months she spent in the village. She too had been unhappy at the family move. She never did go to the grammar school and when she returned to Leavesden I would not see her again till my mother and father took me to the Festival of Britain in 1951.

All I recall of this bus trip was a thick white mist lying across the fields in the early morning and rabbits playing in the field, an abundance of rabbits, more than I had ever seen, even though they had all supposedly been stricken by myxomatosis. My Uncle Bill and Aunt Flo had now moved from Leavesden to Watford, but we would return to Leavesden aerodrome for a sports day. I had entered into one particular race and this I had won and it had gone down well at my grammar school when I told my sports teacher.

Margaret had been moving from childhood to womanhood, tall and willowy and blonde as ever, and when we had gone to the Festival for a day I had taken little interest in the shows and exhibitions but had thought of Margaret and had wanted to return to her home to see her. We would fight again in her bedroom, heaving and battling, grappling, flinging ourselves around the bed, laying into each other as apparently we had done as children on the grass ring before our house.

She would return to my village for a holiday when she had been sixteen, staying with another aunt, but I recall walking with her across the fields from my house, summer in the air, the sun warm to the touch of our skins. She would be wearing a dark costume with yellow trimmings, open at the neck, a beautiful young woman now, the same blonde hair caught and held by the sun, tressing around her neck, holding herself well, tall and slim, a wind rustling through the trees in a coppice by the burn, the burn hastening from the colliery through the fields.

She had seemed full of assurance, of confidence, a woman from the city, whilst I had felt shy and awkward

168

and backward, still the village lad. I neither held her hand nor felt the touch of her wrist. All other memories fade and I would not see Margaret again till I was looking for a job in Fleet Street, when my Uncle Bill and Aunt Flo persuaded me to abandon my board and lodging at Wood Green and come to stay with them at Watford. In a sense, my uncle and aunt were repaying my family for having looked after Margaret and Sylvia during and after the war, but I would not stay long in Watford, no more than ten days, Christmas was coming and I had prudently bought a return ticket to Newcastle at a cost of two guineas and threepence, as my diary tells me.

My Fleet Street venture had not gone well.

'*I grasp wraith-like for a shadow which is employment,*' my diary would say. I had already seen the Editor of the *Weekend Mail* because I had written to him from my council home before leaving for London. The Editor had replied that they were unable to offer me a job but had suggested I should go and see him for advice when I was in London. The most optimistic advice he had been able to give was that generally you had to be twenty-three or so before being taken on in Fleet Street.

I was, after all, only eighteen.

I had written to the *Exchange Telegraph*, a news agency rival to the *Press Association*. I had spoken with them and I had written to the *Daily Express*. I had written from my home whilst turning out another piece for the *Weekend Mail* entitled *Ghosts Robbed Bank* – and why not indeed? I had wanted to write about the charismatic film star Rudolph Valentino, a favourite of my mother's, famous for the part he had played in *The Sheik*, but who had died young; and I had also prepared an interview with a brewer's son called Jimmy Deuchar, who had turned from the family brewing business to become a jazz player.

169

'I suppose I'm a damned fool,' he had said.

The family business no longer exists.

I had been advised to get myself a job on a weekly paper, not the kind I had known in the North-East, that is the *Blaydon Courier* or *Consett Guardian*, slim and modest compared to those prosperous weekly newspapers in the Thames Valley owned by the Dimbleby family of television fame. Indeed, I had travelled to Hounslow at the end of the Piccadilly line to be interviewed for a job there, but I had no great yearning to live so far from the West End of London and even less to go back to weekly papers.

I was relieved not to be offered a job.

I had worn out the leather on my new shoes, they were no longer tight and circumscribed, but it had become clear staying with my relatives at Watford that I had been somewhat naïve in seeking a job in Fleet Street with such rudimentary skills, hardly a year behind me as a newspaper reporter, slow at shorthand and typing, and that I might have been motivated more by desperation than by arrogance.

Perhaps I should return to my pit village, not to stay, but to regroup my thoughts and energies, return to London in the New Year, to seek out those basic skills, get myself a job in gainful employment, and begin again. Or as the French would say: *Reculer pour mieux sauter.* After all, if a newspaper reporter did not get into Fleet Street till the age of twenty-three, I had some five years ahead of me to achieve this noble aim.

My cousin Margaret had by now married and left home.

She would work in the evening as an usherette in a Watford cinema and for me to see her again I would need to go to the cinema. She was coming up to twenty now, still slim and beautiful, her brow cream, perhaps the hair less blonde, her accent sharp and Cockney from her mother, the humour lively to her eyes as she halved the ticket of her cousin and showed him to his seat. Her life had begun to take shape, as had my own, and she knew that she must treat me seriously.

'What's yer plans, Stu?' she had asked.

The film I had seen that night had been *Istanbul* with Errol Flynn.

Errol had fallen out with Warner Brothers, who had been making pictures since 1934 with him in a starring role. Errol wished to go to Rome and begin making his own pictures. His first would be in Cinemascope, the saga of *William Tell*. But while Errol had sunk almost half a million dollars into the film his Italian backers did just that – they backed out. Errol had made forty-five films in all, he would be diagnosed as suffering from a hepatitis that would kill him; he would go broke, if not bankrupt, and make a further two films in England.

Eventually, he would spend three years on his schooner off Palma de Majorca, increasing his vodka intake from – in his words – a fifth of a bottle a day to more. His bible had become a kit that he carried around with him containing a bottle of vodka, two or three glasses, and a bottle or two of quinine water. The vodka would later come in cases and by then Errol Flynn was living like a beachcomber.

He returned to Hollywood to make *Istanbul*, not a foot of it being shot in Turkey, but he had rescued his film career and would make a number of films before the vodka and hepatitis overwhelmed his liver. The film would be remembered not because of Errol Flynn but because of his co-star Nat King Cole. He would sing a wonderful song called *When I Fall In Love, It will be Forever; Or I'll Never Fall in Love.*

All that I recall of the film was a great deal of violence, explosions and flames, all in Technicolour; there was also an actor who said every time he heard Nat King Cole sing this song in his bar it cost him a phone call to his wife in New York. Perhaps the song has cost me more than the price of his calls, for over the years each time I hear it I am reminded of my cousin Margaret and I too call her on the phone.

'Perhaps you should settle in Watford,' Margaret had said.

'What would I do in Watford?'

'They have local papers here too.'

I did not return to settle in Watford, nor did I try to keep warm the hot-cross buns I had bought fifty-one years later in Newark but would have them with my family in Middlesbrough over tea on Good Friday. They were better garnished than the first hot-cross buns, richer with fruit and lemon peel, the glaze along the surface melting into the bun itself, the cross more lightly delineated. The buns could be toasted too and I would feel the richness of each nibble.

I called Margaret again at Watford.

She had been to hospital with a blood clot to her brain, she had been back to hospital that day because of kidney trouble, but she had not complained, neither of her heart nor her kidneys; she had not even told me she had been ill. She explained that if you ask about someone's health you don't really want to hear what they have to say.

'There's nothing worse,' she said.

She and Brian her husband had been together since the day she had married, they would have three children and she was now a grandmother. She never did return to the village. She had worked in a betting shop and she and Brian had lived in the same street as they had forty-three years ago when they had married. Brian had been born in Great Ayton, outside Middlesbrough, he had worked his passage

172

through life, but both were now retired, except for looking
after the grandchildren.

'I want you to come to the House of Commons,' I said.
'After the Election.'

'How can I come to the House of Commons?'

'Take a train from Watford Junction.'

'I mean with the grandchildren?'

'Come for tea,' I said. 'On the terrace.'

'How many times have you asked me?'

'And still you don't come.'

'There's my hospital treatment.'

'But I miss you so much,' I said.

I thought of the young girl who had stayed at my house
during the war, whom I had visited at Watford, whom I had
fought on our ring or in her bedroom, who had returned to
my village as a teenager in the splendour of her youth, the
young girl in the black coat and the teenage girl in the dark
outfit with the yellow trim. The days were as fresh to my
mind as the hot-cross buns on the tea tray before me.

A sigh soughed all the way down the years from my
pit village.

'You're such a liar,' she said.

'I'm a politician,' I said.

The hot-cross buns tasted nicely all the same.

How to Spell Hemingway

I asked my literary agent how you spelt Hemingway.

'You tell me,' Sonia Land said. 'How do you spell Hemingway?'

'Look at the panel on the wall. Do you see anything wrong with it?'

We were awaiting a *kir royale* at the American Bar in the Savoy Hotel.

The bar had been crowded in the early evening, not a happy hour but happy enough for those young upwardly mobile City men encroaching past Ludgate Circus who came into the bar to listen to the pianist, to chat over the day's deals, to meet girl friends as young and alluring as they were themselves. Few of them noticed the panel, perhaps they had no view of it from alcoves stretching back towards the main foyer; but the panel depicted American writers of the twenties sitting around a bar, not particularly this bar, perhaps Harry's New York Bar in Paris, with the names of famous authors such as Hemingway and Scott Fitzgerald engraved upon the panel.

'You've spelt my first name wrong for years,' Sonia said.

And still do, she might have remarked.

Upon the dissolution of Parliament, before my drink at the Savoy, I had called by the offices of Goldman Sachs

174

in Fleet Street. They had taken over *The Daily Telegraph* building, splendid clock and all, its solid brick and staid facade contrasting with the darkened glass of *Express Newspapers* that I had first walked past when seeking fame, if not fortune, as a newspaper reporter. The taxi had left me at the entrance of the *Telegraph* building, but when I marched into the entrance I was told Goldman Sachs were now round the back in Peterborough Court.

'You mean where the printing presses were?'

'I don't know about that,' the receptionist said.

As a putative Minister of the Crown, in the event Labour won the General Election, I had been given a tour of Goldman Sachs' trading floors: bonds, stocks, derivatives, currencies, dealing not in one single country but in all the countries of the world, with television screens showing particular dealing rooms in Frankfurt and Paris and the dealing room of the Federal Reserve Bank in New York.

Yet the entrance to the *Telegraph* building was no different than it had been forty years ago.

There were the high ceilings, monumentally high you might say, as high as any ceilings in Orson Welles' film *Citizen Kane*; as high as any ceilings in Gotham City where Batman and Robin, when you could find him, sped through the sky. There was gold too, gold leaf, gold carpets, gold walls, as if the gold represented the distinction of *The Daily Telegraph* throughout the ages from its days as the original *Morning Post*.

Had it really been forty years since I had taken a bus from Tufnell Park to Aldwych and run past the Law Courts and into Fleet Street to be interviewed by the *Telegraph*? I had returned to London in the New Year, only this time I had no money; the savings I had put together through my free-lance work had gone, exhausted in my three-week stay trying to get a job in Fleet Street.

The YMCA had a notice board which had addresses pinned upon it, essentially for students but also for young men such as myself who, having arrived in London, did not find the streets paved with gold, but rather hard on a new pair of shoes. I recall visiting one prospective flat opposite St Pancras so horrible and ugly that I almost threw myself from the balcony, but telling myself that if I were to start again in life I would have to put up with such miseries.

My common sense rebelled, I would not settle opposite St Pancras, and eventually I found lodgings in Tufnell Park, north of Camden Town, with a senior couple who owned a boarding house. The husband had been a celebrated cartoonist in India, working for a national newspaper, and they had invested their savings in this boarding house in Anson Road where they also lived.

Upon my return to London, I had thought the best way to keep in my journalistic hand would be to become a copytaker for one of the newspapers. I had written to *The Daily Telegraph* and the *Star*, a London evening newspaper owned by the *News Chronicle*. The *Star* would write to say that they had no vacancies but when one occurred they would write to me again. The *Star* closed as an evening paper, as did eventually the *Evening News*, though the title still remains with Associated Newspapers.

The *Daily Telegraph* had offered me an interview on a Saturday morning.

I was conscious that I came from a pit village with a strong Northern dialect. The dialect would change from village to village, from one part of the county to another; but though it might be noble, its roots in the Angle and Dane invasions, it was embarrassing not to be understood, to be looked down upon because of the way you spoke in an age before television made regional dialects and accents acceptable.

176

I had hoped, too, that once in the *Telegraph* building I might be able to move from copytaker to reporter; I held a National Union of Journalists' card, but a copytaker was required to be a member of a different union; and were I to be given the job my NUJ card must be torn up. Should this happen I never would become a reporter, since there were in the *Telegraph* building a variety of closed shops.

I would be incarcerated as a copytaker.

The beauty of copytaking, however, was that I would be free during the day, working evenings to be sure, but able to seek out my free-lance stories either by way of features or hard news. There was also the prospect of a new weekly paper, to be called *The Weekend Star*. I saw the creation of this as 'a first journalistic opportunity', but I would in the meantime try to get a job as copytaker.

I would be twenty minutes late for my interview with the *Telegraph*.

This was a Saturday morning, the manager of the copytaking room was on his own, surrounded by newspapers, but relaxed about my tardiness, not finding it unusual in such a busy city as London. I recall him as a dark-haired kindly man with a thin pitted face and dark eyes and moustache; he wore no coat but the customary cardigan. I had apologised for my late arrival, feeling slightly flustered and anxious, the interview meaning so much to me. He had settled me down before a typewriter and given me a test of some description, but he had not been satisfied either with my typing or my spelling. The traffic heaved down Fleet Street as he studied my work in the white light from the window.

'Neither are up to standard,' he said.

He had given me a week's trial.

The interview had clearly not gone well and I would write that evening on my typewriter: '*I am on a week's trial with the Telegraph, which means that next Saturday at this time I shall know where I stand. If I think correctly I shall in all probability be weeping again, as I was last Saturday evening. It seems remarkable that a young man of eighteen should cry for his mother who is three hundred miles away – and after only two days in London too! It is absolutely ridiculous, isn't it?'*

Perhaps it was not as ridiculous as all that.

Truth to tell, I had been homesick.

I construed this as a form of self-pity but felt sufficiently wretched to go to King's Cross Station on my first Sunday in London and buy a copy of the *Sunday Sun* brought down from Newcastle on the night train and sold from a trolley on the platform. I would read the *Sunday Sun*, which made me more miserable, and I remember saying to myself that if I felt this way in a week's time, I would use the return portion of my ticket and return home, this time for good.

I had felt sufficiently better the following week to buy a copy of the *Sunday Sun*, but to walk from King's Cross to Leicester Square, following the Underground map, the church bells pealing, the streets empty, the day dry but cold, being well wrapped-up with my scarf and gloves, but content and reassured to find myself again in the West End, my homesickness receding like an emotion spent.

My return ticket I would give to a school friend who was studying at the London School of Economics.

'I think it was loneliness,' I typed. *'Frustration, despair at its height, the knowledge that there could be no future for me which made me cry. Of course there is no harm in crying; it is only a human weakness like parsimony, anger, or any other individual characteristic you would care to name.'*

I had thought my typewriting skills would have been adequate, but I would spend three hours this Saturday night at my typewriter, sitting in my partitioned room in Tufnell Park. The owners of the boarding house had cleverly partitioned one big room into two. Their speciality had been putting-up Indian students, given their lives in India, and the boy in the other half of the room had been studying in London, his life even lonelier than mine, for he had neither friends nor family, only his books. He was, however, no trouble or problem, except when he had bad dreams and I would hear him sigh and turn and sometimes cry out.

Certainly he never complained about my typing.

I declared this Saturday night my typing to be '*a little off*' and '*the speed is bad to what I can really do: I only hope the hours of typing tonight – I was thinking of three but since I am doing so badly up till now, I think four will be more beneficial – will do some good for Monday. The number of advantages The Daily Telegraph will bring me are too many to number. To begin with such a prestigious newspaper – even as a copytaker – can only lead to better things.*'

I had not been aware then of the problem of a union card.

Copytaking consisted of sitting in a large room reading the newspapers and waiting for a phone to ring in one of the booths with a red light flashing above the booth. The hours would be from four o'clock in the afternoon till two in the morning, though I would begin at four and finish at half-past nine. The pay would be eleven pounds a week. I had been paid six in my first week in London, working as a temporary typist in a shipping office.

There would be a typewriter, you would put in two or three sheets of paper to make carbon copies, and take dictation from the reporter calling in. There would be four or five of us in the *Telegraph* copy room, all male, each taking turns to enter the booth and register the copy,

179

though I would not be there long enough to get to know them well. The conversation would be friendly if banal and I recall once expressing my surprise at how low the *Telegraph* circulation was when compared to the more popular newspapers, now known as tabloids.

'But think of the advertising revenue!' I was told.

I did befriend one copytaker who would take me for an evening meal in the cafeteria down the long editorial corridor where the Editor and Assistant Editor and Diplomatic Correspondent had their names on prestigious-looking doors. My friend would spend his days as a photographer looking for good pictures to sell to the newspapers. He felt I could spend my days writing my free-lance stories and selling them as he did his photographs.

'You must never give up your NUJ card!' he said.

I had been encouraged by my new-found photographer friend and had enjoyed our chat in the staff cafeteria before returning to my duties in the copytaking room. I recall one call from a full-time staff reporter at Heathrow Airport with a story about a tin of paint. The story had not been written, only dictated, it had been filled with errors and inconsistencies, but the reporter had left for the evening, disappearing into the local pub as the copytaking manager surmised.

He had not been pleased.

There was another call from a Prospective Parliamentary Conservative Candidate who phoned in the copy of a speech, stating that but for NATO the Russians would be at the ancient gates of Paris, so wild and emotional it never did see the light of day; and I recall that there was too the trial of Dr Bodkin Adams, a Bournemouth doctor alleged to have murdered his patients. In those days, there were committal proceedings where all prosecution evidence was typed by the clerk to the magistrates' court for onward

180

transmission to the Crown Court where there would be a
trial by jury. I had followed such proceedings as a reporter
on the *Blaydon Courier* when attending the Magistrates'
court sitting in Gateshead. They had been long and tedious
and it did not surprise me when they were abolished.

It meant, however, that all prosecution evidence would be
given in open court whilst the defence reserved its position
for the full trial. All the incriminating evidence against Dr
Bodkin Adams was revealed and the country and the press
made up their minds he was guilty. Even to this day, his
case is often referred to and he is always named by those
reporters not around at the time as the doctor who murdered
his patients.

'He'll get off,' the copytaking manager said.

I had been surprised by this.

I would often reflect on his statement and even when
I had left the *Telegraph* and followed the case before
the Crown Court I would wait patiently for the verdict
to see whether it justified the manager's judgement. Dr
Bodkin Adams did indeed get off, though the evidence
against him appeared overwhelming; the jury, however,
had heard it all and thought differently. The judgement
of my copytaking manager had been right and that of the
press and public wrong.

My instincts told me I would not get the *Telegraph* job
and again I would find myself in the West End, walking
from Leicester Square to Piccadilly and to Trafalgar Square
with its spraying white fountains. I would be on the verge
of tears, but when the news was broken to me, that my
week's trial was over, that I had not got the job, much
to the disappointment of my photographer friend, I walked
out upon the Embankment, '*my brain quite tranquil, utterly
content in myself, already making my plans for the future
with every confidence of carrying them out*'.

181

The manager had told me my fate in the washroom.

'It's your spelling really,' he said.

I did not know how to spell accommodation or occasion or Spanish or leisure, and reviewing my diaries they are filled with such mistakes, not knowing how to spell Charing Cross, all inconsequential till you are applying for a post as copytaker on *The Daily Telegraph*. I have been a stickler for spelling ever since, the first name of my literary agent excepted, and I am often amused at how such simple words like exorbitant or targeted or benefited or Teesside or Middlesbrough or *Alfa Romeo* are being mis-spelt, even in such reputable and articulate newspapers as the *Financial Times*.

All this did not help me, however, notwithstanding my mood, as I walked along the Embankment feeling the cold Thames air.

I had not been entirely alone in those first weeks in London.

Alan High had been *Victor Ludorum* at Hookergate Grammar School. He came from my pit village and had been six years older than myself. He had qualified as a dentist and was now working as a locum in Woolwich. Alan would have a great influence on my life, I would often visit him in his home at the top end of the village; he would be kind enough to take an interest in me, notwithstanding that I was callow and immature, and probably boorish and arrogant with it.

Eighteen months previously, he had talked of a Warsaw Youth Festival and had suggested that he would like to visit a second Festival to be held in Moscow in the summer of 1957. He showed me pamphlets and photographs taken at the Warsaw Festival; he had not been himself but he had heard it had been an excellent holiday and experience; and he said he intended going to Moscow when the time came. I had wanted to go too and we had discussed the possibilities of my getting there, but the conversation had come to an abrupt end when he reminded me that I would have to do my National Service.

'They wouldn't give you leave,' he said.

I would forget about Moscow till I had gone on holiday with my school friends to Butlin's Holiday Camp in Filey. Somehow the subject had come up again and I would write to a girl I had met at the camp, who came from Mansfield, that the following year I had hoped to go to Moscow. No doubt I had written to impress her, since I had yet to attend my medical for National Service and there would be no holidays for two years, but she had not been impressed at all.

She had not written back.

Now in London, with Alan High urging me on, staying with a friend who was also a dentist and who would be going to Moscow – in the end I would arrange it for him – the idea had several attractions. It would be an ideal opportunity to travel and to write free-lance stories. But who was organising the Festival? How much would it cost? The details were scant, no-one quite knew the answers, not even Alan High. I would have to find out for myself.

I rang the Russian Consulate.

They gave me the name and address of the organisers, who were also organising a British Youth Festival, and though I would not attend this I was told that the Moscow Festival would be in July. This was January and I had no money. Where would it come from? I would work for it. How would I work? Well, somehow I would find work.

And I would save my money.

I thought I might become a part-time secretary to a Member of Parliament, learning Parliamentary practice, sitting in the Strangers' Gallery of the House of Commons, studying the 'etiquette and procedures' of the House; but if this was an idea, a stroke from my imagination, I had no knowledge how to go about it. In the meantime I was jobless and went back to the Lawsen Employment Agency who, before the *Telegraph*, had arranged for me a week's work with a shipping firm.

I was sent to an insurance firm near Eastcheap.

This was not a typing job, rather one of manual book-keeping, logging off premiums as they had been paid, using an old-style calculating machine which I promptly jammed, much to my fear and chagrin and embarrassment, feeling a fool, but time lying so heavily that constantly I looked at the white face of the clock ahead of me. This caused irritation to at least one secretary who thought I was checking the time she went for lunch and the time she came back, or the time she took to powder her nose, making tart comments that embarrassed me further.

I recall 5 February 1957 sitting at my desk at two o'clock in the afternoon.

I wondered what I had been doing a year ago, where had I been and how had I felt. I had been working at the *Blaydon Courier* office, with its grimed windows and no heating or facilities, only a desk and a telephone, but at least a full-time job as a newspaper reporter; yet about to be moved to the *Consett Guardian*, against my will, so that in my diary I would call the move '*my impending doom*'.

What would I be doing in another year?

'*That is a question I cannot answer*,' I would write.

The clock said two minutes past two.

Why, I wondered, thinking of these dragging minutes,

is success not swift or fleet of foot? Why not immediate? Why should talent be squandered? Why cannot life be enriched by happiness and contentment in the years of youth, when the sky is a deeper, purer blue, the sun a shining animated disc, its rays on the Thames, shimmering like vibrant wedges of colour, when beauty and nature stir the soul and warm the heart? Why not add the ingredient of happiness by acclaiming talent with success? Why should I be idling my hours in tedium, cherishing an ambition, yet having to wait for its fulfilment?

I looked at the clock again.

I could hardly believe it.

Four minutes past two!

I went back to my reflections. Why should the summer sun of a man's life fade to the west, autumn leaves fall from the trees, the cold winds of winter rustling through foothills before a man's peak is reached and contentment found? I pondered still further. The hands of the clock had moved but reluctantly, yet keeping a constant pace, the seconds following the minutes, unaffected by the hustle of life, the hurrying of man in his quest for the invisible, as if seeking out the wind.

There are those who succeed early in life, who in their youthful years attain a rapid success and are promptly acclaimed genius. They have never known failure, the river of life for them has been broad and placid, no dangerous undercurrent tugs at their soul and threatens to drown them. Their standards are set. They are happy. They have measured the time by their watch and are content to keep its pace through life. There is for them no worry, no furrowed brow, no empty pockets, no empty stomach. They are a moderate success in their chosen field.

The sum total of it all would be happiness.

But still the hands of the clock hardly budged.

185

Now it was only six minutes past two.

And here was the tarty secretary back from lunch!

The real success in life would be one which laid its foundations in patience, faith in one's talent, in the confidence to go forward, the ability to turn the other cheek when failure has smitten the other, to react positively. That is why the declining years of a man's life are not dull and lonely. They are enriched by success, enriched by the years of patient if despairing youth, a success built as a lasting beacon, pervading a man's soul with its light, the light of God if you like, but a success that could only be built on foundations not only of patience but of failure.

In the last forty years, each time I look at a calendar and see the date, each time I hear 5 February mentioned on the radio or television, I see myself back in the insurance office in Eastcheap, logging the premium income, jamming the calculating machine, looking at the hands of the clock, dreading the secretary passing my desk, reflecting again my deep philosophical thoughts and thinking that perhaps – but only perhaps – they would be among the truest I had put to paper, since I had written them all in my diary.

Soon I would be out of work again.

After the insurance I would work in a bank, though my diary tells me that my banking experience had been *'disastrous'*, whatever that might have meant; but the fact I had no work began to affect my morale: *'The storm is gathering. The problems are pressing down upon me with such weight that I do not know if I can shoulder their weight any longer. It is Friday tonight and I have as yet no job. Today I rang up the coffee employment bureau and drew a blank cheque.'*

Coffee employment bureau?

Nothing would come of this either and I would write: *'It is approaching ten o'clock on Monday morning and I have no job. I wonder what the succeeding hours will bring. I am trying to spin the coin of fortune in such a fashion as to be able to say: "Heads I win; tails you lose". The coin is in the air, spinning upwards, but soon it will fall'.*

If there was no temporary work perhaps I should work full time.

'Today,' I wrote 15 April 1957, *'I have been for an interview for a £10 a week job. £10 a week! Imagine it! £10 a week! But will it come off?'* My temporary work had paid me six pounds a week, but though the ten pounds a week job did not fructify I did get myself work with Swift's of Chicago in their mail department at eight a week. I would be on my feet all day, from quarter-to-nine till six o'clock.

'Personally,' I wrote, *'I think it will be more than a job. It will be slavery. I get £8 a week and a grey coat to wear and luncheon vouchers. It is at London Bridge. If I can keep it for three months – and that is at the moment very uncertain – I can save up the money to make my Moscow trip a little easier; otherwise it is fairly obvious I shall have to borrow from my parents.'*

I had been trying to save whatever was left from my six pounds a week to pay for the trip to the Moscow Youth Festival, which would cost all of fifty-five pounds but would mean three weeks in Moscow. It was the thought of this, the goal of travel, of free-lance story writing, as well as my ambition to get into Fleet Street, that would keep me going as winter turned to spring and the nights grew light again: *'The days will lengthen and infuse gladness to many hearts. The refreshing, sunlit mornings will be a source of joy to those so delicate of spirit and sensitive of nature to feel the impact and the happiness the warmth can give.'*

After breakfast in the boarding house, I would live on a bowl of tomato soup and a bread roll for lunch with a cup of tea and a Lyon's fruit pie after work. By Thursday

187

I would be so hungry my resolve would fail and I would treat myself to fish and chips at Archway. I wanted to save all the money I could for Moscow. This life-style would continue until Whitsuntide when I returned to Newcastle. I arranged a meeting with the Editor of the *Sunday Sun* for whom I wanted to write articles.

'I'll bet you're starving yourself in London,' he said.

I had always been on the lean side and perhaps I was leaner still.

'It'll not do you a bit of good,' he said. 'All you'll do is fall ill.'

Upon my return to Tufnell Park I had taken his advice and have eaten properly from that day to this. Nor would I ever be able to face tomato soup again. I would leave Swift's of Chicago and their mailing department as soon as I could, but in all this time I would continue my newspaper writing. I arranged one Saturday morning an interview with *Alcoholics Anonymous* and would write a story to send to *Everybody's* and *Reader's Digest* entitled *Ten Years of Saving Souls!*

The story would not be accepted.

I had wanted to visit a Bob Hope Youth Club in Camberwell and a Freddie Mills Sporting Centre. I wanted also to interview Bob Woof of colliery office fame who had now become an MP. It would be my last piece for the *Blaydon Courier*, and though I had written it without expecting payment Jon Lander would send me a cheque for ten shillings and sixpence – being half a guinea – which had been gratefully received, though with no bank account now I had trouble cashing the cheque.

I would visit the newspaper reading room at Colindale, an annex to the British Museum, in the hope of repeating my success from Newcastle City Library, where I had found past news stories which could be converted into *actualité*.

I turned out such stories as *Pirate Wore Panties*, the story of a woman who had gone to sea as a pirate but who had disguised her identity – till she fell in love with the captain!

Another entitled *Spent Honeymoon in Nude*, more pulsating than prosaic but not successful; or *Married in Prison Cell*, unusual in those days though commonplace today. There were other stories too – *Bought Wife for a Herd of Goats* – turned down by Reveille, and though the *Evening News* wrote to say they would accept outlines of stories from me for their *World's Strangest Stories* nothing would come of this.

However, *Forged Inside Jail* would get me five guineas from the *Weekend Mail*.

I would write my final football story during my week at *The Daily Telegraph*, visiting Millwall Football Club to interview the manager because Millwall were playing Newcastle United in the F.A. Cup. Newcastle had a glorious Cup record in the fifties, they would win the Cup three times, but in this match they would be beaten by Millwall 2–0, a Cup upset since Millwall played in a lower league and thus became so-called giant killers.

I had filed my pre-match copy to the *Evening Chronicle* but it was never published.

I had always been strong on football stories, writing of such boy wonders as Duncan Edwards, who would lose his life at Munich when a plane carrying the Manchester United team crashed in 1958; of Louis Rocca, the famous Manchester United chief scout – he would hold the post for thirty-eight years – who would declare that to play a good game of football '*takes sixty-five per cent courage and thirty-five per cent ability*'. I would write of Stanley Matthews, who had been the youngest England player, recounting how at the age of six he had begun kicking around a ball in the town – and a paper ball at that.

None of this would be published.

My last newspaper story I had written before leaving the North-East had dealt with the death of a two-year old boy who had wandered into the River Derwent. In my enthusiasm or through a lack of sensitivity, I had visited the parents in their home; it had been an extremely sad experience and one I should not have had. I should not have disturbed them in their grief. This had not gone down well with the Newcastle *Journal* for whom I had written the piece; I regretted it, but I would be astonished years later to find that intrusion into private grief became commonplace, the new technique of door-stepping introduced alike by newspaper and television reporters.

My last hard newspaper story I would write when I had returned home for Easter in 1957.

I had not intended to return home, I was saving my money to get to the Moscow Youth Festival, but I received a letter on Thursday from my sister asking me to return, to please my mother and father, and impulsively I had paid my week's rent in advance at my boarding house and made my way to King's Cross Station. I had been received home like the Prodigal Son, my visit being unexpected, but on Easter Sunday I heard that a man had been murdered at Chopwell.

I would spend the day checking out the story, of a man who had been found dead in the street, his head badly gashed. Four national newspapers would carry the story, the *Express* on its front page with the headline: *Murder Rumours Sweep Village*. When the inquest came to be opened it was ascertained that he had died of natural causes; he had probably keeled over when drunk and struck his head against the kerb. He had not been hit over the head with a bottle after all.

190

So much for the murder rumours.

It might be my last hard newspaper story but it would be my finest, my most sensational, my most newsworthy, and would pay for my trip north to see my family and help me on my way to Moscow. By living each day on my bowl of tomato soup and bread roll and Lyon's fruit pie, I had been able to set aside some thirty-eight pounds by Easter and on my return home my mother had offered to put up another twenty-five pounds to ensure that I would meet the full cost of getting to Moscow. I would write in my diary, quoting the words of John Gay written on his tombstone: '*Life is a jest and all things show it; I thought so once and now I know it*'.

Sadly or otherwise, my week with *The Daily Telegraph* would be the closest I would get to Fleet Street for thirty years.

When I became Member of Parliament I went to see Bill Deedes, Editor of the *Telegraph*.

The printing ink had yet to dry from my veins and I wanted to know what would be the prospects of my writing articles for the *Telegraph*. The first letter I had written as Prospective Parliamentary Candidate for Hexham had been published in the *Telegraph*; I had been reading the newspaper since my days in the colliery office, when it had been brought in by the colliery under-manager when he could no longer work underground because of damage to his spinal cord; and it had been the *Morning Post*, fore-runner to the *Telegraph*, that had written of Chopwell as Little Moscow.

It seemed a fitting enough place to start for a Labour MP who would claim to be New Labour even before Tony Blair.

'It'll not do your reputation any good,' Bill said.

Garland came into the room with his cartoons for the next day's edition, two of them if I recall, and Bill Deedes with hardly a glance chose the one that pleased him best. I had long been a fan of Garland and later, when the former Prime Minister Harold Wilson died, Garland had sketched a truly wonderful cartoon of a young Harold Wilson in cloth cap and short'uns, hurrying away from Number Ten with a farewell shake of his hand. Harold, as a young man, had had his photograph taken on the steps of Number Ten.

I had written to congratulate Garland on the cartoon and reminded him how we had briefly met in the Editor's office. He had written a kind reply which I would pin to the wall of my study, but on the day I had met Garland and Bill Deedes, looking out beyond the windows to Fleet Street, thinking of the prestigious offices I had known for the Editor, the Assistant Editor and the Diplomatic Correspondent, I mentioned to Bill that I had once been a copytaker with the *Telegraph*.

'You should have stayed with us,' he said. 'You'd have made more money.'

Fleet Street had still been the home of the national press, but new technology and high costs had begun to push the newspaper into new buildings, scattering them around London as far as Wapping or Battersea. *The Daily Express* went, as did the *Press Association*, leaving behind only its Edgar Wallace plaque; and so eventually did the *Daily Telegraph*, decamping to Canary Wharf. The *Evening Standard* changed its location from Shoe Lane and only *Associated Newspapers*, owners and publishers of *Weekend Mail* and *The Daily Mail* and *The Mail on Sunday*, and now too the *Evening Standard*, would cling to their building near the Embankment, before they moved to Kensington.

I had written several articles for *The Daily Mail* and *The*

Mail on Sunday on the Cleveland child abuse crisis, *The Sunday Times* would serialise my book *When Salem Came to the Boro*, but when the crisis drew to an end with the 1989 Children Act I was commissioned by Nick Gordon to write a series of articles for *You* Magazine. This was *The Mail on Sunday*'s colour supplement, now a women's magazine, but then covering general features.

Nick had been Deputy Editor of *The Daily Mail* during the crisis and when he had become Editor of *You* Magazine he had called and asked me to go, at a moment's notice, to Ankara to interview a Turkish weight-lifter who had won an Olympic gold medal. Later I would go to the Sea of Galilee and write of St Peter's fish. I would go to the South-West of France and write of a village owned by an English cricketer, and to the European Parliament to write about Otto van Habsburg. I would write a satire of senior colleagues in the Labour Party, imagining what careers they might have had had they not gone into politics.

The articles would appear under my own name and I would regularly visit Nick in his office. It occurred to me on one visit that I had made it after all, writing my features, visiting the Editor, seeing my name in print, that the journey I had begun from my pit village to Tufnell Park, that had seen me running down the Aldwych past the Law Courts to *The Daily Telegraph*, that had taken me through loneliness and frustration and despair, desperation even, that had seen me live through poverty and deprivation.

That journey had ended.

I would write for the *Financial Mail*, another supplement to *The Mail on Sunday*, and my first article would be sent to me at my hotel in Newcastle when I had returned midweek to attend a football game at St James' Park. United were playing Liverpool in the F.A. Cup. The journey had begun from Newcastle Central Station at ten minutes past eleven

193

one Tuesday evening thirty years ago and on arriving back, there in my hotel room to be proof-read would be the copy of my article. My coverage of football, my early newspaper reporting days, my stories for the *Weekend Mail* all came back to me.

I was in Fleet Street at last.

After my visit to Goldman Sachs I would have supper with Sonia Land at the Savoy Grill, but before the Grill there would be a *kir royale* in the Savoy Bar. I looked again at the panel with its roll call of famous American writers from the twenties. It took a little while for the *kir* to arrive, so great was the crush of the young upwardly mobile, accountants and lawyers and dealers from the old newspaper buildings.

'Tell me what's wrong with the spelling of Hemingway,' Sonia said.

'They've added an extra "*m*"', I said.

'Do you think anyone here cares?' she asked.

'Maybe not,' I said. 'But I know one thing.'

'What's that?'

'Whoever wrote that would never get a job as copytaker with *The Daily Telegraph*.'

The *kir* arrived and Sonia gave me one of those looks that Tony Blair often gives me.

An Arthur Scargill Story

Arthur Scargill had a problem.

The National Union of Mineworkers had lost staff as the coal industry had shrivelled rather than shrunk. There had been a million men working eight hundred pits 1 January 1947 when my father had asked me to look out of our bedroom window to see fluttering from the colliery headstock the blue flag of the National Coal Board, its white initials etched into the blue. By 1992, with a hundred-and-thirty pits and hundred-and-forty thousand miners laid off since the 1984–85 pit strike, only nineteen pits would be left and another forty thousand miners lose their jobs.

There had been more than a blue flag flying that first day of 1947.

There had been plaques on the pithead depicting that property had passed from the coal owners. The pits had been nationalised. They belonged now to the men who worked in them. The National Union of Mineworkers had been created to cater for their needs, to see that pithead baths were erected, safety equipment issued, pensions organised, concessionary coal granted, aged miners' cottages built, proper medical treatment arranged for those suffering from nystagmus or pneumoconiosis.

Under the rules of the old Iron and Steel Community, then the European Community, now the European Union, subventions had been paid to local communities where workers engaged in winning coal had lost their jobs; but this had not applied to those white-collar workers within the National Union of Mineworkers, since they had not been employed in a productive capacity.

As President of the NUM, Arthur Scargill had taken this up with Tim Eggar MP, Minister for Energy in the Conservative government. Tim had given the matter a thorough airing but to no avail. The rules of the Community were explicit: subventions or windfall money could only be paid where there had been a loss within a productive industry by those who did the producing, and even then to their communities, so that they might build anew; not the white-collar workers within the Union.

Arthur had brought the problem to New Labour as the future government.

When in Opposition, a meeting would be held under the chairmanship of David Blunkett MP, future Secretary of State for Education. The meeting would be held at the Old Labour headquarters in Walworth Road with Robin Cook MP and Martin O'Neill MP and myself as members of the Shadow Trade and Industry team. I had promised, as the son of a miner, coming from a pit village, to look at the matter and give Arthur a definitive response.

As front bench spokesman for New Labour, I would do all that I could to help.

After the meeting Arthur Scargill and I had talked of the 1957 World Youth Festival we had both attended in Moscow. He would recall the splendid night around the Kremlin and in Red Square, with some three-hundred thousand young people, the arcing searchlights; he would recall dancing and singing, the Hull City Crescent Jazz Band setting itself up in the Square, its syncopated rhythms and harmonic idioms if not lilting in the air, certainly exciting young Russians who had never before heard jazz.

Arthur had actually compèred the show.

'How had that come about?' I asked.

'I cannot remember myself,' Arthur would recall.

For his efforts he would receive as a souvenir a model air-liner. The concert and festivities had been so successful the police had difficulty clearing the Square; they had thought the young people should move by one o'clock in the morning; but since no-one would move it would be quarter-to-three before Arthur began to make his way back to one of the hostels where the youth delegates were staying.

Arthur would recall a visit to the Agricultural and Industrial Exhibition where he had seen *Sputnik*, a Russian spacecraft, the first man-made satellite to orbit the earth, emitting its own harsh signal, irritating the United States, so that they would launch a satellite programme of their own. *Sputnik* had been the centrepiece of a whole section at the Exhibition devoted to the Soviet space programme and I recall visiting it myself, on a Sunday afternoon, somewhat daunted by the heat, having my photograph taken on steps leading to the fountains.

Arthur had been a member of the Young Communist League.

He had been its industrial organiser and sat on its National Executive Committee. He had sat on the National Festival Committee. He had addressed the Communist Party Conference at Scarborough earlier in the year. A number of delegates from the Festival Committee were invited to have dinner with the Soviet leaders, Nikita Sergeyevich Kruschev, Anastasy Mikoyan, Nikolai Bulganin and Mikhail Andreyevich Suslov, and other members of the Politburo.

Arthur would listen to Nikita Kruschev whilst sitting next to Communist Party ideologue Suslov.

Newspapers would later recount how Arthur had engaged in a debate this historic night with those at the top table; the subject had been whether Stalin's embalmed body should be removed from the mausoleum beneath the Kremlin walls where it lay permanently in state alongside the body of Vladimir Illych Lenin, founder of the Soviet Union. They had yet to make a decision, since I would stand in the long queue tapering to the edges of Red Square, the people in the queue respectful, having come from all parts of the Soviet Union to see the embalmed remains of both their past leaders.

Later they would indeed remove Stalin's body.

Kruschev had been First Secretary of the Communist Party. At the Twentieth Party Congress of the Communist Party, he had denounced Joe Stalin as a mass murderer. Arthur had not approved of Kruschev's Twentieth Party speech. The speech had lasted four hours and had been given behind closed doors, but substantially leaked to the Western world to indicate a turning point in the history of the Soviet Union.

Kruschev had recalled how Vladimir Illych Lenin had called for Stalin's removal from the General Secretaryship. He had been a blunderer as well as a killer. He had failed to anticipate Hitler's invasion of the Soviet Union, he had deported ethnic communities such as the Chechens, he had developed the cult of the personality and destroyed internal Party democracy.

Arthur, however, had a point.

'You can't get rid of Stalin by removing him from the history books!'

Nor had he thought it a good idea to change the name of Stalingrad.

Arthur had been born in Worsbrough pit village two miles south of Barnsley where pitmen had amused themselves with whippet and pigeon racing. Arthur would recall, too, bare-knuckled boxing matches on a Sunday afternoon with side stakes of half-a-crown. He had been born in a home identical to my own, one room downstairs and one up, a single tap of cold water, a netty in the garden, but whereas I would leave this home at nine months Arthur would spend four years before moving to a council house.

At fifteen he would go down the pit, leaving his secondary modern school, seeking a job in engineering before ending as his father had ended, working underground. He had not begun in his own village pit but rather at Woolley colliery eight miles away. His first day had been like many a first day for young pitman, working on screens where stone would be removed from the coal, the coal broken up before being loaded onto wagons that would take it by rail from the colliery.

Perhaps he would recall the rhyme of *bait, bottle, candle, matches* that I would hear so often in my own home, my father patting the pockets of his fustian jacket, cap to his head. Arthur would have as his bait – snap as it was called in Yorkshire – bread and jam sandwiches in a bait tin. He would carry too a tin water bottle. He had gone to his first branch meeting of the NUM at sixteen and he would work in-bye at seventeen. He would have his own pit pony.

He would join the Barnsley Communist Youth League.

His mother had worked in a local bobbin mill, though during the war she had worked full-time in a munitions factory; she was a religious woman who played no part in politics. She had died a year before Arthur had attended the Youth Festival and he would say that he had a more vivid recollection of her than anything else in his life; it had been a devastating period when she died and for three months he had been unable to focus. As he revealed to Sue Lawley on *Desert Island Discs*: 'I was very close to my mother because

199

my father had been in the RAF during the war and so my mother and I became inseparable.'

If his mother had been Christian, his father had been Communist, one the antithesis of the other, 'a marvellous contradiction,' as Arthur would recall. His father had taken Arthur to his first political meeting at the age of twelve: 'It would always be up to him whether he came with me or not, but from the first meeting he was always with me, and we heard many a famous speaker and took part in many a debate.'

It would be the pits, however, that would be the reality of his life.

The trip to Moscow took three days by train.

I had visited the grave of Karl Marx in Highgate. Where else would one begin a journey to Moscow? The cemetery stood on a steep slope, the grave stones chalk-white, protruding like tablets from the earth, *'pinnacles of respect to the dead but not forgotten'*, as I would write in my diary. Flowers on some of the graves were fresh, others encompassed by grass and weeds; there was a silence to the graveyard, seeping out of the ground, perhaps from souls at rest, bodies at peace, minds no longer alert, brows no longer fevered; the past and the present would coalesce in a tranquillity few in the graveyard would have known in their time.

The grave of Karl Marx would stand out.

The gravedigger had done his work in March 1883, few had mourned the day Karl Marx had been interred; his friends had wept, but the earth had not trembled to embrace him; there had been no thunder or lightning, no portents, no pathetic fallacy as there had before the

200

death of Julius Ceasar, at least in the mind of William Shakespeare, when there had been *'tempests and scolding winds and threatening clouds'*. The grave, however, would be as impoverished as the life of Marx itself till the huge headstone had been restored with Soviet money, the daubed paint of malefactors washed away.

I thought I might learn Russian before I got to the Festival, but I did not get beyond the phrase book.

The train would leave Victoria Station with Dover as the first stop. I would see the white cliffs and green harbour water for the first time. I would stand upon the deck of the ferry like others before me, not waving goodbye to my country, as the poet Rupert Brooke had waved goodbye, slipping from his troopship to give a handkerchief to a young girl on the quay so that he would not feel alone, but I felt the freshness of the sea breeze on a lengthy but calm journey to Ostend. It would be a hard train from Ostend to Brest Litovsk through Berlin and Warsaw, some pulling out sleeping bunks from the wall of the carriages, some sleeping on the floor. I had not known how to pull the bunk from the wall and had asked an Australian in the next carriage.

'It's the Jairke System,' he explained.

'What's the Jairke System?' I asked.

'I'm all right, Jairke.'

I had slept on the floor.

Only when we reached Brest Litovsk and had transferred to a Russian train did we become guests of the Soviet government. We were given comfortable sleepers and tea from samovars; the flat countryside would roll gently over the famous Russian steppes, the train travelling so slowly that I would often wonder if they had really dispensed with the man carrying a red flag who in the past had marched before each train.

Arthur Scargill would remind me that Robin Corbett, MP for Birmingham, Erdington, had not only been on the trip but had been in charge of a whole train. There had been at least two train-loads of young people making their way to Moscow from London, some of them Communists, wearing red shirts, others fellow travellers, some pure Marxist students, one of whom explained that it was perfectly all right in China to kill two million of the population for the greater good.

'So long as one of them's not your mother,' I replied tartly.

We had been held up in Dover whilst the authorities, whoever they were, listed our names and passport numbers, registering each and every one of us as potential subversives. It would often cross my mind that if ever I were offered a place in government a Permanent Secretary would ask what on earth I had been doing with so many Communist reprobates and fellow travellers on a Youth Festival trip to Moscow.

'You shouldn't worry,' Arthur had said.

'Why's that?' I asked.

'Just tell them in 1978 I went to the World Youth Festival in Cuba with Peter Mandelson!'

My mind was filled with the stories I would write from Moscow.

I had already seen the Editor of the *Sunday Sun* at Whitsuntide. He had promised to consider one article, though I had offered him five: *Ivan The Terrible*, *Archangel – the Forgotten City*, *Paul the Mad Czar*, *the Russian Drought of 1946* and *The Man Who Built the Moscow Underground*. I would write to *Weekend Mail* and the *Daily Express* and I rang *Reveille*. I would consider *The Sunday Times* as a possible market.

A week after my arrival I had visited a film studio. The

studio had not been far from the hostel where I had lodged.
I explained that I worked for an English newspaper and
desired a tour. I was introduced to a young girl about
twenty-five, medium height and pretty face, and as my
dairy records, '*an excellent personality*'.

Her name was Leica and she gave me a genial reception.

She told me she was married but had no children and
that she worked at the studio adding Russian sub-titles to
foreign films. I asked many questions about the Russian
film industry, its actors, its technicians, its studios. She
took me through the studios and in one particular studio
they were filming a scene from *Puss and Boots*, the King
upon his throne, the studio entirely silent for the short scene,
my one and only attendance at the shooting of a film.

In another studio she pointed out certain of the more
famous actors whose portraits graced the walls and gave
me a few facts concerning each one, how many films they
had made and the like. Halfway along she stopped before
a portrait of a young man with regular features and hair
brushed back. A seductive smile hovered around the corners
of his mouth; his eyes had a sparkle which women might
have found alluring.

'He's in the studio at the moment,' she said.

'I'd like to meet him,' I said.

'I shall see if it can be arranged.'

I reflected perhaps at last I had a story that would be ideal
for *Weekend Mail*, perhaps *Reveille*. A full feature piece
on the Russian film industry built around this charismatic
young man might perhaps be attractive for *The Sunday
Times*. I wondered if there would be a photographer in the
studio so that I could take pictures back with me, not only
of the actor but of Leica.

Perhaps she might be able to arrange this.

203

I sat down by a table and gazed again at the handsome face. Leica had told me he was one of the most famous and popular actors in Russia. He attracted audiences not only because of his looks but because he had a pleasant voice. Most of his popularity came from his singing. I could imagine him on the screen, young, expressive, creating the same hype as the American singer Mario Lanzo, though slimmer and younger.

Leica returned with a short dumpy middle-aged man. He had a pouch, *embonpoint* as the French call it, a double chin and fleshy cheeks. His skin lacked colour, as drab as Ukranian granite; there were wrinkles around his eyes and deep creases to his brow. His ears were over-large and, when you came to think of it, his hair too thin. His handshake was strong and sincere, his palms not calloused by manual labour, but he seemed short of breath and when he spoke his voice was low and laboured.

'I'm sorry you couldn't find your star,' I said.

'He speaks English,' Leica said.

'You mean this is the star?'

The star not only smiled but grinned.

He pointed to the picture on the wall.

'Do I still look like that?' he asked.

'You've not changed a bit,' I said.

The actor hugged me and pounded my back and said that I was a friend for life. Did I need a lift anywhere? Perhaps if he visited England he could come and see me? Leica would give me a full list of his films and songs. I could write what I liked. He would be popular in the Western press. The portrait on the wall beamed as he beamed towards the portrait.

His podgy body turned and he bundled himself off.

'How long ago was the portrait taken?' I asked Leica.

'About ten years,' she said.

204

'Time has changed him,' I said.

'Not if you're a famous actor,' she said.

'And I have a story to write.'

Except there would be no story.

Perhaps out of sympathy, Leica did arrange for me to visit television studios where I was given a photograph of a young Russian singer which later found its way into *Reveille*; he had been strumming a guitar and I had described him as *'Russia's answer to Elvis Presley'*. My diary tells me the visit to the studio had been *'highly interesting'* and had delivered me *'the most newsworthy story'* of the whole trip, but this had passed me by unless it was the Russian Elvis Presley.

I came to the conclusion I had not used my time wisely.

The articles I had wished to write were never written, and I would not make a single penny except, I suppose, *Reveille* paid me two guineas for the photograph they had used of the Russian Elvis Presley. I blamed my *'sheer frivolity'* and reproached myself where days had been wasted *'because of laziness'*; and there had been only a little culture, with a single visit to the Lenin Museum and an Art Gallery.

There were, of course, my memories.

The Festival had opened in the Lenin Stadium beneath the Lenin Hills.

I had been studying the paintings of Claude Monet, the facade at Rouen Cathedral, a single motif painted at different times during the day, the paintings reflecting the different light; and in a stadium filled with a hundred-thousand spectators, in the bright sunlight, so the images of the spectators would change as the light changed, a rustle of

205

colour, a mosaic creating and uncreating itself before one's very eyes.

The stadium stood by a river and the upper parapets beyond the spectators were ridged with red flags, the flags limp in the heat; they were meant to reflect the proud achievement of such a glorious stadium, but it had been the spectators, relaxing in their bright shirts and caps, arms open to the sun, that were the achievement. They might be privileged to be in the stadium at all, to await the arrival of Nikita Kruschev and other members of the Politburo, but they were happy.

I had met two students from London University and we would become friends.

The students were neither Communist nor fellow-travellers. Perhaps they were history students, or there out of curiosity, a desire to travel, a sense of adventure, cheap at the price, for once across the border at Brest Litovsk we were guests of the Soviet government. The only cost to the trip had been the travel from London to the border. One of the students would fall ill with bronchitis and be sent to hospital to recover, so that he did not return on the trains with the rest of us.

He and his friend would be good companions.

We had taken a bus trip to the Russian Orthodox monastery at Zagorsk.

The monastary has changed its name, but stands upon a hill surrounded by a stone wall, and as you approach you can see only the beautiful blue and gold towers thrusting upwards. There is a cobbled square before an archway leading into the grounds that reminds you of Red Square. I had read of Zagorsk and had pictured a small village, alone as it were, severed from the rest of the country, because this was an athiest state that closed churches and was hostile to believers.

The monastery would be an anachronism in an age of dialectical materialism, but Marx could no more extinguish religion than he could convert the world to scientific socialism, either in his time or from the grave, and when Communism collapsed the towers of Zagorsk would still be standing, as forthright as they had been the day I had visited the monastery and shared the prayers of the Russian Orthodox Church.

'How many divisions has the Pope?' Stalin had once asked.

It turned out the Church had more divisions than Stalin.

There had been a visit to the Bolshoi Ballet and to our astonishment and delight there had been a performance of *Swan Lake*, the likes of which I am not likely to see again, those beautiful young ballerinas flapping around on the stage with broken wings as the music of Tchaikovski reached its crescendo. I had taken the programme around to the stage door and waited for the ballerinas so that they might sign the programme. I would keep the programme for years, proud to have been there, proud of their signatures, the ballerinas so fragile, so petite, their dark hair swept back, but now the programme has been lost.

I hope it will one day reappear among my papers.

There had been student festivities at Moscow University and I had found myself dancing with a Russian girl who spoke no English. We had danced the night away, as it were, enjoying each other's company, and as a gallant Englishman I had accompanied her home. This extravagant journey had been undertaken by bus and when we had left the bus we had walked up the street, hand-in-hand or arm-in-arm. She suddenly stopped and smiled and nodded towards the darkness of an alleyway.

This was no invitation.

This was where she lived.

She pumped my hand and called:

'*Dasveedanee-ya!*'

I returned into the small hours of the morning, full of the joys of the University, the music still to my ears, the rhythms of the dance floor, feeling warm still from our dancing, flushed with excitement, thinking still of the young girl I had just met, whom I would never see again but whose image I was sure would not fade from my mind.

Then it occurred to me.

I had not the slightest idea where I was.

I might discern the Red Star over the Kremlin but even this stared indifferently. I had no fear and stopped some road sweepers. Moscow is a clean city, its cleaners work in the night, out of sound and sight, as they do in the Metro. I spoke to them in English but they did not understand. There was some discussion, their cigarettes glowing scarlet in the darkness, and one of them hurried away across a bridge. I remember their boiler suits and twig brushes, water rushing down gutters, but still I had no fear.

The man returned with police officers.

They politely invited me into the back of their van and we drove across the bridge. I was taken to the Metropole Hotel where a man at the desk spoke English. I explained I had been to the University but had become lost and did not know my way back.

'I want to go home,' I said.

'You want to go home?'

'Not home,' I said. 'To the hostel.'

'How do you get to the hostel?'

'I know the number of the bus and where to catch it.'

'In that case, why not sleep over there?'

I would sleep my one and only night in the Metropole Hotel, the poshest and most expensive hotel in Moscow, though I would sleep not in any of its spacious rooms, rather on a sofa in the lounge, awaiting the first light so that I could slip from the hotel down the road to Red Square and from the edge of the Square to the bus stop where I knew my bus would take me to the hotel.

I would never even know the girl's name.

Arthur Scargill might recall a dinner where the Young Communist League members had sat at the top table, but I would recall the Kremlin ball, wandering by mistake into the Palace of the Czars. The Palace had been all that it should be: thick red carpets, eighteen and nineteenth century furniture of stained wood, chandeliers poised above your head, wall lights as elegant and graceful as the chandeliers.

The night of the Kremlin ball – 28 July 1957 – had also been the night Arthur Scargill had compèred the jazz show. I had found myself alone in the Kremlin grounds gazing towards the river. Moscow had never seen such a night, not even when it had been celebrating May Day or the anniversary of the October Revolution. The Kremlin towers were draped white in the lights of searchlights playing upon them from across the river, the moonlight a gentle crystal, but overwhelmed by the blinding sweep of the searchlights as they arced the sky.

In contrast to the white brilliance of the searchlights, I would see the river curving reluctantly towards the Smolensky Hotel, as if afraid of moving forward, unlike history, brooding over some dark secret, afraid that a little haste might reveal a tragic past, secrets as dark as the waters were deep. The river might be wide but it would flow quietly as the Don, curving under the arches of bridges so slightly, so gently yet without menace or hostility.

There was gaiety and colour all around me, the Kremlin ball spilling onto the cobblestones around the Palace of the Czars, into Cathedral Square and the gardens with their limp lime trees and ever-greens, down into Red Square where by now the Hull City Crescent Jazz Band had assembled. I felt empty and alone, my spirit abandoned among such gaiety and colour, such joy and happiness.

I contemplated my own life, my ambition, my destiny, my past in the pit village, at the grammar school, in the colliery office, as a newspaper reporter, now working as a shorthand-typist in London. My future might not be as darkly hidden as the deep waters of the river, yet it would be as uncertain. Perhaps I romanticised, my imagination getting the better of me, losing me in reverie, neither waking nor sleeping, so that I ignored the calls of those I knew as they hurried past, intent on pleasure, following their enthusiasm and vitality into the softness of the night.

I wondered if I might trace my future as the searchlights traced the sky. Where would my ambition take me? Would it take me anywhere at all? Had I a true ambition and a perseverence to achieve that ambition? Did I have talent or ability? Would there be for me a tide taken at the flood or would this be omitted? Would I spend my time in shallows and miseries? Or as Oliver Cromwell said, would it be the case that no man goes furthest than he who does not know where he is going?

Standing by the wall of the Kremlin gardens, listening to the music from Red Square as the searchlights filled the darkness, I could be certain only of one thing: that I had be going somewhere, even if as tonight I would be cut off from the joy and gaiety and pleasure of those around me. Mine might be a full life but it would be a singular one.

Below me Arthur Scargill would see the searchlights.

The laughter and the tap of feet upon cobbles would be submerged by the jazz. There were other bands in the square that night, some of them oriental, their sounds intermingled,

210

and those who danced would feel the softness to the air, not crisp nor muggy either; they would be lost to their own sweat, their own joy that the whole of life lay before them. If they had a past it was forgotten, if they had a future they did not care, at least not tonight. If they had aspirations they might be set aside.

If there was a destiny to fulfil it was not for them.

Except, that is, for Arthur Scargill.

I would return to Moscow forty-one years later.

There would not be the sultry heat Arthur and I had known, this would be September, the first touch of autumn to the air, yet Moscow warm still, enjoying its own Indian summer, the clouds high and relaxed, as were the people in the streets, notwithstanding a financial crisis, the rouble devalued against the dollar.

I would look for the Metropole Hotel, not on Red Square as I had imagined but on Teatralny Lane off the Square, rising away from the Kremlin, turning right past the National History Museum. The vestibule had changed, there were no horse-hair sofas, only people in a hurry across the marble floor. I had wanted a coffee in the Metropole, for old time's sake, or rather tea from a samovar, but there were too many people and no samovar, and I had come back into the wide street, squinting into the sunlight, changing tack towards the Gum store.

I would find the store easily enough, with its white marble-like walls and blue slate spirals, filling a side of Red Square opposite the Lenin mausoleum and Spasskaya Tower. The ground floor had been filled with Western-style boutiques selling Estee Lauder and Christian Dior, the stores empty, the collapsed dollar driving customers

211

away except for women queuing for cheaper tights and cosmetics.

Silver teeth were out and aesthetics in.

The Soviet Union was no more.

I was back in Moscow to attend the hundredth conference of the Inter-Parliamentary Union, a Parliament of all peoples, some with democratic governments and some with governments who had democratic aspirations. The inaugural ceremony had been held in the Grand Kremlin Palace where Arthur Scargill had dined with Kruschev and Suslov; only now it was Boris Yeltsin who would welcome the world's Parliamentarians. He had been head of the Russian Federation, his health had not been good, his skin sallow and liverish, but he had worn an electric-blue suit that sharply accentuated his blue eyes and white hair.

The Inter-Parliamentary Union plenary meetings would be held in the State Kremlin Palace and I would speak to the Conference for all of four minutes. The Palace had not been built at the time of my first visit to Moscow. It stood by the Troitskaya Tower entrance to the Kremlin, its auditorium of red and gold and corrugated wooden panels; all seats had been fitted with special electronics so that there might be simultaneous translation into at least thirty languages.

There would be too a Kremlin ball.

The Archbishop Sergei Solnechnogorsk, Chancellor the Patriarch of Moscow, had been at the ball. I had met him with the Bishop of London when a few months earlier he had attended a lunch in the House of Lords. On being asked to say a few words, I had described my visit to Zagorsk, the monastery reposing in the shadow of tall lime trees, monks with flowing beards and ringlets to their waists, wearing silver crosses, some big, some small.

'But you must visit Zagorsk again!' he said.

Except that it had changed its name.

212

At the Kremlin ball I would remind the Archbishop of our conversation, but it would be too late to make arrangements for another visit to Zagorsk, and we exchanged greetings before he and his entourage moved on, the Orthodox Church re-established at the heart of Russian life, churches not only reopening but whole cathedrals being transformed. I would pass one in the heart of Moscow.

One reason I had not been able to get to Zagorsk was because I would spend most of my spare time at the Conference studying Russia's financial crisis, writing for the *Financial Mail on Sunday*, filing copy not by telephone or telegraph but by e-mail from the computer room at the Marriott Hotel. A Polish friend had warned me that hotels in Moscow would be cockroach-infested and damp, but the Marriott was entirely new, it had been used by the staff of President Clinton only a week earlier, when the President had visited Moscow; it had its own Russian and French restaurants, its breakfast rooms and foyers, as well as the ultra-modern computer facilities.

But as I had spent too much time on journalism on my first visit so I would spend too much on my second, calling accountants and lawyers in Moscow, speaking to British Embassy staff, speaking to the *Reuters'* correspondent, also to members of the Russian Parliament, even to Yuri Primakov who, within an hour of addressing the Inter-Parliamentary Union, would become Prime Minister of the Russian Federation. I would reconstruct the crisis and interpret this for readers of the *Financial Mail on Sunday*.

I would spend my day off in the hotel room preparing my copy.

The *Depeche Mode* rock band had been staying at the hotel. They had begun their career in 1980 and had sold some thirty-five million albums. One afternoon, returning from the Conference, there had been fans outside the hotel,

213

having waited all day for sight of the band. The band had settled around a piano and as one of them played, to the exasperation of their manager, they had got in a little singing practice, enlivening the foyer where I took my cappuccino and sliced cake.

After making my speech to the Conference, I had strolled around Cathedral Square through the gardens towards the wall where the river ran beneath, walking on the allotted footpaths to avoid the whistles of the Kremlin guards, who wished to keep the cobbles free for official limousines.

The gardens had not changed in forty-one years, with their lime trees and ever-greens, and I was able to pause with my hands upon the balustrade overlooking the embankment, feeling the sun warm to the cheek, closing my eyes and reflecting back to the night of the Kremlin ball, the gaiety and joy, those quiet thoughts of a future as well as a past, a destiny to be fulfilled, whatever that destiny might be, deep and unrevealing as the river.

How had it all turned out?

Had it been as I had expected? What had happened to my career in journalism? Had I fulfilled my career as a writer? Had I indeed fulfilled my destiny? Or had all this been romantic nonsense, neither here nor there, flotsam and jetsam, of little concern to me and less concern to the world? Would my life have been led without the same motivation, the same ambition, the same sense of journeying onward, of seeking not one goal but several, the desire of the moth for the star, of the night for the morrow, as Percy Bysshe Shelley had once written?

Had Oliver Cromwell been right after all?

Below me to the left they were setting up the stand for the *Depeche Mode* concert that evening. The concert would be part of their first tour since 1993. It would be held on the sloping cobbles before St Basil's Cathedral rather than in

Red Square; the seats were already in place and I hoped that it would be as warm and sultry as the night of our Kremlin ball forty-one years ago. Perhaps the crescendo music rippling across the river might equal the jazz stridency of the Hull City Crescent Jazz Band, compèred by Arthur Scargill of the Young Communist League.

I reflected that perhaps if I had fulfilled my destiny had Arthur fulfilled his?

As President of the National Union of Mineworkers, he would lead the greatest strike in history.

He would fight for a dying industry as other energy forms moved onto the economic stage. Power stations became gas or oil-fired and there would no longer be a conveyor belt of coal from ground to surface to power stations. Pits might close and miners lose their jobs, yet each time a finger flicked a light switch, there would be electricity.

An entire industry had been made redundant.

But if the Conservative government perceived this to be a class war, a struggle fought on Marxist principles according to a Marxist reading of history, so too would left-wing groups. They would organise meetings up and down the country and those who organised a rally in Middlesbrough would not allow me to speak on a platform within my own constituency. I would invite myself onto the platform anyway and speak in support of the miners.

I would write for an NUM magazine covering the Northumbrian coalfield. I would meet miners when they lobbied Parliament and I attended the Durham Miners' Gala where Neil Kinnock would share a platform with Arthur Scargill. He had only recently been elected Leader of the

215

Labour Party. I would write to *The Times* and say on *BBC Newsnight* that I supported the miners. But which miners, an exasperated Jon Snow wanted to know.

'Those on strike or those not on strike?'

'All the miners,' I would reply.

'In Durham they are striking. In Nottingham they are not.'

This was because there had been no national ballot for strike action, it had been left to local mining areas, and Neil Kinnock would be hampered in his support for the miners because the strike lacked the legitimacy of a ballot. My support, like the support of the Labour Party, would never be enough and if hampered by the lack of a ballot it would be hampered still further by violence on the picket line. The worst conflict had been at the Orgreave coke works in Yorkshire. There had been a mass picket organised to achieve the same result as at Saltley twelve years ago. More than a thousand pickets had shown up the first day, among them Arthur Scargill, but this time the police would not be overwhelmed.

More than five thousand miners now joined the picket line but they would be met by police deployed in riot gear; some eighty-two pickets were arrested and more than a hundred police officers and twenty-eight pickets injured. Pickets had moved in to prevent thirty-five lorries from entering the works, but the gates would not be closed as they had been at Saltley.

There would be missiles and firecackers, mounted police would charge with batons and long shields, arrests would be made, but the convoy would get through. More lorries would arrive, the pickets would charge again; the police would charge the pickets and the pickets would scatter. Three weeks of picketing and confrontation did not close the coke works, but in the eyes of the Marxist left for the

216

Labour Party to condemn picket line violence was the same as condemning the miners.

The striking miners would be defeated because not every coalfield had been on strike, coal stocks had been too high, electricity supplies had been maintained, there had been no power cuts and no three-day working weeks; secondary picketing had been confronted and beaten off, there had been no national strike of workers in other sectors. Popular support had been weakened by picket-line violence. The establishment too had closed in through the courts and the NUM were fined for defying the law requiring a union-wide ballot before the strike.

The strike would end in hardship and deprivation.

Miners had moved from linoleum to wall-to-wall carpets and central heating and sometimes not one car in the street but two. They had done well in their pay settlements after the 1972 and 1974 strikes. There would be money in the bank, but their savings would go and with them their livelihood. Their cars would go if not their wall-to-wall carpets and central heating, but some would lose their homes if they had been bought on mortgage.

They would lose their jobs too.

Many of those on strike would be sacked, there would be no amnesty when the strike was over, and in Scotland no sacked miner would be reinstated. The strike had begun 9 March 1984 and would end a year later on 5 March 1985 when those men who had not been sacked marched behind colliery banners like their fathers before them, marching in the early morning, sometimes a fine mist seeping through the colliery yard, sometimes a light etching to the sky. They would make their way as one to the pithead, to the headstock, to the cage, to the drift mouth, their womenfolk alongside them, as they had always been, at the time of a colliery disaster when they would wait for news at the

217

pithead, now at the time of tribulation, bringing their children with them, but proud still that their men had endured.

They had been defeated but they had not been destroyed.

Except that the men would march once more, a final march, not a funereal march, a march of hope and encouragement that perhaps – only perhaps – a tide might turn, pits might be saved and with them men's jobs.

After the 1992 General Election had returned another Conservative government, Michael Heseltine as President of the Board of Trade had announced the closure of thirty-one pits with the loss of thirty thousand jobs.

Some of the pits would be closed within days. The announcement had been badly received on both Conservative and Labour benches and after a short debate I had seen the Prime Minister, John Major, in the Commons corridor running parallel to the library.

'I saw something was not right,' he said.

The reaction had been more forceful in the country. There were marches in Cheltenham against the Heseltine announcement; three thousand took to the streets. They wanted John Major sacked not the miners. Major called an emergency Cabinet meeting and Heseltine would announce a freeze to his pit closure programme. There would be an investigation into whether new markets could be found for coal.

There would be for Arthur Scargill a final flickering moment of glory as he led miners through the London streets. He had marched them through Chelsea and Kensington. Citizens would come out upon their hotel balconies and cheer and there would be white chrysanthemums offered in Kensington. On Sunday there would be a march of a hundred thousand, beginning on the Embankment, moving slowly through the West End to Hyde Park Corner.

Margaret and Malcolm had come from Middlesbrough, it had rained heavily that day, but we had marched under unfurled colliery banners, black anarchist flags swirling among the marchers, though for what purpose had not been clear. The tail of the march would only arrive at Hyde Park when the speeches were over. Even the Liberal Democrat leader, Paddy Ashdown, would address the miners. Arthur Scargill would have friendly and positive talks with John Smith.

He had become the new Leader of the Labour Party.

Arthur would recall that a hundred-and-forty pits had closed since the miners' strike with a hundred-and-forty thousand redundancies. But the last pits would close despite the marches and the flowers and the rhetoric; if thirty-one pits had been listed for closure in the original proposal thirty-three would close; and if thirty thousand jobs had been threatened forty thousand would be lost.

Some pits would stay in private hands but the nationalised industry of which the miners had been proud would be no more. The assets of the coal owners above and below ground might have been turned over to the people in 1947 but the people did not want them anymore. Only rusting plaques declaring that the pits now belonged to the people might be found in disused pit yards, if even they can be found, so complete had been the devastation of the coal industry.

Except that Arthur wanted help from New Labour's front bench to get compensation for those NUM officers who had lost their jobs. I would take up Arthur's cause, I would read the rules and regulations and statutes of the European Community. I would speak with lawyers specialised in these matters, but if Tim Eggar MP as Minister could find no loophole nor could I. It was with sadness that I wrote to Arthur and told him a future New Labour government could be of no assistance to him.

Arthur was nothing, if not persistent.

He raised the matter again after the 1997 General Election, when Margaret Beckett became President of the Board of Trade, a title she would inherit from Michael Heseltine. Her political advisor Dan Corry called me to say that Arthur was seeking money from the European Union for the NUM because the white-collar staff had lost their jobs with so many pit closures.

I explained that I had thoroughly investigated such a possibility, that it had been raised with the former government, that I had checked it with lawyers, that I had read the regulations and statutes and that Community law was clear. No money could be paid to the NUM because of staff losses. Money would only be paid to coalfield communities where there had been a loss of productive labour.

'I'm sorry,' I said.

'Why are you sorry?' Dan Corry asked.

'Because I couldn't help Arthur. And I couldn't help the miners.'

The blue flag of the National Coal Board fluttered still in my mind.

A Story of Seven Loaves

I had wanted to thank Angelica for the work she had done arranging my Parliamentary delegation to Saudi Arabia.

'It's worth a cup of tea,' I said. 'When I get back.'

Angelica was personal assistant to the Deputy Ambassador at the Saudi Embassy; she had worked there for twenty-two years; she was Greek but she had lived in London most of her adult life. She had dark hair and brown eyes, a pleasant manner and sufficient patience to enable fifteen Parliamentarians to visit Saudi Arabia as a guest of the Sura Council.

The 1997 General Election might be imminent, but it had been important that I lead a delegation of those Members of Parliament interested in Saudi Arabia so that we might explain New Labour policies to the Sura; we would talk also of constitutional change which Tony Blair would seek to bring about as well as listening to members of the Sura, who would tell us how they were enhancing and buttressing their own democracy around the King.

The Sura was a new Consultative Council – the *Majlis Al-Shura* – set up to advise the King and at our first meeting Sunday afternoon one Sura member let drop he was a Manchester United supporter. I said that although we were pleased to be their guests on this day we were actually missing that afternoon a Manchester United–Blackburn Rovers game.

Janet Anderson MP, who would later become Minister of the Crown, had been a Blackburn Rovers fan. She too said she had made a sacrifice. She would also become Vice-Chamberlain of Her Majesty's Household, writing a letter each evening to the Queen on the day's Parliamentary proceedings; and on the day of the Queen's Speech she would be held hostage at Buckingham Palace until the Queen safely returned from Westminster.

A tale which the Sura members found most extraordinary.

Getting back to football, a member of the British Embassy staff slipped out of the meeting on my mentioning the football game and returned discreetly to pass me the score. We would discuss the more weighty matters of British–Saudi relationships until at the end of the meeting, profusely thanking our hosts for their hospitality, I was able to read out the score, to the pleasure I hoped of the Sura supporter of Manchester United.

They were astonished all over again.

They wondered if I had some modern apparatus on my person that had allowed the score to be communicated so quickly. Was it the latest new-fangled mobile, an international bleeper, or some minute receiver hidden in my ear? I kept to myself the secret of the piece of paper slipped around the table from the Embassy secretary, nothing more nor less than an old-fashioned hand-written bush telegraph.

We had dinner that evening in the grounds of the Sura Palace and I had been able to recount the story of how in the thirties when the Kingdom had been short of money King Abdul Aziz had asked his Minister of Finance and three advisors from the civil service to devise a scheme that would rectify this unhappy situation. They had returned to his presence and the King had asked:

'What do you suggest?'

'Half of all government employees will have to be dismissed,' the Minister of Finance said.

'Since you are all civil servants,' the King replied. 'Which two of you will go?'

The four retired and after a while returned with a policy that would maintain full employment, at least within the civil service, a practice that has not changed in any country in the world over many years and many administrations. It also showed that simplistic solutions may be practical but hardly efficient and give rise to more confusion and uncertainty than living with the original problem.

I had been to Saudi eleven years earlier and met His Royal Highness Prince Mohammed Bin Fahd only a year after he had become governor of the Eastern province. There had been the Gulf War and he had come to the House of Commons to thank Parliamentarians for the efforts of the British forces in the Gulf.

One evening, during my visit eleven years ago, I had been invited for dinner in the desert, and for a few moments I had walked the desert sands as William Kinglake had walked before me. He had written a travelogue in 1844 called *Eothen*, which meant *From the Early Dawn* or *From the East*; he had described how the endless sands had yielded nothing but small stunted shrubs. Even these had failed after the first two or three days and from that time forth there had been sand, sand still sand and only sand and sand and sand again.

Now I stood upon the same timeless sand, with its creases and rucks, its slight wind across the surface, the small stunted shrubs, aware that turning one way or the other I had already lost sight of the air-conditioned fully-modern mobile homes that had replaced the tents of the Saudi princes, but feeling no fear, safe in the knowledge that I had only to retrace my steps a hundred yards to be back to the company of my fellow Parliamentarians, before the wind had sifted over my tracks.

The delegation eleven years ago had been led by Julian Amery, son of Leo Amery who had served under Winston Churchill during the war. Julian had also been in the war on special missions; he had married the daughter of former Prime Minister Harold Macmillan and had been a Member of Parliament since 1950. He would lose his seat in 1966 but return to the House in 1969 as MP for Brighton, Pavilion till his retirement in 1992, when he had gone to the Lords as Amery of Lustleigh.

Julian has since died.

He had been offered by Prince Mohammed Bin Fahd a splendid sword in a gold-bejewelled scabbard; the sword had been long and curving and shining, like the sword King Abdul Aziz had used to show his power in the film *Lawrence of Arabia*, his part played by Sir Alec Guinness. During the film a silk square had been thrown into the air and had come down upon the upraised blade of the sword, the blade so sharp and fine the silk had been cut in two simply by falling upon it.

I had wondered how Julian would get the sword through Customs on his return to London, but in our evening in the desert we had been given heavy sheepskin cloaks that would keep us warm through the coldest night under the stars, the wind chill across the sand, sighing beyond the dunes as it curved its fingers to tress the sand into disparate curves.

Julian would simply wrap his sword and scabbard in the sheepskin cloak and barge through Customs into the arrival hall, his luggage ensconced upon a steel trolley, his head down, his chin tucked in, pretty much as he would speak on the floor of the House, standing below the gangway, hands in his pockets. But perhaps I need not have worried, the sword and scabbard had been a gift anyway.

On this trip we would again meet His Royal Highness Prince Mohammed Bin Fadh and I would present him with the original programme of eleven years ago. I would remind him of our lunch together in the House. I would compliment him on the progress in his Eastern Province, and indeed the whole of Saudi Arabia, and say how much we were looking forward to visiting the petro-chemical complex at Jubail Industrial City.

There would be no sword and bejewelled scabbard for me upon my return, but I had invited Angelica for tea at the Cavendish.

'Where is Middlesbrough?' she asked.

'In the North-East,' I said.

After tea I would take a train to my Middlesbrough constituency.

'Anywhere near Whitby?'

'Beyond Whitby.'

'Do you come from there?'

'I come from Newcastle.'

'Anywhere near Scotland?'

'Sort of.'

'When I was at shorthand school,' she said. 'I met a young man who came from your part of the world. He wanted to work in the House of Commons.'

'You're looking at him,' I said.

She smiled and continued her story.

'I'm sure this young man liked me,' she said. 'We both worked in the City and went for a walk together one lunch time down Petticoat Lane. We were looking through a window and he stood very close. My brother-in-law spotted us and when I arrived home that night there was an almighty row.'

'You were staying with your sister?'

'My brother-in-law was very Greek. He did not like my being seen with an Englishman.'

'You're a Greek-Cypriot?'

She nodded and sipped her tea.

'When I was at shorthand school,' I said. 'I met a Greek Cypriot girl. I used to tease her about Turkish Cypriots. She would say there were some very nice Turkish Cypriots.'

'I settled my brother-in-law by saying *"I know this boy looks English, but don't you think he resembles Seven Loaves – Eth Epta Psoumis?"*

'*"He's a Greek boy?"* my brother-in-law asked. *"He doesn't look Greek."*

'*"Neither does Seven Loaves,"* I said. *"Tall and slim with blond hair. But Seven Loaves is Greek – is he not?"*

'*"I would never have dreamed he was Greek,"* my brother-in-law said.'

'Who was Seven Loaves?' I asked.

'Just someone we knew.'

It was time for me to leave the Cavendish to catch my train.

'Were you ever at Pitman's College?' Angelica asked.

'Southampton Row,' I said. 'January 1957 until July 1958.'

'I was there at the same time,' Angelica said. 'A hundred-and-twenty words a minute.'

'I saw you the day before you left,' I said. 'You went back to Cyprus.'

'You took me to lunch,' Angelica said. 'At some kind of emporium – very large but not expensive.'

'We had no money.'

226

'And your hair was darker,' she said. 'Less blonde.'

'You mean not so handsome?'

'Your hair was longer.'

'It was shorter in those days.'

'This is true?' she asked. 'We did meet forty years ago?'

'Every bit of it,' I said.

All this flowed like a film we had seen, the images running before our minds, taking us back like stepping stones across a stream. We were together at Pitman's College in Southampton Row, taking dictation in a first-floor room looking out beyond the huge square clock, or perhaps overlooking gardens at the back, not sparing each other a glance, but there all the same, the two of us, as we had been, but as we were no more.

I still have my Pitman's shorthand *New Era Edition*, known as a shorthand instructor, probably the most valuable book I have owned after the *Bible* and the *Works of William Shakespeare*. It had cost me seven shillings and sixpence and provided a complete exposition of Sir Isaac Pitman's system of shorthand: grammalogues, half-lengths, hooks and arches.

I had begun my love affair with shorthand at Blaydon Grammar School when I had begun working in the colliery office. I would take shorthand and typing lessons and gain a rudimentary shorthand that would be sufficient but would not be easy to read back. As a *Blaydon Courier* reporter I had covered a speech one Saturday night at Blaydon Grammar School by Clem Attlee, Leader of the Labour Party. One of my former teachers at Hookergate Grammar School had asked me to send him a transcription, but truth to tell I had not been able to read it back.

I had been too mortified to tell him.

In London, having set myself the goal of one-hundred-and-fifty-words a minute to get me into Fleet Street, as a court reporter if nothing else, or possibly a *Hansard* Parliamentary reporter, I would walk in the evenings after my day's work in the City through Ludgate Circus along Fleet Street up Kingsway, past the Methodist Hall where Dr Donald Soper preached, and into Southampton Row where I had enrolled at Pitman's College.

Later, when I walked from the City I would come from St Paul's along Holborn Viaduct past the *Daily Mirror* Building rearing out of the ground, taking five years to build, pausing for a hard-baked cheese bun and cup of tea, having abandoned the Lyon's fruit pie, sometimes cutting behind Gray's Inn where, in the autumn, the leaves would grace the lawns and the lights from barristers' chambers glow through a hazy fog.

In my first week in London I had worked for a shipping firm for six pounds five shillings; after my week's interlude with *The Daily Telegraph*, I would return to the shipping firm with an increase of ten shillings. With the *Telegraph* behind me I enrolled at Pitman's College, paying three months' courses in advance, uncertain whether I could afford this without dipping into the money I was already trying to save to pay for my trip to Moscow.

I would enrol for four nights a week, two hours a night, come winter, spring, summer or autumn, beginning in reception class, moving through theory and onto the foothills of speed tests. From April to July 1957 I would advance from fifty words a minute to a hundred words. I was obsessed with '*the idea of progress, passing test after test after test, rising higher, destroying failure, initiating success, sacrificing style, fluency – all the finer points to give me speed*'.

I warned myself I must pay attention to detail, to the

small grammalogues, to punctuation and in particular to half-lengths, hooks and arches: '*I must cut down my haste in writing and concentrate on improving the quality of my notes. If I do this, I will simplify the task of reading back and thus give impetus to my speed writing. I have considered the possibilities of a new shorthand pen to improve my writing and facilitate the legibility of my hooks and arches, but on consideration I have decided that better pen control will prove just as effective.*'

Each Tuesday there would be a speed test, read at the appropriate speed for five minutes by one of the teachers at the College. The teacher would check the speed against a stop watch. I recall a distinguished man in his fifties with blond hair but glasses with dark frames; he would leave after a while for another job. There would be a young woman in her twenties, blond and attractive, who one day had allowed herself the extravagance of exposure to an ultra-violet sun-lamp, and who came to give the speed test exceedingly red in colour and embarrassed because of it.

Our job would be to take down the one-hundred-and-twenty words a minute for five minutes and transcribe it back. I would progress quickly to a hundred-and-twenty words a minute, when it all began to slow down. One of the difficulties in passing a speed test at shorthand is nervousness. I suddenly became nervous, my hand trembled, and it became almost impossible to read back the shorthand outlines. Even when I passed one-hundred-and-twenty it was because it had been a very easy examination, a text on business, but even then I had become nervous half-way through and had relied on my memory to read back many of the forms.

I would write in my dairy that my shorthand appeared to be in '*a dark passage, leading to nowhere and to nowhere and again to nowhere, yet I feel that some day, emerging from the gloom I shall see the light. Meanwhile until I do I shall continue to strive and be patient.'* In my impatience I had hoped to reach one-hundred-and-fifty words a minute by the year end, but I would not get beyond one-hundred-and-ten.

I would also, upon returning to my boarding house in the evening, arrange to pay the landlady half-a-crown to use the dining room next to the kitchen and take down the nine o'clock news. This was an almost impossible task, given the speed at which the news was read, but I recall one evening a lady boarder dying her hair black in a huge enamel dish of tar-like liquid; and on another occasion turning on the radio to hear the strains of Rachmananov's *Ninth Variation on a Theme by Paganini.* This would so thrill me I would read of Rachmananov, how he had written the *Variations* in Lucerne, and dream of going there.

Now each time I hear the *Ninth Variation* I am back in the dining room with the lady dying her hair and my waiting for the news.

I would go too to the British Museum Reading Room on a Saturday and one day, wandering through the Museum, I had would come across a glass case of shorthand notes written by Bernard Shaw. The notes had been written on blue paper and though the shorthand had been rudimentary, with appropriate thick and thin strokes, written carefully, it had been perfectly readable. I do not know if this inspired me but it comforted me in later life to know that if I had not become a second Bernard Shaw at least my shorthand had been more advanced. The notes had been no more than scraps, but they were the first lines of Shaw's Play St Joan.

'*No eggs! No eggs!*'

It occurred to me that a hundred-and-fifty words a minute was a self-imposed ambition and that I might get into Fleet

Street with a lower speed. In those early days in London, I would spend whatever spare time available after writing free-lance articles and shorthand studying in a number of different libraries. I would study out of the Westminster Library opposite Irvine Street and the Beefsteak Club and when I enrolled in my shorthand class I would study out of the Holborn Library.

One evening I noticed that a famous journalist, Ritchie Calder, had agreed to come to the library to give a lecture. Ritchie had been Features Editor of the *News Chronicle*. I would attend the lecture and at the end of it I would explain my ambitions and ask him his views. I would tell him of my ambitions to find a job as a reporter in Fleet Street, my shorthand intentions and my ideas concerning Parliament, either to become secretary to an MP or a *Hansard* Parliamentary reporter.

Ritchie warned me not to place too great an emphasis on shorthand; he said one-hundred-and-thirty words a minute might be enough and that I might try the *Press Association*. He said that I might be able to succeed as a telephone reporter, which is what I had been for a week with *The Daily Telegraph*, but breaking into Fleet Street would be 'very difficult'. I referred to the need to have a contact, but he said there was no easy way and repeated that he had got into Fleet Street with a shorthand speed of a hundred-and-thirty.

'You might easily do so,' he said.

My diary recalls that I would pass my one-hundred-and-twenty word examination in February 1958, with only seven transcribing errors, my best result since I had passed at sixty. It had taken me six months, I would pass a

231

hundred-and-thirty the following week, and move into the one-hundred-and-fifty class.

Even before I had reached my new-found speeds I had been able to take my first temporary job as a shorthand-typist with the Indian carpet dealer. My diary records the office of the time, with thick Indian carpets, a telephone with a sharp angry buzz and a typist that would leap to its bidding. There would be an old man with a tea trolley, wearing a silver moustache over-large and drooping, and where time had carved deep lines into his face and pressed a weight upon his shoulders.

Since this had been early summer, an open window would send in a warm breeze to ruffle the loose papers on the desk; and since we were still a cricketing nation someone would enquire of the Test score, no radio or television in the office, no teletext to transmit the score. Our tea cups would huddle together on the tray and rattle as the old man rattled, shuffling forward, his moustache, it seemed, as hunched as his shoulders, his weight heavy to his legs.

Who will wash the tea dishes?

Certainly not I, the young shorthand-typist on his first job as a shorthand-typist, even though his speed might be only sixty words a minute. The young clerk looks bewildered. The task will fall to him. The typewriter clatters again, the typist's excuse for avoiding this menial chore, the old man trundles out with his trolley, forecasting rain the morrow, no good for Test cricket, and though one enquires again of the Test score none is available unless someone can slip out to a local pub where the score might be chalked on a board. Some of the pubs were so fed up with queries they would chalk on their own particular board:

'We don't know!'

232

Angelica had left Pitman's College at one-hundred-and-twenty words a minute to return to Cyprus.

She had been known to me as Eve, her full name Evangelitsa, but hardly had she returned than an English policeman had politely asked for her hand in marriage according to Greek custom and they had returned to England, to the wrath of the brother-in-law, or at least his disenchantment, that she had gone beyond lunch with an Englishman at an emporium, beyond even a stroll down Petticoat Lane, and had married one to settle and raise four children, all of them now grown.

I had last seen Angelica at Bank Underground the day before she had left, walking those long circuitous corridors, a slim girl with dark hair, rising on her toes it seemed to me, elegant and graceful. Had she sent me a card when she returned to Cyprus? Our hands had hardly touched, our lips never, not even a kiss on the cheek, nor the familiar kiss of the French on both cheeks, but our hands had touched across the years and there she was, proposing to drive me to King's Cross Station so that I might catch my train.

'Do you remember the City?' Angelica asked.

'I remember the hottest day of the year.'

It had been eighty-four degrees Fahrenheit.

The buildings had been white and grey and lifted in silent protest to the sky; the windows were opened to relieve the heat. The sky had been cloudless and the sun beat down upon the streets burning them like brass. There would be no such thing as air-conditioning and at lunch time young typists without cardigans, wearing white blouses, looking neat and cool, would find somewhere to settle in the small square of grass in Bishopsgate next to the church; the young male clerks would take off their coats and throw them carelessly over their shoulder. The City man would wear a bowler and carry an umbrella, long and dark like

233

a slim sheathed sword. He would be more embarrassed by the heat because he would remain prim and correct, unable to undo either collar or tie.

Ice cream would be a favourite refuge from the heat, but the shops would be sold out, and where there was mineral water, not yet popular, not yet available in plastic containers, hardly available at all, that was sold out too. There would be nothing to relieve the discomfort, neither ice cream nor water nor shade; the heat would strike like dagger blows to the neck and head; and those with dark hair more prone to sunstroke would knot their handkerchiefs in the corners and place them upon their heads.

Even on the hottest day of the year the sun must pass, as if crossing desert sand, taking the heat with it; but this day the heat remained, oppressive still, so that I felt languid. To stay indoors would be unthinkable, for even with the windows open the heat would linger in my half bed-sit and the sweat would stand out on my brow, runnelling the furrows. In the street I would seek the cool of an evening breeze, but there was no breeze, only the enervating heat: too hot to walk even to one's favourite café, too hot to sit by a wall in the dusty shade of a privet hedge.

The evening would pass and soon it would be night.

In the darkness the foliage on the trees hung limp and pitiful against a mocking crystal sky; there were still no clouds and because there were no clouds, or so one thought, because there was no breeze, the ground had retained its heat; it would linger still so that returning to my room it would await me like a persistent stranger.

There would be nothing for it but to undress and clamber upon the bed and to fall into a restless sleep until, suddenly awaking, I would be soaked in sweat. Perhaps this was pneumonia or influenza? It is only the heat, lingering, still a presence to the room. I felt like a cold bath but such a thing would not be lightly undertaken at one o'clock in the morning in a boarding house where others might be wakened. I would rub the sweat from my body, slip into pyjamas, throw off the bedclothes and leave open the window.

It had indeed been the hottest day of the year.

'And there was the makeshift café,' I said.

'I can't remember that.'

'It stood on a bomb site near Tower Hill.'

The café had stood open to the road and in summer City workers would visit the café and sit beneath the shade of parasols sipping milk out of pint bottles or lifting tea from sloppy saucers. Tame pigeons wheeled above, swooping suddenly to alight on the table where I would be sitting, their yellow claws struggling to grip the iron surface, their wings folded, fluttering as they fought for balance, gazing unafraid and unashamed from their yellow eyes directly into yours, so that you felt guilty, as if you were on their terrain, their territory, the tea you were drinking, the pie you were eating, belonged to them.

The pigeons would whirl away at the clatter of empty bottles being mishandled into crates.

'I remember the pigeons,' I said.

Notwithstanding that I would stay four nights a week at Pitman's College, my determination to pass speed tests at one-hundred-and-fifty or one-hundred-and-sixty would defeat me. '*I intend doing shorthand and nothing else,*' I would write. '*Doing four nights a week, an adequate amount during the day, and sufficient at the weekend. I must thrust forward as never before, devoting as much time as possible without going stale.*'

In the higher reaches, however, I would meet two men who worked for a City shorthand-writing firm. The firm made money attending Annual General Meetings of quoted companies, taking an official record of the statements of board chairman to their shareholders and the questions that shareholders might put from the floor. They would also be official shorthand writers at national conferences.

They too were seeking higher speeds, higher even than one-hundred-and-fifty, and fifteen months after I had left Pitman's I would read of their prize-giving ceremony in the Royal Albert Hall. I would go along to the prize-giving, for old time's sake, because Pitman's College and shorthand had been so great a part of my life for eighteen months.

One of the men had been short and dark with glasses, the other had been younger, tall like myself with red hair and brown eyes. The senior of the two would receive a prize for having attained a speed not of one-hundred-and-fifty nor even one-hundred-and-sixty but two-hundred-and-ten! He had been the last to gain a prize that evening and as his name had been read out, with the astonishing achievement, he had paused on the stairs before climbing onto the platform. I would speak with him and his friend afterwards, in the passageways of the Albert Hall, but I would never see them again.

Our shared experience was over.

I never did become secretary to an MP or *Hansard* reporter, but my shorthand would stay with me all my days. I would write short stories and novels in shorthand, take notes in Court or in the House of Commons, confounding those who would be surprised at my verbatim recall of their comments. The speed might fade but never the ability both to write and read it. I would keep a diary in shorthand and read notes made twenty to thirty years ago, as if they had been freshly written today.

Angelica drove through Trafalgar Square to Aldwych and up Aldwych to Southampton Row. She parked on double yellow lines and the chauffeur of a Jaguar also parked on the same double yellow lines warned us not to tally, the traffic wardens here were ferocious. We assured him we would not be long, long enough to cross the street into the cold and find ourselves not at King's Cross Station but before the old Pitman's College.

Only six months earlier it had become Giles' College of English and the principal had just come out and locked the glass doors.

'I'm sorry,' he said. 'I can't reopen.'

In our excitement Angela and I had decided to revisit the College.

We explained we had been students forty years ago, that we had met again over a cup of tea, fortuitously, accidentally, neither of us knowing we had met before; that it had dawned on us simultaneously, and we had got into the car and driven to Southampton Row to visit again the old college that neither of us had entered these past forty years, talking so quickly we must have perplexed the principal.

I gave him my card.

'What happened to the clock?' I asked.

'It was a bit of a landmark,' the principal said. 'We're getting a new one. Why not come back during the day? When it's less cold?'

'You have to get to Middlesbrough,' Angelica said.

'And you to Croydon.'

She explained she gave Greek dancing classes on a Thursday.

'My dear Seven Loaves,' she said. 'We'll never be back.'

'We'll have our memories,' I said. 'To keep us warm.'

237

A Gordon Brown Story

During the last days before the calling of the 1997 General Election, I sat next to Gordon Brown on the Opposition front bench on the floor of the House of Commons.

'I'll buy you a proper pen, Gordon,' I said. 'When you become Chancellor of the Exchequer!'

He was about to make one of his formidable speeches to attack the Conservative government, but nothing would be more formidable than his onslaught upon the Bic ball-point pen that he twirled in his fingers, that he lifted to his mouth, not to caress his lips with the plastic, but that the plastic be lost to his teeth as he mercilessly bit and chewed.

The rear end of the pen would re-emerge as he scribbled fiercely among the margins of his speech, the top of the pen long since destroyed, the plastic twisted in his fingers, crumpled and bent, shamed to oblivion, and he would cast the top aside as he raised his eyes to the Conservative Minister speaking from the Dispatch Box. The eyes seemed to say that having completed one act of destruction, once he rose to his feet, he was about to embark upon another.

'I'll look forward to the pen,' Gordon said.

Gordon and I had come into the House together in 1983 and I had first heard his name mentioned when entering the members' dining room for my first evening meal in the new Parliament. The dining room stands on the ground floor and looks out through narrow latticed windows beyond the terrace of the House to the river; the evening lights from around Westminster Bridge reflect back a garish yellow, the yellow rippling across the surface of the waters.

I met Nick Brown waiting by the side of the entrance.

'Aren't you coming for dinner, Nick?'

'I'm waiting for my namesake, Gordon Brown,' he said.

Waiting by the entrance to the members' restaurant, Nick settled his own destiny and that of Gordon too, for they became great friends, Nick would be Gordon's campaign manager when he stood for the Shadow Cabinet after Labour's election defeat in 1987, and later still he would run two Shadow Cabinet election campaigns, one for Gordon and one for Tony Blair. He became Chief Whip and then Secretary of State for Agriculture in the 1997 Blair administration.

Gordon had entered Parliament as the Member of Parliament for Dunfermline, East.

As I had fought Hexham in the 1979 General Election, he had fought Edinburgh, South. He had been in his short time rector of Edinburgh University, a journalist and editor of the current affairs department of Scottish Television, and a lecturer in politics at Glasgow College of Technology. He had written columns for the Scottish *Daily Record*. His father had been a Presbyterian minister, he was the son of a manse, austerity would flow through his veins, and I would forecast he would make Stafford Cripps, the most austere of all Labour Chancellors, look like a profligate.

He was also a modest and shy man.

He made a powerful maiden speech, standing at the back of the Commons with the oak panelling behind. This was where he would make all his back-bench speeches, no huddling for him close to the front bench and the seat

239

of most MPs' ambition. A year later, when offered a post on Neil Kinnock's front bench, he declined because he wanted to concentrate on social security affairs from the back benches.

I recall he had an article printed in *The Guardian* which had been based on a particular analysis of Conservative government policy, but where he had been helped by confidential information that had been leaked to him. I saw him outside the members' cloak room and congratulated him on the success of the article, how it had been a serious attack on the government which had hit home.

He seemed mystified by the genuine praise.

'I was only doing my job,' he explained.

His shyness had been revealed to me at one Labour Party Conference after the 1987 General Election when we had left the conference hall simultaneously, he walking a yard or so behind me. I had been aware of his presence and had expected that he would catch me up, that we would walk together up the street, that we would chat and gossip, indulge in small talk; but we did none of these things. We walked for more than two hundred yards with Gordon always a pace behind.

John Smith had been Shadow Chancellor of the Exchequer at the time.

'Gordon's terribly shy,' he explained.

The only pen I could fittingly buy Gordon when he became Chancellor of the Exchequer would be a Montblanc, with its dark skin and silky white top, its slim line, its proud clip, of silver or gold, a pen so recognisable that even the sketch writers in the Press Gallery would pick it up, would notice the change, would understand that not only was there now a Chancellor of the Exchequer to be reckoned with, who could make the Bank of England independent in three days, but a Chancellor who would encapsulate style and grace within the confines of his pen.

~

I recalled my own first pen that my mother had given me during playtime at the primary school.

She had come to the spiked wooden railings, wearing her dark-brown coat, carrying a green-and-red-panelled shopping bag, slipping her hand through the railings so that her wrist showed white against the brown wood, spelks scratching the skin. A few groceries languished at the bottom of the bag but she plucked out what appeared to be a fountain pen she had bought from the draper's shop in the Cooperative store.

'It's a new kind o' pen,' she said. 'A biro.'

The pen had been invented by Senor Ladislao José Biro who would die 24 October 1985 in Buenos Aires.

He had produced the first ever ball-point pen for hand-writing. It had cost two pounds fifteen shillings when first marketed in the United Kingdom. My own biro pushed through the railings had a blue marine body and a shiny steel top, but it did not write well, the ink coagulated before it settled on the page, and when I dismantled the top to peer at the narrow enamel tube the ink stained blue the palms of my hands and bleached my fingers.

'I'm sure ye'll like it,' my mother said.

She had made the discovery before I had.

She knew I was a writer.

From six-years-old I would write short stories, not parables of the kind you find in the Bible, the most beautiful short stories of all, but accounts of fictitious football matches. Perhaps this had been born of a need to amuse myself, with no toys in the war years and little reading; but as I moved into my early teens I would write stories based on the titles of books serialised by *John Bull* Magazine bought by my Aunt Mary and passed on to me.

There would be *Death and the Sky Above* by Andrew Garve and *The Man from the Turkish Slave* by Victor Canning, the titles a sufficient inspiration for me to write entirely different stories, my own *Death and the Sky Above* being about pilots in the Korean War. I would write a fictitious story describing my first adventure with a young girl from the next street, taking her to the cinema in Newcastle, a story which troubled my sister when she read it because she thought it was true.

It would be my first lesson in verisimilitude.

At fifteen I would do the Sunday paper round and notice that *The Sunday Times* were serialising the latest book by Somerset Maugham entitled *Ten Novels and their Authors.* I persuaded my mother to buy *The Sunday Times* so that I could read these extracts. They would be my first introduction to serious reading. I would not be sufficiently mature, however, to distinguish the serious from the not so serious, and I would be determined to read Maugham and Charles Dickens alongside Agatha Christie, Arthur Conan Doyle and Victor Canning.

Ensconced in Newcastle City Library, I would read too Edgar Allan Poe and Rudyard Kipling, but though I might enjoy Kipling's *Phantom Rickshaw* and *East is East*, they did not fire my imagination. I would later berate myself for this. It was my fault. '*I had not matured enough to understand and admire, and I hope the time will come when I shall do Kipling justice by reading his work thoroughly.*'

Edgar Allan Poe would be beyond me.

I would try my hand at a first novel called *The Stars Are My Guides*, the story of a man imprisoned for a crime which he naturally did not commit, who escapes and after a chase throughout the country finally finds himself on a rowing boat to Iceland. *'The stars were my guides on those dark and lonely nights.'* This is the only line that survives from a book which did not get beyond four pages, but it did give me a great attachment to the stars and to this day I look upon them as my companions, if not my guides.

I thought two years' National Service would help me to read and to write what I described as *'saleable fiction'*. My first short story would be entitled *Counterfeit Charge* and sent to *Weekend Mail* because they were taking my free-lance news articles. I would create a new character, called Alfredo Bugetti, a barber who had his shop in Northern Italy. My first – and last – story would be called *Alfredo's First Client*.

I thought this would be a smash hit with the *Evening Chronicle*, but they told me all their stories were bought from an agency in London. It had been a kindly encouraging letter which inspired me to believe that, if I changed the opening, I might send the story directly to the agency. I would also write a ghost story called *Deadly Secret* and a story for *Women's Own*, neither of which appeared.

Alfredo still works out of his Italian barber shop without fame or fortune.

I would enroll for an English course with Newcastle University and I have still the original notes of the course. They deal with language and sentence structure and characterisation, but I would not get into the course before leaving for London. Nor would I make any great hit with the professor who did not appreciate my free-lance journalism. Newcastle would always be a part of my life, the spans of the Tyne Bridge had been seen from the highest ridges of my village; and as part of my writing I would describe the city as it had been in those days.

The bus from the village would always take you along Scotswood Road.

Lord Graham of Edmonton, formerly the Member of Parliament for Edmonton, had spent the first fifteen years of his life on Scotswood Road; he would recall the Road as a happy homogeneous community governed, if not regulated, by the hooter from Vickers Armstrong across the Road, facing the Tyne; for the hooter would go at seven-thirty in the morning, twelve noon and again at five o'clock when the work day ended.

His father had been a meat carrier, serving the cattle market opposite Marlborough Crescent bus station at the entrance into Newcastle; in Lord Graham's view the cattle had been brought in olden days through Cowgate up to Rye Hill and down into the market. His father had a knack of carrying a carcass of beef on his left shoulder, slipping it onto the scales so that the carcass dropped through a hole in its haunch onto a hook on the scales, sliding it off again with equal ease.

I would remember Scotswood Road as a dilapidated industrial heartland. It would eventually be pulled down as slums and I would describe the buildings as '*grey and flaking and pock-marked, grimed and dusty, dirty and damp, decaying and derelict*'; but once into the city I would find the lines of the buildings cold and hard, the spires of the Catholic cathedral '*majestic*'.

The Central Station would be '*a black huddle*' squatting grotesquely opposite Pink Lane.

Then there would be the smell: '*Of the butchers' and fruiterers' stands, the fish market; the smell of dirt and filth and fat and foam; of cooking food and flowers; fried fish and dry fish; fresh fish and meat, meat and fish. The smell never changes; it penetrates the nostrils and seeps into the lungs.*' At least I was learning the art of alliteration

244

as well as describing a Newcastle that might well have been in Elizabethan England.

~

I had also begun my reading, Tolstoy's *War and Peace*, Maugham's *Cakes and Ale* and *Liza of Lambeth*, and also his semi-autobiographical novel *Of Human Bondage*. The first Maugham novel I had read had been *Catalina*, a true introduction to literature, followed by *Theatre*, but it had been the collected short stories that would give most joy. My own short stories still seemed embedded in the detective and the ghost.

My reading of Maugham introduced me to other short story writers and I discovered Guy de Maupassant.

On my first visit to London before Christmas I had found de Maupassant in the bookshops down Charing Cross Road; I had even discovered Foyle's, though overwhelmed by the shelves and shelves of books, stacked over many floors; yet not so many books or shelves or floors as to discourage a young writer. I would not only find Guy de Maupassant in these bookshops, I would describe him as '*my greatest friend in fiction*'.

I would write: '*My old obsession to be a novelist filled me. I left the shop exultant – determined to succeed one day in the fiction field.*' When I returned to my lodgings at Wood Green I began a second first novel. '*The provisional title is To Hell and Happiness, though I have a final title This Fevered World. And I shall finish it, not today or tomorrow; not next week, maybe not next year, but sometime.*'

These were indeed brave words.

Hell and Happiness owed little to my literary reading but to a youth dedicated to writing stories for *Weekend Mail* and *Evening News* and *Reveille*; it was a spy story with Leslie

Krells and Howard West and Pierre Montespan and Elize Pechon, all of them exciting, but never wandering from my imagination to the page and into the real world. I might have written four pages of notes on *The Stars Are My Guides* but would not get beyond a few thousand words for *Hell and Happiness*.

My notebooks are filled with fragments of stories, clay rather than marble, lying around as the broken pieces of the old Forum lie around Rome. *Hell and Happiness* might have been a saga of subterfuge and deception, but upon returning home for Christmas, determined to leave again for London in the New Year, I would also write a series of *Fog Stories*.

I had been feeling sorry for myself, having been alone in London, raising my Christmas wine glass to the unknown many. I would write for *'the diseased and crippled who cannot capture the full vigorous spirit of the season; and finally to myself, for I have an idea this may be my last Christmas at home, with my intimate circle of friends who exchange my love for their happiness.'*

The very first book I would buy when I came to London a second time would be short stories by Guy de Maupassant. I have the book to this day. It is entitled *Tales of Night and Day* and I would buy it in one of the bookshops by St-Martin's-in-the-Fields for three shillings and sixpence and read its first pages on a Saturday morning at a Lyon's tea shop opposite Charing Cross Station.

I would read all of de Maupassant in the years to come, as I would read all of Somerset Maugham; I would read the short stories of H.E. Bates and the American writer O'Henry; and there would be Anton Chekhov and Ernest Hemingway. I would develop, for a short while at least, an H.E. Bates style of short clauses and read a hundred of O'Henry's stories. I would be particularly impressed by

246

Chekhov's '*simplicity of style and economy of words*'; and I would copy tracts of Hemingway's *Snows of Kilimanjaro*.

I might study style at the Westminster Library and when working in the City I would call into the Bishopsgate Library at lunch time and read a Somerset Maugham short story. I would borrow philosophy books from the Holborn Library, reading them over a fish-and-chip supper on a Saturday night at Archway: Professor Joad and Bertrand Russell. There would be psycho-analysis with Sigmund Freud and Professor Jung. I would read too the novels of Charles Dickens.

After my trip to Moscow, whilst I would continue my drive to become a Fleet Street reporter on the back of a hundred-and-fifty-words a minute shorthand, I would begin to feel that I was capable of something better. I could indeed become a writer of fiction. As I moved into my twentieth year, I began spending my Saturdays in the Reading Room of the British Museum, not only studying and copying the texts of my favourites, but also reading John Ruskin and William Hazlett and through Hazlett's essays William Shakespeare.

There would be Friday evenings at the Old Vic and the night after my twentieth birthday I would find myself in the Gods watching Sir John Gielgud and Dame Edith Evans in Henry VIII. I had at least half an hour to spare before going to the theatre and I had spent it wandering through the Festival gardens and having a tea at a café at Waterloo. I reflected on the progress I had made in shorthand since my last birthday, climbing from a speed of seventy to attempting one-hundred-and-fifty-words a minute.

I felt too my spoken English was better, the northern vowels being softened, transformed into a gentler accent, less rough and harsh. I had begun to learn the value of dress, I was beginning to enjoy my work experiences, even though as a temporary, and I began to feel that the confidence that had left me when I had departed from the North-East, when I had failed my medical for National Service, when I had failed as a free-lance journalist, unsettled at home, a teenager no less, all this was coming together to burnish my ambition.

To add gloss and polish.

I had begun to rid myself too of a pernicious acne that had been with me throughout my teens, that had ravaged my features with white-heads and cists and pustules, sapping my confidence, making me not lonely but dedicated to my ambition, so that I would not need the company of others. I had never been lonely in London, rather I had been like a childhood Horatio Nelson who having been lost had been found by the river.

'Where you not afraid?' he was asked.

'What is fear?' he had replied.

I might have been on my own in London but I had never known loneliness.

I had begun having ultra-violet sun lamp treatment at the skin hospital in Soho, taking a bus twice a week from the City, alighting in the Strand and striding from Trafalgar Square to Leicester Square. I would take the treatment throughout the winter months, the consultants telling me to get as much natural sunlight in the summer, so that I would spend any fine weekend day on Parliament Hill, feeling the sun to my face, reading such books as H.E. Bates' *Fair Stood the Wind for France*.

I was being transformed into a different person.

I was planning to travel again, to Switzerland and France, to pick grapes in the wine harvest, travel not for its own sake but because Somerset Maugham had advised young writers to travel; and as Ernest Hemingway had also advised them not to waste their time or talents on journalism the

248

ambition of a career in Fleet Street began to recede. By the time I had reached Easter in my twentieth year I had already written four short stories in my first book of stories.

I felt that '*life was a continually changing substance and we are at once observers and participants of that change; we unconsciously adapt ourselves so that we reach the stage where very often we are not aware change has taken place; and it is only when we pause to think that we realise how different life has become*'. I felt I had made the change from callowness to maturity, from darkness to light.

I was beginning to forget the past and think of the future.

All of this came together in the knowledge that it was time I moved to the second stage of my developing career, the one I had planned all along but had not thought could be consummated in my teens, that of the true and genuine writer, not the newspaper reporter, not the free-lance, but the author of short stories and novels and plays. I might not be sufficiently experienced, my education might never be complete, and all my life I would be self-taught, but the time had come. Or as Somerset Maugham might have written, indeed did write:

I was on the wing.

It is a long time since my mother thrust the biro pen through the school railing.

There would be other pens, a Conway Stewart, a bejewelled biro, miniature in size, that my sister bought me; there would be a Platignum which, when the nib crossed I would give to my cousin, only to take it back from him when the nib uncrossed, much to the disgust of his mother. I would bring back from Somalia in the sixties a specially-carved ivory pen stand and in New York I would take the Lexington Avenue subway from Gramercy Park to Alexander's so that I might buy a Sheaffer because, describing the Park in winter, with its ice, its shard blackened shrubs, I thought only the best pen would do.

J.B. Priestley would type his novels and plays and essays rather than write them long-hand; Ernest Hemingway gave away good pens, as he gave away other possessions, for fear of losing them; and when Victor Hugo sat down to write *Les Misérables* he used not only a new pen every day but also a new inkstand. His mistress Juliette Drouet recopied the novel for him to make it readable for the publisher.

I had typed my first novels and stories, but later I decided to write in long-hand to slow down the text, seek out the right word, build patience into my work. John Steinbeck wrote his novels using a fine pencil and Roy Hattersley, when not speaking or participating in a debate, would sit on the front bench writing his articles. I recall one particularly rowdy debate when as Deputy Leader of the Labour Party deputising for Neil Kinnock, the noise growing around him, Roy steadily wrote an article for a Sunday newspaper on Sheffield Wednesday Football Club.

I have on my desk a Sheaffer that has stood there these past thirty years, a gold pen on a jade stand, and when my eldest son Ian married in Lisbon I bought myself a new Parker. I have a collection of Waterman pens and, from my days learning Pitman's shorthand in Southampton Row, I have some pens with thin nibs, others with thick, that I use depending upon my writing mood, or if I am writing in shorthand. Looking through old notebooks I can tell which pen I was using and when, and the ink like the memory has never faded.

There are my Montblanc pens which Margaret bought me for my fiftieth birthday, one a ball-point and the other a full-fledged ink-consuming pen, no cartridges here, that requires to be filled from the special bottle of Montblanc ink, a curved bottle, rather like the curves in a bottle of Tavel wine, that is as distinctive as the pen itself, the pens black and slim, with their white silken caps like skull caps, but not sinister, as friendly and reassuring as the flow of the gold nib across the page, the pens encased in black silk in a black hard-edged box that reminds you what it is that the box holds.

The wonderment of the pens themselves.

I noticed that Peter Viggers MP used a Montblanc pen when taking a particular piece of Northern Irish legislation through Committee. He had been Parliamentary Under-Secretary at the time. He had entered the House after the February 1974 election as Member of Parliament for Gosport and would write his own name in the history books when he had a Ten-Minute Bill before the Commons on 28 March 1979, the day the Labour government fell.

Conservative whips were not anxious that Peter spend a lot of time with his Bill and thus delay the all-important attack by the then Leader of the Opposition, Margaret Thatcher. The Bill was designed to make further provision for service pensions and in particular to provide pensions for widows of non-commissioned servicemen who retired before 1 September 1950.

Peter offered to shorten his time on the floor if the whips agreed to implement the provisions of the Bill should the Conservatives form a government after the Election. They grudgingly agreed, Peter did not hang around on the floor of the House, the government lost the Vote of Confidence, the Conservatives came to power and those widows of non-commissioned servicemen who previously had been

251

deprived of a pension found themselves the beneficiaries of new-found Tory munificence.

All thanks to Peter Viggers.

Peter had been a safe pair of hands when Parliamentary Under-Secretary of State for Northern Ireland and at the time of a reshuffle, when called in to see Margaret Thatcher, he wondered what promotion lay ahead. Certainly he would rise to Minister of State but at which Department? Perhaps the Department of Trade and Industry or even the Environment.

'You've been such a wonderful Minister, Peter,' Margaret Thatcher said. 'No-one could have done better. I'm very proud of you and the work you've done. But I need you to place your portfolio at my disposal.'

I consoled Peter as best I could.

'At least you still have your Montblanc.'

He smiled and pulled two from his inside pocket.

There are those who when you talk of Montblanc think you are talking of a mountain. I bought a Montblanc pen set for Malcolm on his eighteenth birthday and learned from the service guide that *'in a world where the pace of life is becoming ever faster, we need things to remind us of what life is really all about. To remind us of the meaning of friendship, of the uniqueness of each individual.'*

On friendship and uniqueness of individual I should have bought a Montblanc for Gordon Brown when he became Chancellor of the Exchequer, but whilst this might have pleased the Montblanc company I wondered what the company of Baron Marcel Bich would have thought. Bich had invented the throwaway pen that Gordon Brown systematically massacred when on front-bench duty and no doubt massacred whenever it was he had to have a pen in hand.

Bich had built on the invention of Ladislao José Biro,

they had both come a long way since my mother had pushed my first pen through the railings. Together they had refined and modernised the original biro design and produced the Bic Crystal, a clear plastic tube with a visible ink supply which could, if need be, write a line three kilometers long. They had opened for business in 1953 and today more than fifteen million Bic pens are sold every day in a hundred and sixty countries. Bich would retire in 1993, but the Bic brand name is the best known French name in the entire world for throwaway lighters and razor blades as well as for pens.

Gordon Brown never did get his Montblanc on becoming Chancellor of the Exchequer.

It was not that I wished to be parsimonious, or that I was afraid to be seen being sycophantic to a man who was now one of the most powerful politicians in the land, brown-nosing as it is called; or that he might feel I was seeking preferment, or that I felt he would not already have enough pen stands and ink stands on his desk in his new Treasury office that, settling down to write *Les Misérables* would have made even Victor Hugo blush with pleasure.

It was the memory of how he had chewed at the Bic ball-point pen, how he had destroyed the top, how he had crumbled the slim *jetable* among his fingers, how the more intense he became the more he chewed, and the more satisfied he became with his speech or his notes the more inclined he had been to set the Bic aside, let it roll from his fingers, lose itself in the folds of the green Commons' benches, never to be thought of again, never to be seen again, as another victim was plucked from the inside of his suit pocket.

Perhaps Mont Blanc the mountain could match the formidable challenge of Gordon Brown, but not the Montblanc pen.

After the General Election, with no place in the government, I quietly moved to the back benches and had the honour of putting a question to Gordon at his first Question Time as Chancellor of the Exchequer. He took the opportunity to praise my own work with the City of London that had helped New Labour to win the Election, and though I nodded and smiled at the compliment I did not look to see what pen he was holding, nor what it was he moved to his mouth for a quiet nibble.

The writer in me had won over the politician, but the dignity of Montblanc had been saved.

Name on a Park Bench

Parliament had dissolved for the General Election.

I had a long-standing engagement to fulfil with the Governor of the Bank of France to explain New Labour's policy for the European single currency and had taken my son Malcolm with me to Paris. We had taken the Eurostar to the Gare du Nord and checked in at my favourite hotel on the Ile St-Louis.

We had walked from the hotel in the spring sunlight and crossed from the island towards Notre-Dame, the gargoyles as ferocious as ever, but the bells silent, if bells there had been. We passed a park behind the Notre-Dame, the trees to the park small and close-cropped, the cherry blossom already out, rose petals unfurled; there were pigeons strutting in the dust, moving from the sandy surface to the manicured lawns around the trees, pecking among the dust, lifting their tails with their own particular arrogance.

'I nearly slept in this park,' I said. 'Some forty years ago.'

'Why didn't you?' Malcolm asked.

'Because they had closed the gates at seven.'

'A feeble excuse.'

'We were all law-abiding citizens then.'

I had paused in Paris on my way to the South of France to pick grapes.

Because Somerset Maugham had urged young writers to travel I had gone to the Moscow Youth Festival and now I would be heading for the vineyards. Not only had Maugham advised travel but he had set up a five-hundred pounds bourse that would go to a successful writer provided he spent six months out of the country. I had a forlorn ambition that I would win the bourse, but I never did apply for it let alone win it, and would make my own way to the South of France.

I would work in the *vendange* for two months.

I had seen an advertisement in *The Sunday Times* and made arrangements through *Jeunesse et Reconstruction*. The organisation had offices in the Boulevard St Michel. I would call by their offices, pick up the papers telling me where to report, which farm or vineyard, and make my way to the South of France from the Gare de Lyon. I had little money but enough to get me to Avignon, and from Avignon to Cavaillon where I would pick melons and tomatoes and grapes.

I had been on holiday to Switzerland with two friends from the pit village but had left the train at Boulogne whilst they had gone back to Dover on the ferry. I had arrived in Boulogne at eight in the morning and made my way through Customs to the railway station where I would catch the train to Paris. I had left my luggage and with time to spare I had moved in and out of wharves and warehouses along the quayside, '*a lone figure*' according to my notebook, '*wearing a sweater and carrying a haversack, clambering up a small slope where the shells of former pillboxes and shelters could still be seen, but from where I could see the ferry on its way back to England*'.

The air had been clear but I had been unable to see the English coastline. I had watched the ferries coming and going, moving rapidly through the water, cutting a white foam-flecked passageway to and from the harbour. I had stood a long while, feeling the fresh wind cutting through my sweater, watching the breakers against the shore, wondering if the sea were rough mid-Channel where my friends were on their way home.

Feeling homesick, but feeling too the freshness of the breeze, I moved from the cliff towards the road bridge leading from the harbour to the town. The fishermen had left their catch to the fish merchants; their ice wagons arrived on the quay to pack the fish ready for filleting in the fish factories off the harbour. The fisherman passed over the bridge towards the town, typical Frenchmen I wrote, pushing bicycles, their berets lopsided, young girls and their mothers, each as plump as the other, hurrying arm-in-arm to work at the fish factories.

I found a café by the station where I called for a coffee, eating fruit and biscuits I had taken from the train, a typical third-class café, '*one of those which may be seen on any dockside from Liverpool to Bombay, the tables dirty and unwiped, several rough-hewn fishermen drinking beer even at that hour of the morning*'. The fishermen were having a well-earned *chope* after a night fishing in the English Channel.

I had my first taste of French coffee.

I found it too strong and asked for a little milk, but still finding it too strong, '*thick and black, stronger than beer and with a tobacco taste*'. It had certainly been an odd coffee. Those in the café were friendly, especially the woman behind the counter, short and fat and jovial, wearing an ill-cut black dress which clung tightly, accentuating the loose rolls running from her breasts to her stomach.

One particular fisherman, I noticed, had been large and stocky, with a long face which appeared all jaw. Perhaps one day I would write him up as a character in a novel or short story; he would be the first and last lantern-jawed man I would meet. He had small eyes and badly needed a shave; his cap had been thrust back and he took a cigarette and smoked it leisurely, having been out all night, relaxing on the bench, elbows on the table, chatting to those around him. He talked a harsh guttural French and I watched him sip his *chope* and smoke his cigarette until with the other fishermen he left the café empty now but for me writing my notes.

I arrived in Paris late Saturday afternoon.

The sun had been bright and strong and cast dark shadows across the wide boulevards leading to Notre-Dame. I settled in the park behind the cathedral. My plan would be to find the Boulevard St Michel and pick up my papers the following morning from *Jeunesse et Reconstruction*. I would sleep out to save money. Children played in the park and there were young couples in deep embrace.

It was a trait of Parisian life in those days that couples were everywhere, at any time of day or evening, kissing on park benches, at bus stops, on corner ends, even in the Métro not kissing in the sense of a farewell peck but kissing passionately, all-embracing, like lovers about to be separated, as if there were a war on and they might never meet again. I learned later that because Paris had not been bombed during the war there had been no reconstruction, no new apartments; young men and women lived with their parents and could only express their passion in public whilst the world turned around them.

I liked this park.

It had been enclosed with iron railings of the kind that had graced our school buildings till they had been removed as part of the war effort; it would be nice to sleep on this bench beneath this cherry tree; but as a chill came to the air and the park emptied a park keeper came along and locked the gates. I would not be able to sleep here after all. Besides, it had been too close to Notre-Dame, there had been too much light, I would not have slept and would have been moved on.

I found a small hotel where I could lay my head.

The hotel lay off the rue de Rivoli and would cost five hundred old francs for the night. I can see the woman now, scrawling the price of the room on a piece of paper. The hotel had been small and clean, a dark stone passageway leading to my room, the room small and tidy, the bed neatly made; there had been red curtains at the shuttered windows and a rug on the floor; but the paper had been peeling and a small makeshift set of drawers stood by the bed opposite a wash basin without a plug. There had been a mirror on the wall beside the washstand and I had sat on the bed and brushed my blond hair.

The following day I walked up Boulevard St Michel.

I found *Jeunesse et Reconstruction*, but I had not realised it, I had not seen it, it had not occurred to me. Today was Sunday and the office closed. I went into the Jardin du Luxembourg where again there were the couples. I sunned myself in the Jardin, holding open my nylon shirt, head held at an angle to catch the sunlight, and only later when the sun passed behind cloud had I moved from the green iron chair through the alleyways of the Jardin towards the Eiffel Tower always visible above the rooftops.

I had a spaghetti meal in a restaurant off Chatelet.

I had disliked the coffee that had been served at Boulogne but it was nothing to the coffee in the restaurant. It had been served in an enamel dish with a rubber band around the bottom so that clumsily I had spilt the coffee in transferring it to my cup. It had been my only meal of the day and I had made the most of it. There were rolls and chips as well as spaghetti and another coffee, drinking it slowly, dipping crusts of the roll into the coffee to kill its bitter taste.

I decided to spend another night in the hotel.

It would be another five hundred francs, the price of a meal, and years later I would go by the hotel off the rue de Rivoli and discover to my amusement that it was an *hôtel de passe* used by prostitutes. I would spend two nights at the hotel, with no lock to the door, but unafraid and at ease with myself.

I woke at eight and feeling refreshed, the sun already high, my spirits as high as the sun, I had walked from the rue de Rivoli towards Boulevard St Michel and the offices of *Jeunesse et Reconstruction*. Only they had no papers from the vineyards. They had not arrived. When would they arrive? Perhaps tomorrow but perhaps not. The *vendange* had been put back because of the weather, a late frost or unseasonable rain. Who could tell? All I could do was come back tomorrow and hope the papers had arrived.

I walked back to the Gare du Nord.

I kept walking by the left hand side of the station going north. I walked with Montmartre to my left beyond the suburbs and, feeling tired, I had stopped at a village and sat on a concrete parapet overlooking the Seine. I could see a line of black-painted petrol barges across the water, hugging the opposite bank, lying still, bow to bow, water lapping against their iron-panelled keels.

A church had stood opposite, the bell ringing, and by the side of the church stood a line of dust-flaked houses, their shutters open. There were those who made their way from the houses into church for Mass. Other men and women sat outside the houses on wooden seats as if it were a fine summer's day with the sun to their face and necks, but there was now a chill wind, the sun had not come back from behind the cloud, and the cloud hung low with a threat of rain.

260

A narrow flight of concrete steps led from the Seine to the road near the houses where women were washing, carrying water from the river up steps across the street to the yard where they washed. One woman carried the water, headscarf tied before her throat, the headscarf hiding pins to her hair; another did the washing, sleeves rolled, wielding a rolling pin with extraordinary energy, hurrying to finish the washing before the weather broke.

I walked till I found a spot that lay in a grove of birch trees.

I had lain down a plastic mackintosh taken from my haversack and, stretching it upon the ground, I had fallen asleep. I had been wakened by dogs barking from a house along the road and later by the sounds of a shunting engine. The spot had been safe, the grass flattened, perhaps by lovers, but the barking of the dogs and the sound of the engine kept me awake, and when the dogs had settled and the engine gone the cold had taken over.

I would sleep intermittently, but each time I opened my eyes there would be the Eiffel Tower in the yonder distance, clear in the moonlight, for the clouds now had fled; the red navigational lights of the Tower flickered as they flicker still in my mind, but the plastic mackintosh had not saved me from the cold of the grass. The light would soon change, the darkness dissipate, and by four in the morning it was sufficiently light for me to leave the slope and head back towards the village, my steps echoing back from the houses.

I took a bus back to Boulevard St Michel but still there were no papers at *Jeunesse et Reconstruction* and no likelihood of their coming not for days but for weeks. The *vendange* had been delayed and the grapes would only be picked in September and October. I would have to return to England and if I had slept out one night such now was

261

my fatigue, my desire to be home, I had used the last of my money to take a first-class night ferry through Dunkirk because this was the only reservation available.

Within two days I was back in my pit village.

'Home before us!' my holiday friends said.

But I did pick grapes that year.

My mother suggested I speak to Eva, my sister-in-law, who could lend me the money to return to France. Eva agreed and I still have a copy of the letter I wrote to *Jeunesse et Reconstruction*: '*I have been able to raise the money to return to France to work in the vineyards at Cavaillon and I shall be obliged if you will forward immediately all details to me at the above address. I enclose a stamped addressed envelope for this purpose*'.

The letter had been a long time in the past as I settled on the bench under the cherry tree in the park behind Notre-Dame. Malcolm wanted to know where we might have dinner and I pointed to a restaurant set high upon a building overlooking the Seine, the curtains half-drawn to keep out the sunlight. The restaurant was called the *Tour d'Argent* and would be famous for its duck. Did Malcolm like duck? They put your name in a book, I said, when you order the duck. They put the number of the duck against your name and it is there when you come back.

'That is how it had been when the Emperor of Japan returned to the restaurant after forty years.'

'Forty years!' Malcolm said.

'As many years that I nearly slept on this park bench.'

'A pity you didn't,' Malcolm said.

'Why is that?' I asked.

'Because we could have put a plaque with your name on it.'

'Just like the duck,' I said.

262

Brighton Bell

Before the 1997 General Election, I had taken the train to Brighton to attend a Congress of the General Municipal and Boilermakers' Union.

I had joined the Union on becoming Prospective Parliamentary Candidate for Hexham; they had asked those MPs they supported to come to Brighton to give a Parliamentary report and I would arrive shortly before noon. A Trade Union Congress is not as rumbustious as a Labour Party Conference and when I arrived with my Parliamentary colleagues we were shown into a lounge and offered coffee and biscuits, following the proceedings on closed-circuit television.

Later we would be shown our seats at the back of the hall, but though I had wanted to spend some time at the Congress the usual heavy programme back in the House required an early return. I would spend no more than two hours in Brighton, but time enough to pay my respects to the Union, to listen to the Parliamentary report given by Bridget Prentice MP, to stand and accept a mild applause, to mingle with the delegates before walking along the front, the air soft to my cheeks, a weak sun seeking to penetrate the heavy cloud, breathing the sea air and looking for a bench where I would park myself and use my mobile phone.

263

I had first come to Brighton on a November's evening in my twenty-first year.

Argos Magazine had a competition for short story writers and I had written a short story and taken it to Brighton and posted it in a letter box on the sea front. When I returned to England after two months' grape-picking in the South of France I settled not in London but in my pit village. I had begun my first book of short stories and would return home two years after I had left, not only to complete them but to settle again in the North-East.

My newspaper days were behind me, I had written some eight short stories and had another four I would write before the end of the year to complete the collection. I had read somewhere that it was easier to get a book of short stories published than a first novel and I had written the stories in my partitioned room in Tufnell Park. Though the stories would be centred around my pit village, I would write one based on my holiday in Switzerland entitled *Rainbow Round the Sun*.

One of the unforeseen consequences of my returning to the North-East was that I would fall in love.

Unencumbered by acne, my confidence having fully returned, I had met my first wife Margaret at the Oxford Galleries in Newcastle, venue where most young men met their wives. She worked in the Trustee Savings Bank in Newcastle and, to the bonds of friendship and love, she shared with me a desire to travel; for whilst I might have returned home I did not believe I would stay beyond two years. I had returned bronzed and relaxed from ten days in Switzerland and two months in the vineyards.

To the surprise of my brother Roy, who had urged me to return to the North-East, I would not find it easy to get a job. Now that I was no longer a journalist what had I to offer? Shorthand and typing? I had no managerial skills at twenty-years-old. I went for a job at Avery Scales in the Newcastle Haymarket, but the manager feared I might get 'itchy feet'; my brother had come with me for the interview. I had been interviewed too for a post with a haulage company and had pleased the local manager; but when the woman boss came from Rochdale she found me too young and inexperienced.

I would write other stories, *North of Camden Town*, and *The Coal Merchant*, and would continue my reading: Hemingway's *For Whom the Bell Tolls*, *The Old Man and the Sea* and *A Farewell to Arms*. Ideas for short stories would not only shower my mind but would be converted to paper: *A Street Beyond*, *Night Ferry* and *The White Rabbit*. There would be a final story in the series entitled *The Floweret*.

These might have been happy days as a writer, reading more essays by William Hazlett and short stories by O'Henry, walking the fells with the first chill of winter, the air cold and thin, snow from last winter still lying in ditches along the hedgerows, the snow speckled with black as if penetrated by coal dust even on the fells. The strains on my family relationships caused by my departure for London two years earlier were behind me. I had now the company of a woman a year younger than myself, but I had no money, what little I had left on returning from the vineyards had not lain like snow along the hedgerow but was fast dissipating.

My diaries tell me I would be lucky to have ten pounds by the end of the year.

By now I would have my complement of twelve short stories and with Christmas out the way I intended to make any revisions and submit them to William Heinemann. They were publishers to Somerset Maugham. The stories amounted to sixty-three thousand words: '*taking into account my youth,*' I would write, '*and the maturity some of my stories, if not all, I feel they will be accepted for publication, although of course that can be by no means certain. Like most things in life I shall have to wait and see*'.

With no jobs available in the North-East I did indeed return to London in the New Year, by this time with sixpence to my bank account, and only that to keep it open. I would return to the boarding house in Tufnell Park. I would no longer share a partitioned room at the front of the house with an Indian student on the other side of the partition; he had anyway returned to India. I would have my own room at the back to the left of the corridor leading to the kitchen, small and quiet, but dusty too since the cleaning lady had also left.

And whilst I would return to the City, with plans to marry I decided not to return to a temporary job but one that was full time. This was an error. I had been happy moving from office to office, or if settling in one particular office having no responsibilities, being temporary and not involved in office politics. I took a job as secretary to the head of a chemicals agency who also owned the business.

The chemical samples in the office and the dust at Tufnell Park gave me asthma.

Unaware of the causes, I would suffer for eighteen months with one serious asthma attack after another, the doctor once being called to give me an injection; I would taking ephedrine, the only remedy at the time which might have opened the bronchial tubes but stimulated the heart, so that I would lie awake at night shouting out texts from my novel or short stories, regardless of the affect this might have on other boarders, or if they heard me at all.

I would also work in the evenings.

Since there would be no shorthand toil to fill the hours,

Mrs Garcke of the Lawsen Employment Agency arranged for me to work with her husband at Becks Carnival Novelties, and leaving the City in the evening, on my way home as it were, I would take the bus to Islington and work a couple of hours three nights a week. I wrote in my diary in those early January days: '*I feel almost cocky again after four days in London. Not only have I an excellent place to live but I have the possibility not of one job but two*'.

I might have left home with sixpence but I had borrowed to pay for my trip to Switzerland and to the vineyards. The two jobs would help me pay my family back. With my short stories completed I also began writing a novel. I must still have been doing some free-lance journalism, for I congratulated myself on earning six guineas. I would also continue writing short stories, adding three to the collection, bringing the number of words to seventy-five thousand.

There would be a play too.

I had my typewriter bought in the Newcastle Bigg Market, my father with me, when the owner had opened the shop on Whit Monday, and I would thud away at the keys in my room, sitting by the window, no doubt to the dissatisfaction of a couple who lived in the basement below. One night they flung a stone at the window. They would deny this the following day, but it brought my late-night typewriting to a premature end.

I would try to rise at half-past-six in the morning and write before I went to the office, but this would make me mean and ill-tempered, falling out with the staff, and this too I discontinued. Sometimes I would write into the night, not using my typewriter, feeling the flow of the story, settling to sleep in the certainty that it would all flow again in the morning, but to my astonishment finding that it did not.

I was learning all of the hazards of writing.

I would write a full-length play for the theatre and

send it to *H.M. Tennent*; the writing would take me six weeks. The play had been written under the influence of Graham Green and Bernard Shaw, the literary dialogue broken by colons and semi-colons; Graham Green had *The Complaisant Lover* with Sir Ralph Richardson playing in the West End; and though I would read the plays of Bernard Shaw it would be some years before I saw a performance on the stage.

How could any actor memorise those lines?

There would still be the Old Vic on Friday evenings, seeing the plays from the Gods, a true *enfant du paradis*, as the French might say, but now there would be Queen's Theatre and the Globe when it opened in Shaftsbury Avenue, and the Haymarket too where I would see Sir Alec Guinness playing Lawrence of Arabia in the play *Ross* by Terence Rattigan; there would be *A Man For All Seasons* by Robert Bolt with Sir Paul Scofield; and also at the Haymarket Sir John Guilgud reciting an anthology of Shakespeare entitled *The Seven Ages of Man*. I would allow myself for the price of two shillings the luxury of taking out a set of small red binoculars and watch Sir John seeking to catch in the palm of his hand a small moth fluttering around his head.

My play, incidentally, would be returned.

I would have but a single week's holiday with my job in the City and proposed to keep up my travel by spending it in Paris. When in Paris a year earlier, on my way to the South of France, I had the ideas for a novel, and by the time I was ready to return I had already written a hundred and fifty pages. In Paris I had thought myself a writer, I would contemplate the stories I had to write, and I would think of the future, as I would note, '*with assurances and in terms of my own personal well-being*'.

If my play had been returned so too were my short stories. They were rejected both by Heinemann and Michael

Joseph, though Mrs Michael Joseph wrote me a kindly letter, suggesting I speak with an agent with whom she had had lunch only the day before. The agent also looked at the work. The consensus seemed to be that it would be uneconomic to launch a new and unknown writer by way of a book of short stories and that I should write a novel. The agent also pointed out that one did not open a champagne bottle with a cork screw; this showed my ignorance and lack of depth, though I cannot now recall to which story this referred, since most had dealt with my pit village.

My first full novel *When Tomorrow Comes* was no more a success than my short stories and play and I would write a second novel *The Way and the Truth*. The second novel would be turned down by William Heinemann, Michael Joseph and Jonathan Cape. It would also be sent to New Authors who belonged to the Hutchinson Group. Whilst the novels were simply returned with rejection slips, in the case of New Authors they let me have extracts from their readers' reports.

One criticism by a first reader had been that my second book reflected '*a common enough story about the working class*'; it did indeed command sympathy. The reader declared that my book lacked quality and originality and the plot '*just tailed off*' though the reader added: '*You have obviously someone who has the power to tell a story and to create atmosphere*'. She suggested (I would always presume the readers were women) that I write an autobiographical novel.

The second reader declared that my novel had distinct promise; she then described the story and added a certain perfunctory criticism, and declared the novel had been '*well written*'. A third opinion came from the director of New Authors. He felt he would not publish. And of course if New Authors would not publish, since they were designed for writers such as myself, who else could I consider?

I described this as '*a cold reality*'.

~

Margaret would be transferred from the Trustee Savings Bank in Newcastle to a branch of the Bank at Archway.

She was and remains a fine noble woman with brown eyes and hair. In those days she would wear her hair in a bun and the photograph I liked best was of her standing by her aunt's gate wearing a slim-fitting black dress with a string of pearls showing the whiteness of her neck. The sparkle to her eyes had reached her smile. She would stay at Dalmeny House in Holloway. This was a residence for young women that overlooked Holloway Prison.

It would be half a mile from my own bed-sit in Tufnell Park and I would recall walking Margaret home in the evening, noticing the moon, how quickly it moved across the sky, now crescent, now half-full, now full; how time passed so quickly, one month after another, almost as fast as our steps. I would make a mental note of this as we walked up the hill and down towards Dalmeny House.

The memory lingers still.

Margaret would come to London by the summer and on Sunday we would take a train to Richmond from Kentish Town to visit Kew Gardens. We would also walk by the river and visit the town. One Sunday we had seen a set of Charles Dickens' novels in the window of a second-hand book shop priced at two-pounds-and-ten shillings. This had been a sizeable part of my weekly wage, but I had called the shop the following day and asked them to reserve the books for me.

We had gone back the next weekend and collected them

and taken them back to the bed-sit. The books would follow me wherever I went, generally in an old tea chest with a silver lining, before the lining disintegrated; they would end in my sister Heather's front room for so long she was reluctant to part with them when I wanted them back. They had become part of the furniture. Now they are in my son Malcolm's room in Middlesbrough.

In the summer when Malcolm came to work with me at the House of Commons I would take him for a drive one Friday evening in order to give the car a run. It had stood long enough in the Commons' car park. I had journeyed west and found myself heading in the direction of Kew. I had parked the car in the village square opposite the cricket field and since cricket fields were rare for me now I had spent a moment on the turf, standing by the crease looking down where years ago on a similar pitch a bowler had trundled towards me as I had stood before my wicket.

There would be no bowler this evening, but I recalled to Malcolm how I had taken the train from Kentish Town to buy the set of Dickens that stood now in his own library. We had been looking for a pub but had wandered down a street that had looked familiar. It had been forty years since I had been in Kew, but we passed a row of shops, some vacant, one of them a travel agency, and there on the end, thriving as ever, no dust to the windows now, stood the second-hand book shop.

'You should bring your Dickens back,' Malcolm said.

'You think they might buy them off me?'

'You might get your money back.'

Always, I reflected, the literary connaisseur.

Margaret would buy for my twenty-first birthday a complete set of the plays of Bernard Shaw from Foyle's. The cost would be eight guineas. The plays had first been published by Odhams Press of Long Acre for *The Daily*

Herald. Shaw had written by way of a warning from the author that this was the first time he had ever attached a condition to the perusal of his plays. The condition had been one had to be a reader of the *Herald*, but it had been the binding rather than the plays that had cost the eight guineas.

Margaret had inscribed on the inside page: *A thing of beauty is a joy for ever.* We had been saving to get married, eight guineas had been almost a week's wages, but the book has endured, the inscription too; it has been read many times over many years in different locations; it is read to this day, not only as a gift, a reflection of true love, more than a memory, more than the capturing of a coming-of-age.

It has indeed been a joy for ever.

As I struggled with my two jobs, my writing and my asthma, my health so deteriorated that to recover I returned to my home in the North-East. My weight had dropped to nine-stone-seven. The fresh village air did me good, as did the walks on the fell; I had forgotten my ephedrine and wondered how I would get through the night. I had been relieved when I did, my tubes clear, no constriction and no wheezing.

No tension.

My recuperation coincided with the October 1959 General Election, and whilst in London there had appeared to be no prospect of Labour winning, this perception changed in our pit village. The only Tory voter had been the milkman and when he had revealed this fact he had lost his custom. It was not that I worked for the Labour Party in the Election but I attended the village committee rooms on Election Day when the chairman asked for a volunteer to attend the count for the local MP. I immediately volunteered but this had been met by an unresponsive silence.

The only counts I would ever attend would be my own.

Upon returning to London the ill health soon returned, not only the asthma but a severe catarrh that affected my ears, so that in desperation Margaret and I had taken a train to Brighton on a Friday evening to pass the weekend. We had found a boarding house not far from the station. It had been a quiet November evening, the streets damp, the sea calm, the waves rustling against the shingle, though later there would be a wind that almost knocked us off our feet as we turned a corner.

I had completed my short story for *Argosy* Magazine and Margaret and I had solemnly found a post box, sending off the short story rather like Charles Dickens dropping into a publisher's letter box his first sketches as a writer. They would be published as *The Pickwick Papers.* My breast might have been constricted and asthmatic, but it had been filled with hope as the story bedded down in the box with other weekend letters.

I cannot now recall the short story and if disappointed not to win the competition, nor be placed second or third, I had been angered that the prize had gone to Sián O'Faoláin, the most popular short story writer of the day. It had seemed a great waste to launch a short story competition for young writers and to give the first prize to an established writer. This would be a difficulty throughout my so-called literary career. Publishers would tell me they only wished to publish successful writers who were known. They would never explain how one came to be in this fortunate position without being published in the first place.

This had been Brighton out-of-season and on Saturday evening we had gone to a music hall to see Ronnie Carrol and Millicent Martin. They had just been married, their pictures were in all the newspapers; they were on their honeymoon but they were working too, performing before the Mayor of Brighton no less. The Mayor had arrived with his wife, wearing the chain of office, his wife in a long heavy gown, a necklace glittering to her throat, a tiara shining to her hair.

There had even been a red carpet leading from the car across the pavement into the music hall.

I would be in politics myself when eighteen years later I visited Brighton again.

I had been adopted Prospective Parliamentary Candidate for Hexham. There had been a debate on rural affairs on the Monday and I would make my first conference speech. I had cobbled together a few words at the last moment, unaware that there was to be a debate. I had stood at the back of the hall and waved my speech. I had no idea how a Party Conference would be organised, with MPs or Candidates sitting to the right of the chair, the trade union delegates to the centre, and Party delegates to the right. I simply stood at the back and waved.

I had caught the eye of the chairman.

I would rush to the rostrum with all the enthusiasm of a new candidate, the enthusiasm of a man who had wanted to be in politics, who now had three minutes if not to change the world, move the universe, make the earth tremble, at least to make some ripple on the political scene as the waves would ripple upon the shingle along the Brighton beach.

The Prime Minister, Jim Callaghan, sat behind me.

There were a sea of faces ahead.

I talked of rural deprivation and quickly ran out of text. I looked up at the gallery above the conference hall where the press were gathered. I saw Sir Robin Day, doyen of all political commentators; he peered upon the scene through his pebble glasses, his hair smoothed back, his bow tie immaculate. I waved my hand to the gallery, my enthusiasm returned and with it the rhetoric. Of the rural areas I would say:

'Such is the deprivation, they can't even watch Robin Day on television!'

For reasons known only to those students of Party Conference, this brought the house down. It was repeated on the nightly bulletins covering the conference. I appeared on local television and the *Hexham Courant* gave my speech top billing in that week's edition. Sir Robin Day also became a friend, I see him often around Millbank, in winter wearing a fur hat, heavily overcoated against the cold.

He had been amused by the speech.

'I've been accused of many things,' he would say. 'But rural deprivation!'

My next speech at the Brighton Party Conference had been four years later.

By then I had been adopted Prospective Parliamentary Candidate for Middlesbrough and would speak at the Conference on the Monday morning following a watershed political battle between Denis Healey and Tony Benn, ostensibly for the deputy leadership but in reality for the heart and soul of the Labour Party.

A left-wing victory for Tony Benn would have made the Party a true socialist Party; a victory for Denis Healey meant that the Party might be saved from itself, maintaining its values and traditions and appeal to the electorate. Denis Healey won by only half a percentage point, there had been high drama that Sunday evening, and I had seen Tony Benn walking along the promenade with his wife Caroline.

'It was a great victory!' he said, even though he had been defeated.

The alcohol had flowed into the early hours, I would sleep very little and would rise at six o'clock to prepare my speech. The debate would be on education. I had put in the ritual note to Alex Kitson, that year's Party chairman, and he had said he would look out for me. The mood of Conference could not have been flatter, the day after the night before; the hall was cold, the debate uninteresting, but I caught Alex Kitson's eye and made the long walk to the rostrum in absolute silence.

By the time I arrived I was so nervous I had actually forgotten the name of my prospective seat. I announced myself as Parliamentary Candidate for Stockton, South. Now why had I done that? I also began with a good news and bad news joke, but unfortunately got them in the wrong order, to the mystification of Conference, or those who were listening. My saving grace had been wearing the tie of the General and Municipal Workers' Union, fore-runner to the present General Municipal and Boilermakers'; General Secretary David Basnett had given me a kindly smile when I stood down from the rostrum, but there had been only a somnolent applause from the delegates.

I regretted my poor performance when speaking to Arthur Bottomley, still the Member of Parliament for Middlesbrough. He reassured me as best he could.

'I talked around,' he said. 'It was all right.'

The Conference were indifferent to most things that Monday morning, it had hardly mattered if I had spoken well or ill; their minds were on the impact of Healey's narrow win over Benn and what it meant for the Party. My own confidence had been severely shaken and I would spend the next months speaking as often as I could to any kind of audience so that my confidence would return.

Two years later, another election defeat behind the Party, I would again be at Brighton to attend yet another Labour

Party Conference, this time as a Member of Parliament in my own right, a supporter of Roy Hattersley whom I had campaigned for in the leadership election. Roy would make me his Parliamentary Private Secretary and my political career in the House of Commons had begun.

Another four years would pass and I would make a Conference speech defending my record on behalf of the families caught up in the Cleveland child crisis. The speech went well and as I turned from the rostrum there was Sir Robin Day, older like the rest of us, but following the speech with professional interest, giving me the thumbs-up. Robin would follow my career from that very first Conference speech; we would talk about it when we met at the Garrick Club; he would tell my wife how everyone was watching my political career. I would feel sad that I would not make more of it and let him down.

'That was a fine speech,' he said.

Now, with the General Election almost upon us, at Brighton again, a spectator this time, an observer to the Congress of the General and Municipal and Boilermakers' Union, I sat on a bench on the promenade, setting aside my mobile phone. I thought of all the Conferences I had attended here. I thought of my first visit. I felt like Oscar Wilde's sinner. He would have a past rather than a saint who had a future.

I reflected, too, that even Brighton has its moments, like today when the sea is soft across the shingle, white like morning light; or in the evening when the sun sinks beyond the pier, all wood like the coal staiths of old, the sun small and round, not as powerful as a sun sinking into the Gulf of Mexico beyond Clearwater Beach; but a sunset all the same, with its pessimism, the light and heat going with it; yet with its optimism, too, that it would rise again, like hope in the breast, facing the day as the rest of us face the future.

There had been optimism and pessimism in my many visits to Brighton. I had been upcast and downcast, exhilarated and despondent. The sea drifted white across the shingle, sighing as it went, seething almost, as political careers had advanced and receded. They had made their mark, but then the wind had drifted across the shingle and dried and polished the stones and shells.

It had left nothing behind.

Book Three

Postcard from the Tate

John gave me a postcard from the Tate Britain.

He had been born in 1940 the son of a Swedish planter in the Belgian Congo; his mother had been born in Argentina. His mother and father had been there in the first place because King Leopold of the Belgians could not get enough of his own citizens to emigrate to the Congo and he had looked to other nationalities.

His family had moved to Cape Town in South Africa when he had been three years old and John had lived there till 1946, when they had moved to Belgium. He had come to England eleven years later, when he was fifteen, and he has been here ever since. He has worked in Dolphin Square for thirty years and speaks a perfect French.

He is night porter in the block where I live.

'Why did Ernest Hemingway shoot himself?' he asked.

'His father had shot himself,' I said.

'And his brother too, *n'est-ce pas?*'

'There were the accidents.'

'What accidents?' John asked.

I had first heard Hemingway's name when I had seen the evocative film of his short story *The Snows of Kilimanjaro*; it had originally been entitled *A Budding Friendship*. It astounded me such a powerful film could come from a short story, but as Hemingway himself would say, he had encompassed the material of four novels: '*I put all the true stuff in, and with all the load, the most load any story ever carried*,' it had indeed '*taken off like an airplane*,' as his biographer Carlos Baker would write.

It had certainly taken off in my mind.

The major parts in the film had been played by Ava Gardner and Gregory Peck and Susan Hayward and told the story of a writer who had lost his way. Harry had been attracted to the high life; a rich woman from New York had paid for his latest safari. He had been killing himself by this attraction just as, according to Hemingway in the story, it had been killing another famous writer Scott Fitzgerald.

This had not pleased Scott Fitzgerald when he received a copy of the draft.

As it happened, the character Harry had been dying from gangrene caused by a scratch to his right leg. He should have treated the scratch with iodine but had not, because he never infected; then he had used an antiseptic solution that, according to him, had paralysed the minute blood vessels. The gangrene was moving now from his right leg to his body. He had time to reflect, as he lay on his cot, that he had dissipated his talents and, like the leopard whose frozen carcass had been found on the upward slopes of Kilimanjaro, he had been diverted from his true path, his true destiny.

Only he had not climbed beyond the lower slopes.

Harry had thought of the life behind him and Hemingway had drawn on his experiences in Paris where he had lived with his first wife Hadley. He had drawn on his skiing in the Alps or fishing in the Black Forest. Or the march to Constantinople at the end of the First World War. He had been a correspondent of the *Toronto Star* who had sent him on this mission, much to the regret of his wife Hadley.

They had had their first quarrel.

In the short story but not the film, Harry in his dying dream sees the plane arriving that will take him to safety, clambers in behind the pilot, and flies off leaving the camp and his wife behind. The plane flies towards Kilimanjaro, white in the sun, the top squat, flying through a rainstorm, but flying back into the sunlight, so that perhaps in death Harry attains those upper reaches that had so eluded him in his life.

The film, of course, has a happier ending.

I had seen the film at the *King's* picture house at Chopwell and had walked home down the railway line, not only stunned by the power, the allegory, but wondering if I could ever write short stories like Ernest Hemingway. I was sixteen years old. The stars were out, the night cold, and I can hear still the echo of my steps from the stone bridge ahead as I marched forward, striding across the sleepers, firs on either side, the line dulled in the grudging light, my mind racing ahead of my echo.

Six years later, settling in Paris with Margaret, finding an hotel on a street running parallel to the Gare du Nord, I would notice that the film version of Hemingway's *For Whom The Bell Tolls* would be playing in a small cinema by the station; the film had been a great Technicolour success with Gary Cooper and Ingrid Bergman. Dialogue would be dubbed into French and we might hardly understand a word. Earlier, when I had come to Paris on my own for a week's holiday, I had seen a copy of the uncut novel in a bookshop in the rue Lafayette under the grand French name: *Pour Qui Sonne le Glas*.

It had all nourished my enthusiasm for Hemingway.

'Tell me about the accidents,' John said.

'They were plane crashes,' I said.

I explained that Hemingway and his fourth wife Mary had been involved in two plane accidents in the fifties on safari in Africa. In the first accident the plane's propeller and tail assembly had struck a telegraph wire over Murchison Falls in Uganda; the pilot had been forced to crash land his Cessna but he had brought the plane down safely.

Hemingway had a bruised shoulder and Mary had been in shock.

In the second, the plane scheduled to take them to Entebbe where they might recover from the first accident did not get off the ground at Shimoni. The runway had been like a ploughed field and the aircraft had stalled and burst into flames. Hemingway and Mary and the pilot of the first plane had been able to escape a second time; so too had the pilot of the De Havilland Rapide.

The pilots and Mary would recover but Hemingway never did.

He had butted his way out of the aircraft, giving him severe concussion, and later he would be diagnosed as having a ruptured liver, spleen and kidney, vision loss in the left eye, hearing loss in the left ear, injuries to his vertebrae and right arm and shoulder and left leg. He might have got out of the aircraft but only into the flames and had suffered first degree burns to his face and arms and head.

'He never recovered,' I said.

John produced a postcard from his pocket.

'I picked it up today at the Tate,' he said.

'You went to the Tate Britain?' I asked. 'Not the Tate Modern?'

'The one by the river,' Jean said.

'They're both by the river.'

There would now be two Tate galleries in London, a Tate Britain on the north bank and a Tate Modern on the south bank built inside the entrails of a former power station opposite the Savoy Hotel where Claude Monet had painted at the turn of the century. The Tate Modern would house stupendous works of sculpture and painting; Tate Britain would content itself with the great works of British artists.

'It was the Tate Britain,' Jean said.

It hardly mattered to me.

The card itself was enough.

The card was a reproduction of a painting of Somerset Maugham by Graham Sutherland.

The painting depicts Maugham upon a bamboo stool, the background apricot, his arms and legs crossed. Maugham's head is tilted upward, giving him a sardonic look; he is wearing a brown velvet smoking jacket, red scarf, slacks and tan loafers. To my mind, the portrait reflects Maugham as a writer who had travelled the Orient and written many a short story based upon the characters he had met there.

'What about Somerset Maugham?' John asked.

One of my party pieces at the House of Commons is to take visitors onto the Terrace, not to admire the Thames or the giant ferris wheel called the London Eye that has been erected close to County Hall, but the red brick building opposite, short and squat, its arched windows reflecting pools of shadow. This is the old St Thomas' Hospital standing in Lambeth Palace Road, a listed building now, overshadowed by a better-equipped modern St Thomas' Hospital.

Maugham had studied to be a doctor and would spend five years as an intern at the old St Thomas' Hospital.

He had lived in Vincent Square and walked across the river from Horseferry Road to Lambeth Bridge and down by the side of the Thames to the hospital. Anton Chekhov had been a doctor and John Keats apprenticed to a stomach surgeon. Maugham would qualify where Keats had not, but

285

rather than practise he would leave St Thomas' to become a full-time writer after the publication of his first novel *Liza of Lambeth*.

Liza of Lambeth had been based on Maugham's experience in the midwifery department of the hospital and he would write more about his years as an intern in his novel *Of Human Bondage*. His writing career would last sixty-five years and when I had first visited the vineyards I had penned a letter to him at his villa at Cap Ferrat on the outskirts of Nice. The letter is dated 11 September 1958 and was sent from *Quartier les Fugueyrolles*, the second vineyard in Cavaillon where I had been working.

'*I am a young writer,*' I wrote, '*working in the South of France and I would like if possible to see you for a few moments at your home, for I believe any advice you may give would be invaluable to my own career. I have read your work and it is because of your influence and your encouragement to young writers regarding travel that I am here today.*'

I would go on: '*I am twenty and I am working on a collection of short stories which I hope to have completed by Christmas and perhaps published next year; but as I have none with me there is little fear of me asking you to read my work. I sincerely believe I can learn something from you, if you can spare but a few moments of your time, and I trust this will not cause any inconvenience. My work here is completed on the 20th September and I am free to call upon you after that date.*'

I ended the letter '*My regards and admiration*', but I did not send it, my courage failed, and somehow it has survived all these years among my papers. When I returned a second time from the vineyards of the South of France to settle again in the North-East, as I thought, I had bought a copy of Maugham's last book entitled *Points of View*.

The book had been a collection of essays, including an essay on the short story.

Maugham had been no great admirer of the short stories of Henry James and had discussed these with Desmond McCarthy, a well-known literary critic of the time. They had been sitting after dinner in the drawing room of Maugham's villa on Cap Ferrat enjoying a whisky and soda. McCarthy had admired James and to tease him Maugham had invented, on the spur of the moment, an absurd James-type story.

'*What you forget, my poor Willy,*' McCarthy had replied, '*is that Henry James would have given the story the classic dignity of St Paul's Cathedral, the brooding horror of St Pancras and the dusty splendour of Woburn.*'

The writer and the critic had rounded the evening with a good laugh. They had helped themselves to another whisky and soda. Or as Maugham would write: '*Well pleased with ourselves, we parted to go to our respective bedrooms*'.

Respective bedrooms?

It had struck me as strange, reading these words in my twentieth year. Why had not Maugham simply said they had retired to bed? Why the emphasis on *respective*? It was only when Maugham had died that I learnt the reason for his circumspection. He had been a life-long practicing homosexual in an age when homosexuality had been a criminal offence.

He had used his words carefully to denote that not only had Desmond McCarthy been a charming companion and fine literary critic – though not good on the '*plastic arts or music*' – he had definitely not been sharing Maugham's bed. Maugham would be dead two years before homosexuality between consenting adults acting in private no longer became a criminal offence; he himself would never publicly refer to homosexuality; he would keep it out of his novels and stories, though I had often wondered why his characterisation

287

of certain women lacked verisimilitude, a word I would learn from reading one of his essays.

It had been a surprise to learn that the man who had so influenced not only my writing but my life had been homo-sexual, but it hardly made a difference to my appreciation of him as a writer, just as it hardly mattered that Ernest Hemingway had four wives; Maugham had succeeded as a playwright, a novelist and a short story teller. He had never written poetry; he had left blank-verse poetry to his brother. My attitude had been the attitude that Maugham himself would adopt towards an artist's life and his writing: *'The sexual proclivity of an author are no business of his readers, except insofar as they influence his work. When they do and the facts are put before you much that was obscure or even incredible may be plain.'*

As in the case of the respective bedrooms.

John had walked with me to the lift in my apartment block in Dolphin Square.

'You know so much about Somerset Maugham?' he asked.

'My first wife and I visited his villa on Cap Ferrat,' I said. 'Many years ago.'

Margaret and I had married in July 1960.

I had drafted a novel called *Angel Girl* based on my observation of Islington life, nourished by my three nights a week working for Becks Carnival Novelties; and I had also written another play called *To Catherine*. I had still been suffering from asthma, for the notes to the play I had dictated to Margaret. I had been treated at a doctors' surgery at Tufnell Park and one day fell upon a younger more energetic doctor called Dr Kennedy who sent me to the Orthopedic Hospital in Great Ormond Street.

I had been diagnosed as suffering from a dust allergy.

The dust in my small room in Tufnell Park, the chemical samples at my full-time place of work, the strain of holding down not one but two jobs and seeking to write too: it had all been too much for me. I had been given a number of tests at the hospital which showed my state of mind and developing character at twenty-two: sharp-tempered, obstinate, impatient, up-and-down, aggressive sometimes; untidy, shy, disliking company, but not affected by crowds; yet sensitive to rudeness and injustice.

Conscientious and confident in myself.

I never set foot again in the office of my full-time job and I also left my room in Tufnell Park. I returned to the freshness of my pit village; the brick flats had been pulled down, the ovens closed, the chimney too had long since toppled into the pit yard in a controlled explosion, leaving the air chill and pure as it sighed down from the fells. Only the smoke from the pit engine would linger over the fir forest.

The wedding arrangements had not gone smoothly.

Or perhaps they had gone as smoothly as any other marriage arrangements, banns to be posted, formalities to be completed at a registrar office; there had been suits to hire from Dormie's in Newcastle; pitmatic we might be, but the tradition in our family was that the men be married in morning suits. There were taxis and flowers, a going-away suit made-to-measure, costing all of sixteen guineas; there were photographs to be arranged and wine for the reception to be held in the Eldon Hotel in Newcastle.

There would be tickets to buy so that we might return by train to London – on the three-twenty on a Saturday afternoon – and a hotel room to be booked in Gower Street, so that Margaret and I might spend a weekend together before seeking out yet another bed-sit, this time across the river in Clapham, leaving the north bank of the river, settling only for two months before leaving again for the vineyards in the late summer. There had been the priest to see who would remind us of our obligations both to church and society and marriage and the upbringing of children.

All of which, he pointed out, had little to do with sex.

Margaret had been radiant in a white silk wedding dress, short rather than long, wearing a soft white veil through which her eyes shone radiant as her dress: '*You look wonderful*', I whispered as she stood beside me, following her walk down the aisle on the arm of her father. We had been married in the West Street Methodist Church in Gateshead, Margaret's church near where she had lived and been brought up; I had rehearsed my marriage vows so that they would be word-perfect; there would be champagne at the reception rather than wine, our very first champagne, no more than a glass each; and I would make the customary speech of the bridegroom.

I would thank my bride's parents, who were paying for the wedding in accordance with the custom of the time. I would thank the waitresses and the guests who had turned up, thank them for their wedding presents, some I had seen and some not. I would thank the best man and Margaret's bridesmaid and of course Margaret, radiant still, thanking her for 'coming today and making it all possible'.

There would be best wishes all round before we left not for the train but for our future.

I had indeed itchy feet, as a Newcastle would-be employer had predicted, and early that year I had thought of working in Geneva or Paris after another month or two in the vineyards in late summer. I had thought of applying for a job with the United Nations or the World Health Organisation and I had wanted to contact the Swiss Embassy in London. I had thought of applying to UNESCO in Paris and also SHAPE on its outskirts, the one a health organisation, the other military. I had wanted to talk to the Foreign Office.

But nothing had come of any of this, though we had enrolled for two months at Chateauneuf-du-Pape where we would participate in the autumn *vendange*. In the two months prior to our departure, Margaret would still be working for the bank, my returning to Mrs Garcke and the Lawsen Employment Agency, doing temporary secretarial work till it was time to leave. I had worked for Lloyd's insurance brokers and to their amusement I would use them to insure our belongings on our trip to France.

There would be theatre in the evenings and we had seen *The Aspern Papers* with Sir Michael Redgrave and Flora Robson, based on a story by Henry James; there had been *The Rhinoceros* by Eugene Ionésco, with Laurence Olivier playing the lead role; there had been Bernard Shaw's *Candida* and St Joan, and a play on *Galileo* with Bernard Miles at the newly opened Mermaid Theatre. There had been *The Caretaker* by Harold Pinter and *The Tempest* by Shakespeare in the open air theatre in Regents Park.

My own play *To Catherine* had languished.

I felt it would be a better novel, it was slow and lopsided, top-heavy with women characters who all played the same kind of part, that is solicitous concern for the health of the hero. I felt it might be better as a novel. I abandoned it after drafting a few pages and never did write the novel, as I never wrote *Angel Girl*. Ernest Hemingway had been right all along: '*You put off the writing of it because you could not write it at all*'.

We had taken the ferry from Newhaven to Dieppe.

The chill evening breeze struck us as we carried our cases from the Customs shed along the damp quay to the white-painted ferry lying along the harbour wall. We had heard the rhythm of vibrating engines as the ferry prepared to put to sea. There had been several cars on the coastal highway on the other side of the harbour and the sudden arc of their lamps had flared across the water, the cars so far off they made no sound as we boarded the ferry. We had lain our luggage on the stern deck and after two coffees stood by the rail to gaze across the water to the hill above the harbour.

Seagulls had drifted in the darkness like so many useless scraps of paper.

I had felt the calm of the evening and the water and the hill, the houses shuttered, curtains drawn, doors locked, people watching television, having supper, enclosed, enveloped, content with their lives, comfortable, secure, whilst Margaret and I set out from England, stirred by restlessness but sad to be leaving our home and our country, the comfort, the contentment and the security of those in their homes on the hill above.

Perhaps we would never be back.

We had picked grapes at Chateauneuf-du-Pape in the Domaine de Mont Redon, taking the train from Dieppe to Paris, finding Paris cold, lonely, standing in a doorway on the Avenue-des-Champs-Elysées with the Arc de Triomphe at the top of the Avenue, but feeling no enthusiasm, no excitement, anxious only to be on the train again from Gare de Lyon to Avignon, where the bridge was half-down and where we spent a pleasant night in a hotel before moving on to Chateauneuf-du-Pape.

We had spent two months among the *gros cailloux*, stones polished white by the Ice Age that reputedly made the wine so special, the flavour so deep; and later we had settled in Cavaillon where I had been determined to learn the language. I had used a simple text book *How to Learn French* and had painstakingly written out all the exercises. We had stayed *chez Trompette*, hotel, restaurant and bar combined, and I would speak French with anyone who came into the bar, most times badly, many times impolitely, mixing the familiar and the impersonal, the *tu* and the *vous*, showing more determination than knowledge.

After a month in Cavaillon we had taken a bus to Nice and settled in the *relais du port*, an *auberge de jeunesse* in the *Vieux Port*. I would write of the palm trees, their trunks as sturdy as oak and resilient as cork, topped by fronds hanging in lament, as if over a great sorrow, like Ruth weeping for her children; and of the evenings along the Promenade des Anglais with winter setting in, the lights brittle along the Promenade, and only a few shining from the Negresco Hotel.

Now this was the stuff of writing.

There would be the broad sweep of the Bay of Angels curving towards Cap Ferrat and the flicker of lighthouses from darkened promontories, the light so white and brittle that it reminded me of Keats' poem *On the Eve of St Agnes*. Margaret and I had walked along the coastline with its dripping bougainvillea and cactus and lemon trees; we had walked from Nice to Cap Ferrat where Somerset Maugham had his villa at the tip of the promontory looking out upon the Mediterranean.

One can never write of tidal water at Nice.

There is no tidal water, rather a sea curling in cream breakers against the shingle, sighing against the rocks, rather like Brighton. I would love the sound of the sea upon the shingle, the long sigh it would make, filled with tedium rather than joy, meek without force, but delicious in the sound of the water upon sharp stones, whitening the stones, swirling around rocks, lapping the stone walls of the Nice jetty.

Margaret would take my picture sitting upon one of the

rocks, my notebook open, my pen at the ready, studying sea and sky, a real writer, describing the autumn leaves floating upon sea water, the smell of shellfish, the dampness of the seaweed caught among the rocks and shingle. We had kept walking up the right side of Cap Ferrat till we reached Villa Mauresque, the home of Somerset Maugham, a Moorish sign etched in red into the white plaster, as it would be etched into the covers of all his books.

The world had been different in 1960, the gates to the Villa Mauresque had been open, and Margaret and I had walked up the drive to the square white house. A green shutter had opened at one of the bedroom windows and a maid popped out her head. She cheerfully told us Somerset Maugham was not at home. I was bolder now than I had been two years ago when I had not the courage to post my letter.

'Can we see his library?'

'The house is shut up,' she said. 'But you can see the gardens.'

We walked past clumps of agapanthus.

Gardeners working in the grounds did not mind our presence among the orange and avocado and lemon trees. A swimming pool had been cut out of the rock and a faun had been built with a concrete mouth through which water would gush. We had been impressed by the bougainvillea along the pathways to the Cap, but from the gardens there wafted the soft gentleness of mimosa. And if there was a swimming pool and faun there was a lily pond too in the grounds.

I took Margaret's picture by the side of the pool, looking across the waters, the waters themselves reflecting her image so strongly, so powerfully, that you could turn the picture upside down and see the image as strongly defined. We took our leave of the gardeners and the maid as if we were part of the family, which I suppose we were: a family of writers. We saw the pathway through the trees

294

that led to the sea and the sea itself had been cast in a silver sheen.

We returned to Nice not on foot but by bus, walking again the length of the promontory, catching the bus at the base, waiting in a queue, the bus filled with workers in boiler suits and women with headscarves clutching their bags, the engine of the bus snorting and steaming, the road brittle beneath the over-large tyres, the quietude and splendour of Villa Mauresque lost to the crowded discomfort and Gitanes-smell emanating from the boiler suits and headscarves.

We thought we might cut flowers at Grasse.

Grasse had been the centre for perfumery too, where pressed flowers had provided the conditioning base for all manner of French perfumes. A flower market stood behind the Quai des Etats Unis at Nice where they sold mimosa, carnations, roses and chrysanthemums and violets; but if the sellers had heard of work it was a long way by public transport to Grasse above Cannes. As we pondered the option, I had received a letter inviting me to Paris to see if I might work as a secretary to an American lawyer.

At the *relais du port* we had met a young American from New York, short with dark hair and slim moustache. His name was George Weis, not a tourist, but with a natural curiosity which led him to the bottom of everything, and with sufficient money that would take him to the places along the coastline that he wished to visit. I recall him sitting by the open window in the *relais* writing a letter, his eyebrows as dark as his hair and moustache, and tidy too since he had the habit of combing the eyebrows each morning.

He showed us Old Nice, saying that it would probably be missed by the tourist.

He described the pizzas sold warm and straight from the baker's tray. He introduced us to marc, a distillation from the juice of grapes, and as we walked through Old Nice it was as if we were wrapped in the odours of cheese and chicken and leather and charcuterie, of sardines and herring, the odours sifting along the narrow alleyways ceilinged by the sky. The alleyways had been hemmed by creaking windows and flaking walls and iron balustrades. Linen hung down from the balconies and the creaking windows were open to hang out more washing. There were more shops with poultry stripped and hanging upside down upon iron hooks, tapering baguettes in baskets in the boulangeries, the odour of bread still fresh in the early morning, a patisserie with its window full of rich chocolate delicacies.

George showed us L'Eglise St Augustin, a sixteenth-century church with a plaque to commemorate the war dead, but with defensive, ugly grills to the windows; not a fashionable-looking church but ordinary; not like a church at all. We examined the wide entrance but because L'Eglise St Augustin stood on high ground it gathered the whole of Old Nice around it: the stalls selling hot pastry, the bakery with its glowing ovens, the pigeons and the markets; the egg shop and shoe shop and meat shop, even the store selling woollen garments.

I told George about our trip to Villa Mauresque.

'I shouldn't think too much about it,' he said.

'Why is that?' I asked.

'Because it won't rub off.'

'You mean it won't make me a better writer?'

'Or a writer at all.'

I had been reminded of a short story by Anton Chekhov.

Chekhov had written plays as well as short stories. His stories had caught the languor of Russia, the plains, the hopelessness, like history seeped into the land and the soul, enervating like heat and destructive like cold, wide like the horizon but equally far off; they would come through Chekhov's writing as they would find expression in Russian art and music, in its religion as well as its poverty and serfdom.

Chekhov would write as a bird sings:

'*I just sat down and the writing came. How or about what didn't bother me. It just came of itself – to write an essay, a story, a short sketch caused me no trouble at all.*' One of his stories had been entitled *Three Years*, of a man who falls madly in love but where the woman does not return his love. This is no bar to a bourgeois marriage and as time passes gradually he falls out of love with his wife.

Paradoxically, the more he falls out of love with her the more she falls in love with him, so that over three years the roles are reversed. The story ends with them sitting in a park, his wife making much of him, fussing around him, her hands white and soft and delicate like butterflies; she touches his waistcoat, his tie, while he sits bored, irritated, wondering how all this has come about and how it will end. He does not know the answer, does not seek one, but enjoys the sun to his face as his wife's hands flutter around him. Perhaps I have re-written Chekhov's story but no matter.

I recalled the last line as we strolled through the alleyways of Old Nice.

'Let us live,' I said. 'And we shall see.'

Or as John the night porter said as the lift doors closed around me in Dolphin Square.

'All that – on the back of a postcard!'

Remembrance of Things Past

Michael J. McNulty invited me to dinner with his wife at his home in St John's Wood.

With a General Election now upon us, he had invited lawyers and economists so that we might talk politics, but the dinner had been exquisite, the company charming, the wine flowing, and with the House dissolved and no voting, no return for ten o'clock, I had been able to relax and not only talk of New Labour and the days ahead but those other days that used to be, when I had typed Michael's letters in Paris.

'Do you remember the letters?'

'I remember you typed novels in the evening.'

'Or do you remember me telling you I typed novels?'

'Remembrance of things past,' Michael said.

As indeed I had said to Tony Blair when we had visited together the University of Northumbria and he had not remembered that I had once been a Newcastle City Councillor and governor of the former Polytechnic. A friend of mine had once complimented the explorer and writer Laurence van der Post on his memory. He replied he had a fly-paper mind; every recollection stuck to it. Another friend in New York, rather than marvelling at my memory, would ask:

'How can your mind be filled with such useless and irrelevant information!'

Les Eagleton had been a fellow pupil at Hookergate Grammar School. His father owned a scrap yard and had a passion for stock car racing at Brough Park in Newcastle. One day his father had skidded from the track and into the wall with its tin-sheeted advertising; he had been badly injured. Les had stayed up all night nursing his father, the kind of thing a young son would do. I had written an account of this incident by way of a school essay and this had pleased and impressed Les.

I had called him on the phone and invited him to a reception in Newcastle.

'I can't remember you,' he said.

'I wrote an essay about your father,' I said. 'How you nursed him when he smashed his stock car.'

'I remember my father smashing his stock car,' Les said.

He had sat next to me at English class and I would recall the interest in his face as he had read another essay, one of a Meteor jet glinting gold in the sunlight as it came noiselessly over a hill, the scream of the jet engines following it like vapour trails. He had indeed come to my reception and brought his attractive wife and only the other day I took out their photos, smiling at me happily, two young people very much in love and enjoying themselves.

'I remember you now,' he said.

Or as Margaret would put it:

'You remember what you want to remember,' she said. 'And you forget the rest.'

She and I had taken a bus from Nice, climbing *la route Napoléon*, that is the route Napoleon had taken when he had escaped from Elba in 1815 and marched upon Paris, sending his imperial eagle metaphorically before him so that it would fly from steeple to steeple until it reached the towers of Notre-Dame. Napoleon had followed small trails and mule tracks; our bus had travelled up sharp mountain sides, clinging to ravine edges, pulling around tight corners, so anxious we had no time to enjoy the view, if view there had been through the drizzling mist, finally turning away from *la route Napoléon* down towards the Rhone valley and the vineyards around Lyons.

When learning French at Cavaillon I had read a small advertisement on the back page of the *New York Herald Tribune* inviting applications to be male secretary to an American lawyer in Paris. The post would be ideal for me, it would give me an opportunity to live and work and write in Paris, and I had the shorthand and typing skills to do the job. I had few expectations, so few that I almost did not write at all, but Margaret said I should write, there would be nothing lost, and at least I reflected they might pay our fares back to Paris from the South of France.

There had been a response from SODERI, the firm that had placed the advertisement, that indicated they would not be able to pay my fare back to Paris but should I be returning their way I should call in and see them. I wrote from the *relais du port* in Nice: '*I have received today your letter of the 19th November and would like to inform you that I shall be in Paris during the last days of this month and the early part of December. I shall be pleased to ring your office with a view to arranging an interview.*'

We had stayed overnight at Lyons in a small hotel where the board and lodging was part of the inclusive bus fare to Paris and after an evening meal, when Margaret had retired, I had stayed to talk to the other guests in the hotel restaurant. The restaurant had been a small narrow room with heavy curtains at the window, the tables without cloths, but I had chatted with the guests in my evolving

French. One of the guests had asked if it were true all Englishmen were homosexuals.

'Not true,' I said. '*Pas vrai!*'

'What a pity,' he said.

It had been a full day's bus ride to Paris.

The journey had become tedious, with no mountains to traverse, no icy roads, no sharp ravines, only the vineyards undulating beyond the Rhone valley. The rain was steady, the rivers had flooded, fields were submerged, vines hung drab and dull, and the poplars were dark and spindly by the side of the road, the road straight as if built by the Romans, the houses as drab as the vines, their yellow plaster pealed all the way to the outskirts of Paris.

We had settled in the Hôtel du Nord.

I had written to my mother from Nice asking her to send my made-to-measure going-away marriage suit so that I might be presentable for the interview. I wore only a pair of baggy yellow trousers, a summer shirt and a dark jacket with silken threads that I had bought in Kentish Town and which I had called my Paris jacket. They might have been suitable for the *après-vendange* or studying French in the bar *chez Trompette*, or strolling along the shingle beach at Nice passing those fishing baby-octopus; but they would not be appropriate for an interview with an American lawyer in his suite of offices in the Place Vendôme.

Come 1 December 1960, the day I had arranged for my interview, the suit had not arrived. I had thought I might hire a suit but my French did not extend so far and possibly our money extended even less. Margaret and I had taken the Métro from Gare du Nord to Place de la Concorde and walked down rue de Rivoli in the direction of the Place Vendôme. We had not been certain about this but came across Smith's bookshop, the only English bookshop in Paris.

I had asked the way of an English-speaking salesman.

'Turn left,' he said. 'A few blocks down. You'll not miss the *colonne Vendôme*.'

And so it turned out.

The *colonne* had been built with the cannon taken from Napoleon's victories; it had been pulled down and destroyed at a time of revolutionary effervescence that Victor Hugo would write about in his *Les Misérables*; but it had been put back together again, patiently, lovingly, only a bellicose Napoleon had been removed from the head to be replaced by a peace-loving Roman-like Napoleon wearing a tunic.

The Place Vendôme would become the centre of my life for years to come, but I would not know this as we tentatively made our way through the arches of rue Castiglione till we reached the Place itself. Since we had little money, I had asked Margaret to stand outside the archway of *le numéro huit* whilst I went inside for my interview. I should have asked her to wait in a local café where it would have been warm, but I had no great confidence the job would be mine.

I expected to be in and out and on our way.

The American lawyer had been away in the United States and the interview had been conducted by Joseph Korenblitt. He had been office manager as well as secretary. He had been an elegant Frenchman, small, rotund with a jolly *embonpoint*; he had too a gentle, quiet manner and a pleasant welcoming smile. He would be the first Frenchman to shake my hands three or four times a day, in fact each time we met. This gave me a habit that would last a lifetime and he would always raise his soft trilby hat to Margaret when they met.

I had been embarrassed by my summer clothing and explained what he already knew, that I had just arrived from the vineyards of the South of France. He gave me dictation

302

and settled me down before an electric typewriter. I had never before seen an electric typewriter. The keyboard too would be different. I had not realised that the Continental keyboard would be different from the English and I had difficulty converting the dictation into letters.

To my surprise, Mr Korenblitt told me in his shy, hesitant manner that I was just what he was looking for and the job would be mine, subject to an interview with the American lawyer who would be my boss when he returned from the United States. That would be in a few days time. My mind had been half on the news and half on Margaret standing outside in the cold. Meanwhile, Mr Korenblitt said, I should work in the office and take dictation and type the letters of a young American lawyer who had been working with them.

This was Michael J. McNulty.

There were three offices in the suite and Michael would work out of the office not overlooking the courtyard but rather the Place St Honoré beyond the blue slate rooftops. This was probably his first job out of law school, he worked on a file called Somlo-Oliver that had something to do with a chef and a French restaurant. He would work in his shirt sleeves and I recall that he was probably as nervous as me, anxious to get his letters right, correcting them and changing them even when they looked right to my admittedly untrained eye.

Michael would spend a year in Paris before returning to New York, his departure greatly regretted by my boss. I would miss him too and years later seek him out in New York City. We would have a drink together at Delmonico's. Our paths would cross again when he returned to London and settled as a lawyer with another friend of mine, Elwood Riqless, their offices in Waterloo Place. Later still, we would share platforms on European Union.

In those early days in Paris I would take his dictation with no difficulty reading back, since Americans spoke so slowly, the letters were short and in English, acknowledgements really, confirming or cancelling appointments, and if my writing had yet to pay off my shorthand and typing in London meant that I would soon be proficient on the electric typewriter even with the Continental keyboard.

There still remained, however, the question of my baggy trousers.

Margaret and I had moved out of the Hôtel du Nord into the Hôtel des Académies in the rue de la Grande Chaumière.

The rue stood off Boulevard Raspail in the Montparnasse and we would settle not far from where Ernest Hemingway had lived. There would be opposite the hotel a famous studio where young female students would be painted in the nude; the students would stand stiff and cold and be poorly paid. They did not inspire the artists who would come into *chez Wadja* for their evening meal, carrying their etchings in large folders. *Chez Wadja* too stood on the opposite side of the street from the hotel.

There we would meet many artists.

There would be Red the Painter who showed his works on the pavement in Washington Square. This was in Greenwich village in down-town New York. He had been small and stocky, with freckles and red hair and gentle blue eyes. He would use the money from the sale of his paintings to visit Paris once a year, living not in the Latin Quarter, now old hat for artists, but around the Boulevard Montparnasse, calling by *chez Wadja* for his meals in the evening.

I would one day meet Red on the right bank of the river around Place de la Concorde, a surprise in itself, since artists were not supposed to leave the left bank of the Seine. He would recall how he had seen a furnace all aglow and thought it would make a wonderful painting. It had all been there in his mind's eye. He had come back the next day with his paints and canvas and easel, but the glow had gone from the furnace and with it the inspiration.

Jean la Forêt had also been a painter.

He had been small and slim and good-looking, with a tanned skin and blue eyes; he smoked a clay pipe, like my grandfather in the pit village, and the smoke from the pipe curled beyond his eyes and gave him a wizened look. He did odd-jobs in the morning and painted in the afternoon, driving his *deux cheveaux* out of Paris to the west, painting in the open country around the golf course at St Nom la Bretèche.

There was an American doctor from Milwaukee who came to Paris once a year; there was an author, an expert on the American writer Thomas Woolf, who would explain the intrinsic value of the short stories I had failed to discern whilst reading in Newcastle City Library. There was Patsy, a Hungarian photographer, who had a club foot and withered arm and wore a shabby corduroy jacket. He might well have stepped from the pages of Maugham's *Of Human Bondage*.

Patsy had his own studio in Montparnasse but had been reduced to passport rather than portrait photography. He would be in his seventies, slim, fragile, limping, his withered arm tucked in, his face crumpled, the flesh loose around his cheeks. He spoke English with a strong Hungarian accent. One evening *chez Wadja* we fellow artists debated whether Patsy's life had been a success.

The American doctor wisely intervened.

'It depends whether Patsy thinks his life has been a success.'

Then there had been Gary Belkin.

Gary would be the most impressive artist of them all. He came from a wealthy Canadian family and lived in Paris because he wanted to be a film producer. He would be in his early twenties and had a brilliant mind; he knew Shakespeare sufficiently well to recite any passage you cared to name. He berated another young photographer who looked upon Shakespeare as all flying bats and owls and men in cloaks, who would not understand the moving themes behind Hamlet's soliloquy from the battlements of Elsinor.

Gary spoke French as he spoke English, he was dark-haired and good-looking with a ready smile and happy eyes. He had taken up with a concert pianist called Françoise. They lived together in a small one-room apartment over-looking the cemetery at Montparnasse. He had too an ear for music and would listen attentively as Françoise rehearsed, picking out her false notes. This dispirited and discouraged Françoise.

'No-one can play without any false notes,' she said.

I recall she invited us to hear her play in a concert one Sunday afternoon near the Eglise at St Philippe-du-Roule, and each time I visit Paris and walk past the Eglise I think of Françoise and her fingers fluttering across the keyboard. She had been a tall, well-bodied woman with short blond hair and clear brow and eyes and I recall Gary inviting us back to meet with her in his apartment, only to find she had been naked in bed reading a book.

Gary would later shoot film with Darryl Zanuck when he was making *The Longest Day* on the Normandy beaches. After our meal *chez Wadja* we would have our coffee in *La Coupole*, either sitting in the front looking through the window to the street or in the back behind the rows of tables where the bourgeoisie dined. At least they had

306

seemed bourgeoisie to us. Their evening coats were stacked high upon the seats against the walls.

Gary had joined us at *La Coupole*, looking drained, having spent the day filming with Zanuck on the Normandy beaches. Whatever filming Gary had done would have been minor, his name did not appear on the credits, and when I poked fun at his taking himself so seriously this had not gone down well. This had been an opportunity for him, a challenge, and perhaps he had been right to take it seriously.

Years later I met Gary on an air flight from London to Paris. I had recognised him at Heathrow airport and reintroduced myself. I shared a taxi with him to his apartment in the Montparnasse. We exchanged cards. He told me he was now settled with a family and making children's films at studios in Boulogne-Billancourt, though not surprisingly I never saw any of his films or even heard of them. By then I was no longer in the world of artists.

The strange thing was he did not remember me.

'We would meet *chez Wadja*,' I said.

'I can remember *chez Wadja*.'

'You would recite Shakespeare. You had a friend called Françoise. We heard one of her piano recitations near the Eglise St Philippe-du-Roule.'

'I remember Françoise,' he said.

I had offered to take up a legal query Gary had and dropped him a note at his Paris apartment, but he did not reply. *Chez Wadja* was now a long way off and I never did hear from Gary again. Except late one evening in the eighties, watching a televised Frank Sinatra concert beamed from Latin America, I saw Gary's name among the credits at the end of the programme.

I had been pleased at his success.

In those early December days, staying at the Hôtel des

Académies, finding new artist friends *chez Wadja*, we had walked up to the American centre at the top of Boulevard Raspail and seen a Eugene O'Neill play called *The Rope*. This had been a one-act play of some length dealing with an American homestead run by an Irishman and his wife, with an ageing Bible-besotted father, old in years but strong as an oak, gnarled and bent so that he carried a stick.

I had been much taken by this play and its dramatic ending, it had brought home to me the joys of being in Paris with fellow artists, for the most part American, adding a new dimension to my life. I could hardly believe that I would be working in Paris. Before the interview, writing in the Hôtel du Nord, I had not believed I would be offered the post; I had looked upon my future as '*stark and heavy and as doom-laden as a painting by Turner in the Tate Gallery*'.

I would write that these were '*my private thoughts, my half-conscious thoughts, but they will not intervene in my interview*'. I would be confident in my ability, though I would not swagger. I would have around me the quiet certitude of success. '*I shall place my credentials, by word of mouth, by appearance, by certificate, before my employers and I shall hope they will receive the cordial reception they deserve; and then I shall hope that their conditions will be in accordance with my own wishes.*'

All this came about, the salary offered would be adequate, the working conditions suitable, and '*I would indeed like the gentlemen with whom I would be required to work and the atmosphere in which I would be working*'. But it might never have happened if my suit had not arrived on time from England, a Customs notification arriving at the Hôtel du Nord that it was at the Gare de Batignolles awaiting collection.

My future boss was due to return from the United States.

308

Alan Salter Hays had come from a distinguished cine-
matic family but he had been a Harvard-trained lawyer with
his own eau de cologne, his own brandy at the *Taillevent*
restaurant, and his initials stitched into the pocket of his
hand-made shirts. He had lived in France from 1945 when
the war had ended. He had met a perfumery manufacturer
on the boat and the perfume manufacturer had been his
client ever since. He had specialised in United States
Customs law and represented not only perfume houses but
Régie Renault.

He had offices in New York and Washington and his
Paris office stood on the fifth floor of the inner courtyard
in *le numéro huit* Place Vendôme. His own private office
had double doors, the walls were lined with silk and against
one of the walls stood a book-case filled with law books;
there were too Louis XVI desks and chairs and a divan. I
recall that the law books were back numbers of the *Harvard
Law Review*, bound in red and embossed with his name;
there were sketches on the wall by Daumier illustrating the
French legal profession and the humour of the last century.
I recall a chandelier of gold and crystal that tinkled with
the air stirring through the open window.

The wall-to-wall nylon carpeting matched the silk of the
walls and if he had style and grace he had too an eye for
detail; and though we had never met, looking around his
office, listening to the tinkling crystal, I knew full well
what his reaction would be when he walked in to see his
new male secretary wearing baggy trousers and summer
shirt and Paris jacket. Coming to know him as well as I
did in the years ahead simply confirmed to me what his
reaction would have been.

I would have been out of the office never to return.

Catastrophe struck, however, when Margaret went to
seek the suit from Customs. There would be Customs duties

to pay and we had no money. In those days duties on suits coming into France had been levied at twice the value of the suit in order to protect the French woollen industry. Since the suit had cost me sixteen guineas there would now be thirty guineas to pay, or the French equivalent thereof; and since there would be no receipt perhaps they would mark the value higher.

Margaret had called me at the office.

'The suit is not new,' I said. 'There should be no duties.'

I had taken time from the office to collect the suit myself at the Gare de Batignolles. I had explained to the junior Customs officer that the suit was not new, but the box had been opened before me. My mother had put in a shirt and tie and wrapped the suit in its original box and soft tissues and since I had only bought it in July it did indeed look new even to me let alone the Customs officer. I still suffered from asthma and had been highly-strung. The thought of losing the job because of a suit, of having to pay duty on a suit that was not new, though it might look new, sent me into a flood of declamatory rhetoric in bad French.

I shouted that I had been married in this suit, that I had worn it to leave home after my marriage, that I had spent some months in the *vendange* in the South of France, that I had a new job in Paris, that it was cold and wintry, that I could not be expected to walk the streets dressed in my baggy trousers, let alone wear the baggy trousers to the office. How would the Customs officer like to wear these trousers and this jacket? How would he like to feel the cold?

How would he like to step into the Place Vendôme dressed as I was dressed?

A crowd began to gather around me in the Customs

310

shed. I had been taken by the Customs officer to meet his supervisor in his office encased in glass windows. The crowd had followed me to the office. I knew I was now before authority, real authority, I sought to contain my indignation, my sense of injustice, my desperation; I sought to speak slowly, more eloquently, more persuasively, even if in bad French, but making the same points, demanding to know if the senior Customs officer would like to stay dressed as I was dressed and work in an office without a proper suit.

He did not rise from his desk but smiled up at me.

'*Il pleut chez vous?*' he asked.

Does it rain a lot in England?

He signed over the suit without Customs duties.

I gathered the suit in its tissue and its box and left the shed. I had not only a suit, I had a job. The entire course of my life would change, my French, my writing and who knows what else, working for an American lawyer, at the beginning of the sixties, possibly the finest decade in the century, at least in its early years, a young man in Paris following in the literary steps of Somerset Maugham and Ernest Hemingway, filled with ideas for stories and plays and novels, with a young wife who shared his desires and his ambitions.

But I had learned something else this day.

My theatricals might have impressed the Customs officers, they might have attracted a crowd, I might have spoken sharply and angrily, gesticulating, my hands flying about, but neither Customs officers nor the crowd had been put out. I had acted as they might have acted, I had been indignant as they might have been indignant. They had seen I had been right. I had spoken my mind and the Customs officer had responded.

Il pleut chez vous?

I would get on well with the French and the French would get on with me.

I returned to the office to type the letters of Michael J. McNulty.

Thirty-seven years later, prior to the General Election, we sat in Michael's home in St John's Wood with economists and lawyers, New Labour policies bright as the candelabra, not boring ourselves with reminiscence, yet looking back with some satisfaction that, in the words of D.H. Lawrence in one of his poems: '*Look! We have come through*'. Michael might have been fresh from law school sitting in the office in Place Vendôme, but he had been a successful trial lawyer in New York and a successful commercial lawyer in London.

He and I had a final night-cap before I returned to my apartment in Dolphin Square.

I reminded him that when Alan Salter Hays had first strode into the office from his trip to the United States I had been sitting with Michael taking dictation. Hays had been wearing a shiny dark-brown suit, white shirt and a tie to match the suit; he thought a lot of his ties and had his own favourite *teinturier* where they might be cleaned in the Boissy d'Anglas, a side street running off rue Royale. I would spend many a Saturday morning seeking out the *teinturier* across the shiny cobbles.

Hays had been slightly hunched, his large head bent forward, his baldness reflecting the light that had been white from the window. His suite of offices stood on the fifth floor where the light would always be bright. He might have flown in from the United States but there was no sign of jet-lag, only a massive enthusiastic energy, his work load as great in Paris as it would be in New York. He had not been entirely bald and wisps of grey-white hair were pulled back from his forehead.

He had pale blue eyes that stared at me as he talked to Michael.

I had sat quietly in my seat facing the desk, wearing my immaculate going-away marriage suit, also wearing a white shirt and slim tie with a single knot. I had looked up from my shorthand notes as he had entered the room but had not stood. Only after a moment or two did Michael realise that we had not been introduced, the boss and I were strangers to each other, and only when we had been introduced did I rise modestly from my chair to take Mr Hays' hand. There was no grip, the fingers podgy, the back of the hand stained with brown flecks.

He and I would get on well.

'I'm glad he likes me,' I had said to Michael.

'You're so smartly turned out,' Michael had said.

But had he really said that?

'It wouldn't be surprising,' I said. 'If you didn't remember me at all.'

I thought again of Tony Blair, being with him when he had attended the University of Northumbria, when he could not recall that I had been a Newcastle City Councillor or governor of the former Polytechnic. There had been a French television crew awaiting him when he had left the train and I had carried his bags so that he might be unencumbered, serious and statesman-like, moving gracefully from the platform to the station exit. The television crew had been there because Tony would be going to Paris shortly to meet with President Chirac.

I had been to Paris myself only a few days earlier to make a speech on New Labour policies and it had been suggested to me by the French Foreign Office in the Quai d'Orsay

313

that Tony might like to speak to the President in English and that the President would reply in French, since both perfectly understood each other's language. This would cut out the formality of the translator, if not the note takers. I had mentioned this to Tony on the train up.

He had given me one of his quizzical looks.

'I'll raise it with your office,' I said.

'If you can remember,' Tony said.

First Day of Spring

We stood on the terrace of the House of Commons looking out upon the Thames towards the new St Thomas'
Hospital.

It had been the first day of spring, the sun warm to the
cheek, the chill gone from the balustrade; the sun reflected
back from the river with hope rather than hostility; but the
waters were wary, fast-moving, unafraid and unashamed
that the season might be changing. The terrace can be cold
in winter, the balustrade merciless to the touch, the wind
can raise white tufts to the Thames, sharp too and cutting
to the cheeks.

Now the cold had gone and there had been a softness
to the air.

'Life is beginning all over again,' the *Hansard* girl said.

'The sun climbs higher,' I said. 'But takes with it a little
more of our lives.'

'The sun is bringing out the philosopher in you.'

'You mean the writer.'

In my maiden speech to the House, I had recalled my
days at Pitman's College in Southampton Row when I
had pushed my shorthand speed to a hundred-and-sixty
words a minute, though my final examination result had
been at a hundred-and-thirty. Charles Dickens might have
begun his writing career as a *Hansard* reporter in the

Parliamentary Gallery and for a while I had wanted to do the same.

I had mentioned this in my maiden speech.

There had never been a *Hansard* reporter who had made it to the floor of the House, I had been the next best thing, and the Editor of *Hansard* had invited me to lunch. We have kept up the tradition ever since, only the lunch had been broadened to the *Hansard* reporters as well as the Editor, those who covered the House and those who covered the committees, and always it would be held on the first day of spring.

Today would be the day of our lunch.

'How about poetry as well as philosophy?' the *Hansard* girl asked. '*"And see how dark the backward stream a little moment passed so smiling"*.'

'You've been reading my speeches.'

'The rivers flow to the sea but the seas are not full.'

'The future belongs to no-one,' I said.

'*Non, Monsieur*,' she said. 'The future belongs to God.'

'Victor Hugo,' I said.

On our first spring day in Paris, Margaret and I had visited the home of Victor Hugo in the Place des Vosges. A Paris winter would begin after the *Prix de l'Arc de Triomphe* at Longchamps, rain and cold would follow the autumnal haze, and in our very first winter the clouds had been low like a curtain that would not rise till springtime. The actor Sir Michael Caine would say that it rained more often in Paris than it did in London.

Certainly it had rained often in our first winter.

I still suffered from asthma, but this would be the last winter I would endure severe and persistent colds that since childhood had given me catarrh or sinusitis. I had been referred to Dr Valerie Radot, who had been an allergy specialist; his grandfather had discovered allergies during

316

the First World War and the French writer St Beuve would suffer from a dust allergy all his life without knowing it. He had worked in a room with cork walls. The cork had held the mites in the dust that caused the allergy.

I would visit Dr Valerie Radot twice a week in his surgery rue de Longchamps, coming out of an evening to walk towards Trocadéro with the Eiffel Tower beyond in the Champ-de-Mars. You knew spring had been coming as the nights grew lighter. Dr Valerie Radot would give me injections to neutralise my allergy, and though the dust allergy might remain in dust-filled rooms the asthma attacks would cease.

Margaret and I had settled at 213bis Avenue de Versailles.

We had found the apartment *chez Wadja* when we had met an American couple sitting opposite us on a narrow table in the corner. They knew of other Americans who shared the apartment but who were returning to the United States. There had been a scarcity of apartments and successful executives would be living in one-star hotels as well as the younger more penurious artists. Indeed, in the hotel around the corner from where we would settle, I would always be amused by a couple coming out of the hotel and getting into a giant DS19 Citroën car before powering away.

Margaret had not known how to type but an English lawyer in my office had a friend who had been senior partner with accountants Peat Marwick Mitchell; they had worked together in the Sudan. The accountants worked out of rue Louis-le-Grand running into Avenue de l'Opéra. She had been placed in the typing pool and had shown great fortitude in settling down to learn on the job, as it were, typing audited accounts and letters for the partners.

Her office had not been far from my own in Place Vendôme.

I would be paid eight hundred francs a month, Margaret would get less, but because we had no expenses, no car to run, no flat to buy, no telephone bill to pay, not even a television, we were able to set aside Margaret's salary and a part of my own for the day I would set up in Paris as a full-time writer. We would eat frugally too, with never a restaurant but for *chez Wadja*, often looking with some wistfulness at the people entering the restaurant opposite our apartment building for their Sunday lunch.

The writer Robert Graves had called upon young authors to avoid '*a gainful occupation*', but the days when a writer could live in Paris and starve in a garret were over, if they had ever existed. Margaret and I needed our gainful occupations if I were to be able to launch myself at all; but the long hours I worked did not help me even being a part-time writer.

The office in Place Vendôme opened at nine o'clock six days a week, there would be a two-hour lunch break, and I would leave at half-past six in the evening. On Saturdays we would leave at half-past one. There would be little time to write in the evening and less desire to write at weekend. Or as I would write in my diary, I would feel extraordinarily tired, unhappy with myself, depressed, dispirited, the writer in me finding no outlet:

'*The art of the novelist, in my view, is to create life,*' I would write. '*And though one may apply words by an effort of will, I am not sure the same will create life.*' I would point out to myself that there would be many occasions when even the best writer does not feel like writing; he can afford to miss a day. '*But for me, if I have a heavy working week, and if there is a weekend that I do not feel like writing, then the whole movement of my work is lost.*'

The only work I could do would be by effort of will.

The two-hour lunch break might be useful, except one

hour would be taken with lunch, leaving only an hour to browse through the books at Brentano's American book-shop or Galliani's or Smith's in the rue de Rivoli; or to go down to the Louvre to examine and describe the paintings there. The Louvre would always be farther than I thought, but I was able on one occasion to study a Rembrandt *Self-Portrait*, the painter standing before a reflection of himself, pallet in one hand, brush in the other, dressed in a shabby coat and a shirt stained with paint.

I would spend some time in the Tuileries Gardens.

I began developing novel-writing techniques, bringing together physical, sensory, character and story description; I would aim for character, pace, story. I would bring together in a single paragraph sight and sound and smell and taste, too, if I could manage it. I would sit on a green bench in the Tuileries studying the dust around my feet, the broken twigs, the shrivelled leaves, the burnt matchsticks, the useless cigarette ends, gathering them together as a *still life*, observing the sparrows, fascinated how bored they became hopping in the dust, a peck here, a peck there.

Little eyes alert in their narrow vision.

I would also describe people around me, sitting in a café, waiting in a railway station, riding on the Métro, writing my notes in a spacious 1960 diary. I recall taking a ferry across the Channel when writing a novel. I described a man leaning over the rail, the spray rising around him as the waves were high; a short man with a round face and brown skin and neat colonel-like moustache. He wore a brown suit and waistcoat and had short hair neatly plastered to his skull.

I developed a whole character around the description in the novel. Some time later, walking past Auteuil racecourse, he came striding towards me with no recognition at all, since we had never met; I had only seen him leaning over

319

the rail of the ferry. He had gone striding past me towards *la piscine Molitor* but also through the pages of my novel without knowing that he would always live on.

As perhaps he himself lives to this day.

I had required a *permis de travail* to work for my boss in the Place Vendôme.

Mr Korenblitt had suggested that Margaret and I return to England and await the *permis* there, as the law required, rather than continue to work unlawfully pending its arrival. I would think later this had been unnecessary, but it had meant our returning home for Christmas and starting again in London in the New Year, without money, finding another bed-sit on the south side of the river, working temporarily in the City through the inestimable Mrs Garcke and her Lawsen Employment Agency.

It would take three months for the *permis* to be issued, but since Mr Hays would spend most of this time in New York he had been prepared to wait for my services. I had returned to my studies at the British Museum and there I would write a television play called *Rainbow Round the Sun*; there would be other television plays – *The Sin of Pride* and *Death by Misadventure, The Fall of Samson* – and though I might have in Christopher Mann of Mayfair my own agent my plays fared little better than my novels or short stories or theatre plays.

When the *permis de travail* did arrive and we had returned to Paris, I had wanted to write radio as well as television plays and listened in the evenings to BBC medium-wave that had been carrying a twenty-six week series of the best plays produced in the fifties: plays with such titles as *Royal Foundation*, *A Hospital Case*, *Cold*

320

Harbour. I would listen to historical plays such as *Henry of Anjou* and true story plays, all encompassed within a series called *Mid-Week Theatre.* I thought my mother might send me copies of *The Radio Times* and *The Listener* so that I might keep abreast.

My determination remained to be a full-time writer.

Margaret and I had discovered French state theatre at the *Odéon*, where not only could we see a play cheaply but buy a copy of the text. We would study the text and return to see the play again the following week. My French improved all the time. My spoken French, learnt through the ear, had improved most of all but my written French improved too through reading *Le Monde* and *Le Figaro.* Sometimes I would write out *La Chronique* from the front page of *Le Figaro* and would remember a line written by Jean Guehenno:

Le temps passe comme tombe la neige, impitoyablement.

Time passes as snow falls, without pity.

The line lives with me to this day.

Hardly had we settled in Paris than I learned the planners had decided to close our pit and destroy the colliery houses in my village. I was so angry at this news I wrote a letter of protest to the *Evening Chronicle* in Newcastle. Even from Paris I had wanted to launch a campaign that would save the colliery and the village, now to be classified Category-D by Durham County Council. That meant not only would colliery houses be pulled down; no houses would be built in their place.

The closure of the pit and the destruction of the village would become a major theme for a novel.

I devised a story which required that I split myself in two, one part of me angry that the past should be so wilfully destroyed, the other accepting that in the name of change or progress, whichever you preferred, the colliery had to be destroyed and the village with it. The novel would deal with pit and village life, past and present, a confluence of the two; it would draw on the characters I had known from a life I had understood.

It would be a story of conflict against a background of social change.

I would return to my village during my holidays and go down Chopwell colliery to spend a few hours with the men. I would be taken down by the safety officer, whom I had known from my days in the colliery office. There would not only be the drop in the cage, the walk along the rolleyway, but a struggle along the number nine seam, the lowest in the pit, no more than eighteen inches, damp too, the men stopping work, my pit helmet dislodging blue post from the roof.

I would soon be black with coal dust but the men recognised me.

'I wish I had your job,' one of them said.

'What is that?' I asked.

'Following him around.'

It would take Margaret and me two years to save up the money so that I could become a full-time writer.

My salary would climb to fifteen hundred francs a month, Margaret would earn nine hundred and we would save twelve hundred a month. We would save ten thousand francs in all, enough to see us through two years of writing before the money ran out. We would need to spend no more than two hundred and fifty francs a month. There would be no social security if I were not working, so I had better stay healthy, and taxes would need to be paid on our salaries, not taken out of the pay packet as in England.

We had been pushed too by an additional circumstance.

Margaret had fallen pregnant with our first child Ian, with the likelihood that she would have to give up her own typing job, thus depriving us of her income. I might never get round to writing my novel. I had resolved that the novel would be written in long-hand rather than typed, that each word, each sentence be crafted in the manner of Gustave Flaubert writing *Madame Bovary*, that I would write six hours a day five days a week.

As Hemingway would recall in *A Moveable Feast*, you had to be lucky to be a young man – or woman – in Paris. Margaret and I had been lucky. We had married young but we had the whole of our lives ahead of us. We had our own personal destinies, me as a writer, she the wife of a writer. We would live cheaply, not meagrely, never going hungry, never doing without, no restaurants other than *chez Wadja*, making our way on only a few hundred francs a month, enough to cover Margaret's pre-natal expenses.

I would write in the spare room of our fifth floor apartment. There was no lift to the fifth floor and no heating in the apartment; the wallpaper had peeled from the walls in the spare room and I worked on a table honeycombed with woodworm. I would use yellow legal pads and if I looked up at all from my work it was to stare at a grey concrete gable often damp with rain.

Margaret and I would spend our weekends, unencumbered by my writing after a week's work in Graves' gainful occupation. We would visit the azalea exhibition in the Bagatelle gardens in the Bois de Boulogne or the flea market at Batignolles or the Louvre or Orangerie in the Tuileries gardens. We would walk by the river and watch the black-painted iron-studded barges go by, or even spend a Sunday afternoon at the races at Longchamps or Auteuil.

And we had been happy.

It had taken nine years but I had become a full-time writer at last.

~

In our first full winter in Paris there had been neither snow nor frost, only the greyness of low cloud and rain or drizzle, no fog or mist from the river, but the damp and dankness would eat into the soul.

One Sunday we had taken a bus to Orly Airport which had been opened by President Charles de Gaulle. There had been hundreds of Parisians taking the same buses, visiting the airport, milling in the concourse, looking at the majestic plaque the President had unveiled, some of the people clambering up the moving staircase to reach the roof where the whine of aircraft had been shrill to the ears, the winter light reflecting cold from their fuselages.

Parisians would not become cheerful again till the cloud curtain rose, the sky became a deeper blue, and beyond the cloud the sun strode high into the heavens. On this first day of spring Margaret and I had come out of the Métro at the Bastille. They were selling triple-decker ice creams and the first flowers of the season: daffodils and narcissi and sunflowers and tulips. It had been the first time we had seen the Place de la Bastille in the sunshine and we had wanted to walk to Victor Hugo's home in the Place des Vosges, through the streets of old Paris filled with frayed hotels, as I would describe at the time, the walls of the narrow streets flaking and dirty, iron shutters thrown back against the walls, and all with the starkness of a painting by Bernard Buffet.

Margaret and I had found Victor Hugo's home pretty much as he had left it, with its Gothic and Renaissance furniture, its cracked plates and vases, its Venetian chandeliers, the pictures that had been painted by his friends and given to him in his lifetime. The Place des Vosges had been known in those days as the Place Royale. Hugo's home had

324

stood on the second floor of an *hôtel particulier*, almost as ancient as Paris, since it had been built in 1604. Already the trees had been out in their finery and the red brick edifice and blue slate mansard roofs had made their own portrait against the drifting cloud.

There are also Hugo's manuscripts and the letters he had written to his wife: *chère Adèle, Adèle mon amour, mon Adèle la plus chère*. I had known nothing about Victor Hugo when I had visited his home this first day of spring, but reading the letters in their carefully-crafted handwriting I had known he had been unfaithful to his wife. No-one who had been faithful could have been so fulsome.

Hugo had been a politician as well as a writer.

He had been exiled to Guernsey for nineteen years. There he had written *Les Misérables.* I had read an abridged version when as a child I had been laid up with measles. I am a regular attender at the musical in Shaftsbury Avenue. His publisher had not been too assured of the book's success when he had received the manuscript. He had wanted Hugo to cut out the philosophical parts and make the book shorter.

Perhaps I had read the abridged version, for I recall only that a nun who had never lied in her life would lie when asked the whereabouts of Jean Valjean; and that a Monseigneur from whom Valjean had stolen silver candle-sticks had said that, on the contrary, he had given them to him. Hugo had refused to accommodate his publisher: '*the quick-moving surface drama will be a success for twelve months. The deeper drama for twelve years.*'

And so it had turned out.

Hugo had believed in a United States of Europe.

In his later years as a politician, he had visited Lausanne and addressed what he called his '*fellow citizens of Europe*'. As the German Chancellor Bismarck prepared for war against Napoleon III, Hugo had been planting an oak dedicated to the United States of Europe. This had been 14 July 1870. He claimed such a United States would outlive all wars and all Popes. The oak still stands but wars and Popes are still with us.

After visiting Hugo's home in the Place des Vosges, Margaret and I had taken the Métro to the Champs-Elysées where the trees were coming out in blossom. There had been couples and families strolling along the Avenue, they too liberated by the sunshine. There had been a deep rich colour to the awnings above the cafés. In rue Marbeuf red parasols were out with white-laced fringes, standing upon green iron stalks, and cleaning the gutters water ran fast and crystal, sparkling in the first spring light. We had felt the joy of knowing that the long winter was over.

We had walked from the rue Marbeuf to Avenue Victor Hugo.

My boss had lived on the Avenue and often I would visit him, taking his papers, picking him up from the airport when I had learned to drive, sometimes waiting for him Saturday morning as he dressed. He would introduce me to whisky and Perrier, an elitist drink popular both with the *tout-Paris* and the legal fraternity in Wall Street. Later Perrier would become famous world-wide, bought by the crate in down-town Los Angeles, but then it had been served in small neat bottles and mixed with Scotch whisky to make it an aperitif.

Victor Hugo would live out his days in a street called Avenue d'Eylau.

A friend would pay the rent on a house and he would live with Juliette Drouet, his companion of fifty years, who would die of cancer in her eighties. I had been right about Hugo when I had first visited his home. He had been unfaithful to his wife with many different women;

326

the French would call him *un homme vert* in his old age; but he had stayed with Juliette Drouet as he had indeed stayed with his wife Adèle.

A truly French idyll.

On his eightieth birthday the name of the street would be changed to Avenue Victor Hugo, though another would be named after the famous battle at Eylau; an arch would be built across the Avenue and the whole of Paris had been invited to march under the author's window. Some eight hundred thousand people would see Victor Hugo on the balcony, hunched now, his white hair matching his white beard, smiling and waving, even though his sight was failing.

A plaque had been placed on the street corners:

Victor Hugo, Ecrivain, poète , homme politique.

This first day of spring on the terrace of the House of Commons, the sun to our cheeks, I had lunched with the Editor of *Hansard* and the *Hansard* reporters in the marquee facing the river. When I had first became Member of Parliament the marquee had been temporary, thrown up after the Easter recess, without heating for the chillier summers, but so popular it had become a permanent feature with windows and heating and air-conditioning, spacious and properly-carpeted, its awning as colourful as any I had seen along the Champs-Elysées.

The food had been fresh, the wine sparkled as had the Perrier water, the sun through the glass catching the effervescence of the water and the dull richness of the wine. MPs brought their guests to savour the atmosphere, to spot the famous faces, those they had seen on their television screens. The balustrade had been warm to the touch, the sun high and untainted by cloud. We too had been part of the ritual, brought together for our annual lunch.

'I brought you this from Paris,' the *Hansard* girl said.

327

She handed me a replica of the plaque on the walls of Avenue Victor Hugo. She had been an amateur photographer and she had photographed and developed and enlarged the plaque to make the replica. She had framed it too. It would be a gift from the *Hansard* staff. I had not made the Parliamentary gallery, some of them no longer wrote shorthand, they had their own steno machines, but I was still one of them. I would always be one of them.

'You should write poetry too,' the *Hansard* girl said.

'And I should take you to see *Les Misérables*.'

'You politicians are all alike,' she said. 'Promises, promises.'

The plaque stands on the wall of my office where I see it each time I raise my head.

I Knew It Was Prewitt

I had met the Governor of the Bank of France in his office opposite the Golden Gallery and now I would meet the French Minister of Trade at his office in the rue Bercy. I had been his homologue on the Labour front bench and should Tony Blair win the Election on 1 May I was expected to be a Minister in my own right.

'I shall fly over to see you!' the Minister said.

'And I shall be happy to receive you.'

As it happened, we would never meet again.

President Jacques Chirac called a snap legislative election and to the astonishment of all, including himself, his party lost and his government fell. The Minister would lose his job. We had talked about completing the European single market, of the United Kingdom joining the single currency, of the unpopularity of the European Union, but the political stream would flow forward without either of us.

I had arranged the meeting for the morning, when it had been convenient for the Minister to see me; Malcolm had still been asleep when I left our hotel, crossing the Pont St-Louis to the Ile de la Cité, catching a taxi from the rank by the side of the Notre-Dame Cathedral. The Minister had been kind enough to have his chauffeur drive me back to the Ile St-Louis and I walked around the island in the early morning sunshine.

329

The writer James Jones had lived in the Quai de Bourbon in a town house not far from the *brasserie de l'Isle-St-Louis*, and from the top floor, in his own words, he looked out upon *'the back of Notre-Dame, with its soaring buttresses, and the high wedding cake of the Panthéon on its hilltop floating above the old Left Bank houses; and always the river and the barges, a never-ceasing source of interest to the eyeball'*.

I might admire and respect the Panthéon with its cupola, the tall cross above it, Corinthian columns below, but it would be a grey wedding cake on a grey day with the cloud low. It had been built along Greek and Roman lines and with its interior the shape of a Greek cross; it would house the remains of great politicians and artists such as Victor Hugo, Emile Zola, Voltaire and Rousseau. Indeed, on the interment of Victor Hugo the following words had been inscribed:

> *Aux grands hommes, la patrie reconnaissante.*
> To great men, from their grateful fatherland.

James had bought his house not from the proceeds of his world-famous book *From Here to Eternity*, made even more famous by the film with Burt Lancaster, Deborah Kerr, Montgomery Clift and Frank Sinatra, all in black and white, but from the money Darryl Zanuck had given him for helping to write the script of *The Longest Day*. The film came from the book by Cornelius Ryan describing events on D-Day 6 June 1944 and it would be Ryan who would take credit for the script when the film appeared, but it had been James who would help out, changing one line of the script and receiving for his pains fifteen thousand dollars.

James had come to Paris in 1958 and he and his wife Gloria had lived in Quai aux Fleurs before moving to the

Ile St-Louis, where they had decided to stay permanently. I had met James, working as I did for Alan Hays in the office in the Place Vendôme; Hays' firm specialised in Customs matters and James had asked that we arrange for his household possessions to be brought from his former home in the United States.

I personally ensured they would pass safely through Customs.

The inventory had been a mile long and included a massive library of American novels and poems in their first editions and a collection of books on the Civil War. There had also been listed many cases of guns and silver, all manner of guns and all kinds of silver, both causing problems with French Customs. Some of the guns were as ancient as Methuselah and could be classified either as antiques or weapons.

His possessions had arrived at Orly Airport and I took it upon myself to visit the Customs sheds and speak with *l'inspecteur des Douanes*. He had on his desk a round golf-ball that was also giving problems. It was no golf-ball, rather the new IBM revolving set of typewriter keys, the latest in modern technology. *L'inspecteur* had not read James' novel but he had seen the film and had cut through his own bureaucracy and released the household possessions, guns and all.

Except the silver needed to be stamped according to French law.

I had brought with me a French lawyer as well as the *agent en douane*, but the lawyer had given up, saying that he should be in the Palais de Justice not in a Customs' shed, especially one that was cold and windy. He had left me and the *agent* stranded among packing cases and straw and silver; to make progress, the *agent* would pass many a five-franc coin across the palms of the hands of Customs' handlers, but I too gave up and returned to the office. It had been late in the evening when the *agent* had called to say that the task had been completed.

The silverware of Monsieur Jones had been *poinconnée*.

The guns must have found their way to the fourth floor of the house, for his biographer Willie Morris would recount how one day a friend found James teaching his maid's lover how to load powder into cartridges. The house had been bought one floor at a time; James would write on the fourth floor where the guns were to be found; but he had filled the rest of the house with refectory tables, straight-backed chairs and overstuffed sofas, Greek and Roman sculptures, and of course his library.

His biographer would make no mention of the silverware.

I would buy James' books at Smith's bookshop or at the Shakespeare bookshop near the Odéon, a famous bookshop going back to the days of Ernest Hemingway and Scott Fitzgerald. James had signed copies of his latest book, *Some Came Running*, and I had felt *chagriné* as I had wanted him to sign my copy personally; I did buy a novella called *The Pistol*, set at the time of Pearl Harbor, and I would read it lunch times in the Tuileries Gardens, studying it, analysing it, savouring it as if it were a vintage wine.

There had been great excitement in the office when James Jones and Gloria had called for the first time. John P. Gorman, an English lawyer, had told James of my own writing ambition and when he left, being a small man, he had looked up at me with a curious expression, neither smile nor grimace. Willie Morris would describe James as '*the rough, two-fisted beer and whiskey man*', but when he came to visit his lawyer he wore a check shirt open at the neck and a crumpled mackintosh.

Another day he would come rushing into the office to

sign a document, saying he was very busy, and John Gorman would ask: '*How can a writer be busy?*' There was a time too when another document needed to be signed and I artfully arranged to deliver this to him at his house on the Ile St-Louis. It had been a rainy day and if I had been shy with him he had been shy with me. After all, I worked as a secretary in his lawyer's office, I was no more than twenty-three years old, but so much in awe that when I departed his house I left behind my umbrella.

I had to go back and get it.

I would take any opportunity I could to talk with him on the telephone. I recall telling him that *From Here to Eternity* was playing on the Champs-Elyéees at a small cinema near the top, the cheapest cinema in the Avenue; he called the film *Eternity*. I would tell him of my own writing difficulties, struggling with a novel, seeking to find time in the evenings and at weekends after my gainful occupation all day in the office.

'It can't be done,' he said.

When I set up as a full-time writer in our apartment on the Avenue de Versailles, James Jones would be my model novelist.

Not only had he written five hours a day but he had written long novels with strong stories and characters and epic themes. *From Here to Eternity* had been based on his own experiences as a combat soldier, enlisting in the United States Army in 1939, spending three and a half years first at Pearl Harbor preparing defences against a putative Japanese invasion, then at Guadacanal, being wounded in the head, and then shipped home after an ankle injury that required an operation.

He would write three famous war novels, *From Here to Eternity*, *The Thin Red Line* that he had been working on at the time I had left my umbrella in his front room, and *Whistle*, incomplete at the time of his death. *The Thin Red Line* came out as a film not so long ago, with Sean Penn and Nick Nolte playing the leading parts; it would have seven Academy award nominations, including one for the best picture. It would be described as '*stunning*' and '*full of poetic grandeur*'.

In our apartment I would not only read the paperback edition of *From Here to Eternity*, I would study it too.

It would take a couple of months for me to settle as a full-time writer, but I would rise in the morning, dress and seek my croissants and fresh bread from the *boulangerie* on the corner of the Porte de St Cloud, reciting the passages from Shakespeare or poetry I had learnt the night before. After a morning's writing, I would go down to the street market along the Avenue to buy groceries and vegetables for the day and make myself a light lunch, working into the afternoon, before going for a walk around the Parc des Princes stadium as far as the racecourse and bus station at Auteuil.

The evening would be spent preparing the meal for Margaret coming in from Peat Marwick Mitchell, and after the meal I would settle to analyse *From Here to Eternity* and *Gone With the Wind* by Margaret Mitchell and *How Green Was My Valley* by Richard Llewellyn, a mining novel situated in the Welsh valleys. There would even be the novels of D.H. Lawrence from *Sons and Lovers* through to *Women in Love*.

I would also learn by heart the Ten Principal Upanishads put into English by Shree Purhohit Swami and W.B. Yeats and published by Faber: '*It lives in all that lives, hearing through the ear, thinking through the mind, speaking through the tongue, seeing through the eye. The wise man clings neither to this nor that, rises out of sense, attains immortal life.'* The same spirit might be found in the second verse of Genesis in the Bible: '*And the spirit of God moved upon the face of the waters'*.

One evening, after reading such verses, moving from concentration to meditation to contemplation, a golden light had filled my mind and I had found a total and absolute peace that others might call *karma*. My personal had joined my impersonal self and I had understood what it was that had been sought by teachers old and new, the maharishi in their mountains, seeking to enlighten their pupils what could not be taught, only ascertained through personal experience.

I had gone through to our small bathroom and kitchen to clean my teeth, the golden light still filling my mind. I began to think, to express my thoughts in words, and it was as if my personal self were descending a ladder, leaving the impersonal self behind. The golden light faded with each thought, soon I would be as I had always been, back to the prosaic, the commonplace, the mundane; and though I have sought for the rest of my life this golden light, this perfect peace, it has never returned.

It had been like the glow from a lighthouse, but the lighthouse is now a long way off and the glow dimmed.

I would write in my diary that at twenty-five I had found the secret of life but at twenty-six I had lost it; that the secret of life was the finding and keeping within sight of the self, that it was mind over body, will over mind; and that life was this moment of time, this precious moment, this second, but more than this second, this half-second, this split second; and if you could hold this you hold everything. It would take courage, however, to grasp and hold this second, not flee from its immortality. Yet if you could hold it you held

335

the secret of eternal life; but if you lose it, if it eludes your grasp, you would sink among fouler shapes.

Meditation would be the secret and through meditation you would open the door to peace.

Our son Ian had been born in August.

I had worked steadily throughout the day and taken Margaret to the clinic standing close to the Roland Garros tennis stadium on the fringe of the Bois de Boulogne. I had seen my own son come into the world, flecks of dried blood to his forehead, his brow crumpled, as if to say he had been here before and now he was back, yawning with the boredom of it all. It had indeed been *un accouchement sans douleur* for Margaret and soon she would be back at the apartment in the Avenue de Versailles, returning to work at Peat Marwick Mitchell, leaving me as a day-time father to bring up our child.

All so that I might finish my novel.

It would take eighteen months, five hours a day, five days a week, and in that time our landlords would decide to sell the apartment where we had been living. This obliged us either to find a more expensive apartment in Paris or return to our families in our native North-East. I would work for Alan Hays two afternoons a week doing his accounting, but the money this made and the savings we had left in the bank would not be enough for us to pay the rent on a new apartment and have enough to live on to complete the novel.

I made a decision that at the time turned out to be a monumental error, though it would have more significant consequences in the longer term. I decided with Margaret that we should return home to our families. There I would be able to finish the novel. I had no doubt that it would be a success; the thought of failure did not enter my mind. Margaret's father had died, her mother lived on her own and could do with the company of her daughter and son-in-law and new-born grandchild.

My own family would be glad to see me too.

The strategy worked in that I did indeed complete the novel, and having written in long-hand set about the arduous task of typing it up for the publisher. Even this would take several weeks. Unfortunately, living with someone else is never a success, through no-one's fault, other than the fault of personal chemistry, and I would end my writing career as I had begun it, returning to my own family in my own village, seeing still the headstock from our front window, the flag of the National Coal Board flying still, but tattered, listless, with the pit closed.

I had written of Sir Will Lawther in my novel.

He had worked at Chopwell colliery but risen through the ranks of the National Union of Mineworkers to be its President. He had retired and now lived at Whitley Bay. I had wanted him to read the completed manuscript, since it dealt with the pit and the pit village that he had known, with historical events such as the 1926 General Strike through which he had lived, and because he had been given a mention. I called him from a local telephone box and he gave me his address so that I could send him a copy of the manuscript.

Margaret and I had gone to see him at Whitley Bay.

Sir Will had changed little in his retirement years, a stout man with dark hair, full face and dark glasses. His wife had died and he lived on his own in a bungalow off the Broadway. To my agreeable surprise, not only had he read my manuscript he had made some notes, correcting some of the historical facts, and being lonely we would

337

spend some time with him, my absorbing his conversation, listening to every word. He would show me a book that John Fitzgerald Kennedy had sent him, called *Profiles in Courage*, and would give me a book written by Harold Wilson in the late forties, entitled *New Deal for Coal*.

I would bring the book to the Dispatch Box of the House of Commons on the day Harold Wilson died.

Sir Will would talk of the politicians he had known, of Lloyd George, whom he had called *The Goat*, some said because he had been a nimble Welshman, like the mountain goats in the higher reaches of Snowdonia, others because of his admiration for women. It hardly mattered. What Sir Will Lawther taught me that day, from his inside knowledge and personal observation, was that politicians were human like everyone else.

They had indeed feet of clay.

I had long taken an interest in Labour politics and my diary records my determination to involve myself in the next General Election when it came. I had never personally believed I had the fine upstanding character that was required to be a politician. I had my own feet of clay and assumed that those who entered politics were living saints. I discovered through Sir Will they were not. This would influence me in the years to come. I had naively thought politics were excluded to me.

Now I knew they were not.

We had finally left Sir Will Lawther and walked along the front at Whitley Bay. It had been a fine day, a sunny day, the sea blue rather than grey, and I had felt the warmth of the sun to my face, the slight breeze ruffling my blond hair. I had not rediscovered the enlightened peace of the Upanishads, the spirit of God across the face of the waters, but Margaret and I had been encouraged, relaxed, the novel typed, the work done, not only a novel but nine years of effort that had brought me to such a contented pass.

But would it be published?

I had written to James Jones and sent him a copy of the manuscript.

I had wanted him to give me the name of his agent in the United States both for publication of the book and the sale of film rights. I was nothing if not ambitious. I already envisioned that when the novel was turned into a film we should have the premiere at the Odeon Cinema in Newcastle. James in fact introduced me to Robert Knittel his own editor with Collins in London and who enjoyed a reputation similar to that of Maxwell Perkins, the editor to Ernest Hemingway, and of course to James Jones.

It would indeed be a prestigious start.

However, having an introduction had been no better than not having one, except at least the manuscript would have been read, whereas other publishing houses might not read it at all: there would be so many unsolicited manuscripts flowing they could not possibly hire the readers to get through them. The best-selling *Day of the Jackal* by Frederick Forsyth had been sent to several publishing houses before Forsyth could find one who read it let alone accepted it.

Knittel said he had been awaiting the book with anticipation but that he had been disappointed. I cannot now recall his reasons. It would not be a book for Collins but Knittel did give me the names of other publishers whom he thought might wish to publish. I would consider sending it to New Authors who had read my last novel. Indeed, I wrote in my diary that I would send it to every publishing house in the country.

I doubt that I did.

I would send the manuscript off for the last time 11

November 1965 from the Post Office in Whitehall. The so-called Rhodesian crisis had broken that day when unilateral independence had been declared, and after posting my manuscript I crossed to Ten Downing Street. The Prime Minister Harold Wilson had received Edward Heath, Leader of the Opposition, and also Jo Grimond as Leader of the Liberal Party. Heath had a car waiting for him that scooped him off with the utmost urgency, as if he were the Prime Minister; Jo Grimond came out to walk back to the Commons, no car for him, pausing only to turn for photographers.

The gravity of the event had etched itself into his face.

The gravity of having failed as a writer would etch itself into my life.

I would return to Paris to work again in the Place Vendôme for Alan S. Hays. This time Margaret and I and baby Ian settled in an apartment not on the fifth floor with a balcony overlooking the fountains of the Porte de St Cloud; rather, further up the Avenue de Versailles in an apartment on the second floor enclosed within a dusty darkened courtyard. The apartment had been long and slim, a deep passageway, with dining room and bedroom, bathroom and kitchen and toilet off to the left.

We had no money and this was the best we could do.

One Saturday evening I had left the apartment for a walk, not towards the river or along the *quais* beneath the chestnut trees, but inward along the Boulevard Exelmans. There had been a large *Gendarmerie* on the Boulevard and a huge advertisement for the Foreign Legion on the hoarding outside the *Gendarmerie*: *Pourquoi pas toi!* Why not you? Why not indeed. It was not that my despair had been sufficiently deep to throw me into the Foreign Legion for thirty years, but I did pause before the advertisement, reflecting how three brothers in the film of my childhood *Beau Geste*, the leading role played by Gary Cooper, had indeed joined up and seen action in the desert sands.

I crossed the rue Michel-Ange and came across a bookstore with a book on the artist Eugène Delacroix, published by Larousse, settled on its own in the window. The front cover to the book had been startling, the portrait of a young girl with swept-back brown hair, her white dress from her shoulders, *décolleté*, her neck muscles tight, her mouth slightly open, her face uplifted, her chin in darkened shadow, but to her eye a tear white as light, stark as day, burning around the brown pupil.

The tear would tell me that whilst life might be good, life might be happy, that all might be well within the universe, things could change too; happiness might flee, sadness prevail over happiness, and that the universe might be flat rather than curved. It had not been a cold evening, rather chill and damp, but as I reflected upon the portrait, looking through the window, I knew that I would have years of unhappiness ahead.

I had been a writer since I had decided this should be my career, my head on a palliasse in Scotland; I had written lineage for the newspapers when working in the colliery office; I had become a newspaper reporter. A free-lance journalist. I had moved to London and written from my partitioned room in Tufnell Park. I had written three novels, a book of short stories, plays for theatre and television.

All to no avail.

I had come to Paris to live the life of an artist whilst working during the day; I had studied the works of great authors and poets and painters. I had visited the theatre and studied plays. I had written descriptions. I had examined dialogue, not only in plays but in French film scripts that I would buy from a bookshop under one of the arches of rue Castiglione. I had left my job with an American lawyer to become a full-time writer.

I had no longer typed my stories but written them patiently in long-hand, word for word, sentence for sentence, paragraph for paragraph, seeking pace and character and story, weaving all three together. I had sent my novels unsolicited through the post to publishers; I had contacted an agent for my short stories. I had used an introduction from James Jones, world-famous author. There had been an agent for my television plays. I had written as a true author, of the places I had known and seen, of people I had lived with and understood. I had used great events as a backdrop.

Still to no avail.

I had also left myself without money for the fourth time in my adult life. I had started again three times and now I would have to start a fourth. What could I do with the rest of my life, with a family to keep, a son born, a daughter to be born, Yvonne coming into the world at the same clinic as Ian, myself working as a male secretary with a salary that no longer covered our living expenses, Margaret no longer working, so that we spent more money each month than we earned?

And no writing left in me.

When I had been a full-time writer, Margaret and I would visit the Louvre Saturday afternoon so that I might study the paintings of artists such as Eugène Delacroix. I had studied one afternoon his *Mort de Sardanapale*. I had learnt from Delacroix the need for harmony in painting and I had sought to transcribe the same harmony into my own novel, my great novel, the novel that no-one wanted to publish, that languished with all my other manuscripts.

Now, standing on Boulevard Exelmans, I studied *Orpheline au cimetiere*, a powerful figure, a tragic figure, a gentle face afflicted, yet with youth before her, a life running ahead into the future; but the tear to her eye reflecting her own grief, the turbulence of nature and life, uncertainty to come, years upon years of uncertainty, of anxiety, of seeking to make ends meet, with each passing day moving slowly, silently away from goals and ambition.

I saw my life ahead in that portrait.

And as the orphan's tear would not dry for many a while nor would mine.

In his letter of introduction to Robert Knittel, James Jones had called my work outstanding and praised me as a young and up-and-coming writer with a powerful talent. With such a magnanimous introduction, I had been ashamed to call James Jones when I returned to Paris to tell him that Robert Knittel and Collins would not be publishing. One Sunday evening, however, on an impulse, I would call James Jones at his home on the Ile St-Louis.

'I don't agree with Knittel at all,' he said.

I would not speak to James Jones again.

I would see *Eternity* on the Champs-Elysées.

It had a curious title in French: *Tant qu'il y aura des hommes.* It had not been easy to translate the original title which came from the Whippenpoof Song: *'Gentleman-rankers out on a spree; damned from here to eternity; God ha' mercy on such as we!'* Perhaps James Jones and I had both been gentleman-rankers in our different ways, born outside the establishment, always seeking an entry, but in his case he had made it.

I had not in mine.

Eternity is famous for a love scene on a beach between Burt Lancaster and Deborah Kerr, the first such love scene ever shown by Hollywood. Fifty years later a picture of the scene would be run in the *Evening Standard* attached to a story entitled *Happy hour for beach lovers.* Apparently, on a Spanish beach a mile from Malaga, lights would be switched off for an hour between one and two in the morning, police would cease their patrols, so that young couples might emulate in their own fashion Burt Lancaster and Deborah Kerr.

Hollywood had been left trailing behind.

There is also another scene in the *Eternity* film when Private Robert E. Lee Prewitt loses his friend Maggio, played by Frank Sinatra, a role that would launch Sinatra as a serious film star as well as a singer. Prewitt had been in the Bugle Corps and would play Taps to honour his late friend. He would play so movingly, so filled with emotion, that the soldiers came onto their porches in their khaki shorts at Schofield Barracks to listen in the dim evening light.

'I knew it was Prewitt,' one of them said.

Years later, when my life had taken another turn, I found myself upstate New York in Salem, Westchester County on Memorial Day 1979. This had been main street, middle America. There had been a white clapboard church, chinked white with mortar, as Hemingway might have written, in fact did write in *The Snows of Kilimanjaro.* There had been too an Episcopal priest who bade us welcome.

He had been followed by the chairman of the governors of the local council and the head boy from the local college. The head boy had been so popular with the girls they clapped him louder than they did the college band; he gave a short eulogy to commemorate the American dead in wartime, ending with a soft and noble rendering of the last verse of *the Star-Spangled Banner.*

We had another reading, this time from the Episcopal priest, and then the bugler of the college band on the grass before the church played Taps to the lowering of the flags held by the veterans of the American Legion. We call it *The Last Post* and we play it on Armistice Day to commemorate the eleventh hour of the eleventh day of the eleventh month when peace came to Europe after two world wars.

The bugler had played his lonesome way through Taps and the roll of drums from the band carried beyond the veterans down main street all the way to the cemetery in Bridgehampton, where the ashes of James Jones had been buried 17 July 1977. He had died of congestive heart failure and on his death bed, knowing his lungs were filling with liquid, he had risen and recorded these lines from the *Lake of Innisfree: 'I will arise and go now, for always night and day I hear lake water lapping with low sounds by the shore; while I stand on the roadway, or on the pavements grey, I hear it in the deep heart's core'.*

Later this Memorial Day they would be selling hot dogs and hamburgers and play drowning-the-maiden; they would sell ice cream and strawberry shortcake and fudge, not to mention popcorn and cola and lemonade; and plants, too, and oven mitts and soft toys and pottery in the church hall. They would do that after the chairman of the governors had laid three wreaths before the Cenotaph and said kind words for all those who had participated.

My mind was still on the bugler playing Taps.

The United States Army had flown their best bugler from Washington to Bridgehampton for Jones' memorial service. The bugler had played Taps at the graveside of three American Presidents. He was a serjeant, not an enlisted man, for all the best buglers were now master-serjeants, and he had come to play farewell to James Jones as Prewitt had played farewell to Maggio. They had read out the piece in the novel where the soldiers in their summer khakis had come onto the porch to listen to the Taps.

The bugler could not have given a better rendering than the bugler who stood in for Montgomery Clift in *Eternity*. James' friends from Paris days were there, writers William Styron and Irwin Shaw, and Willie Morris who would write his short biography. His wife Gloria and their children. The apple blossom and lilac were in bloom as his family and friends walked down cemetery road and on future Memorial Days war veterans would lay a flag by the gravestone, set in a corner of the cemetery where the green grass is regularly clipped.

After seeing the Minister for Trade, I could hear the bugler too this day on the Ile St-Louis, some twenty years after James Jones had died, thirty-six years since I had collected my umbrella. I would stand in the sunlight looking down towards the barges that passed his window as they had always done and would always do, the Taps so strong to my ears that I thought the bugler was playing in a corner of the island, from the *brasserie* which James and Gloria had always loved.

I had been reassured about one thing as they had lain James to rest and the Taps had played at the memorial service and they had read extracts *From Here to Eternity*. I had known it that Memorial Day in Westchester County. I knew it now as I walked past his old town house on the Quai de Bourbon and looked at the unknown name plate on the door. They might have laid James Jones to rest, his body might have perished, consumed by flame, but as the bugler had played, he would have known it too.

He would have known it was Prewitt.

346

No Hard-Boiled Egg for Tony

After having seen the Governor of the Bank of France and the Minister for Trade, and before taking with Malcolm the Eurostar from the Gare du Nord back to Waterloo station, I received a call from the Labour Party to say Tony Blair would be coming to Middlesbrough this coming Saturday.

The General Election campaign would officially open that day, Tony would be adopted at Sedgefield, and he would drop down to Middlesbrough to visit the South Cleveland hospital. The hospital had its own show-case cardiac and baby-care units; Princess Diana had opened the baby-care unit some years earlier; but the cardiac unit, now one of the best in the country, had come later.

Tony's campaign had not gone well in Scotland on the issue of devolution, he had made not a slip of the tongue but a somewhat false analogy, seeking to reassure voters that elections for a Scottish Parliament were no more onerous than elections to a parish council. This had caused umbrage in the Scottish press. It would make little impact on the electorate, but the Labour Party wanted some fine photo opportunities of his visiting a hospital that would fill the Saturday night television news bulletins and also the Sunday press.

I would put through calls to the local health authority and ensure everything would be in order for Tony's visit before taking Malcolm to the *Café de Flore* in the Boulevard St

Germain. The café stands shaded by speckled plane trees, their barks peeled and blotched, their leaves upturned, ashen with the dust of traffic down the wide Boulevard, the awnings white and trim, the *Café* terrace open to the pavement, the wicker chairs and round marble-topped tables almost backing into the parked cars.

We treated ourselves to a breakfast of *café au lait* and croissants and *pain aux raisins* and *pain au chocolat.* There had been a tray of hard-boiled eggs in the centre of the table and Malcolm leant over and took an egg and cracked the shell and peeled the shell away to the hard white and pallid egg yoke that looked as blotched as the plane trees. He let the egg shells litter the table among the crumbs from the croissants.

'That'll cost me twenty-five francs,' I said.

'I thought the eggs were free.'

'A hard-boiled egg free in the *Café de Flore?*'

In my early Paris days along the Boulevard St-Germain I had preferred *Les Deux Magots* overlooking the Place St-Germain-des-Prés and the Eglise, the oldest church in the city; the awnings of *Les Deux Magots* were green and gold, the parasols in the narrow garden bordered by hortensia, the parasols themselves a proud white with green edges, the words *Les Deux Magots* ingrained in threads of gold. I might have an apéritif – *un apéro* – at *Les Deux Magots* before crossing the street to dine at *La Brasserie Lipp*.

The waiters at the *Brasserie* dressed in black suits and white aprons and black bow-ties, following a tradition from the end of the century; they wore numbered metal checks in their lapels, showing where they stood within the Lipp hierarchy. The head waiter would be *le numéro un.* One evening Georges Pompidou, Prime Minister, future President of the Republic, would be having dinner in the downstairs room of the *Brasserie*; but when I had dined with Stanley Cohen and

348

his friend Michael Harrington, we had moved upstairs on the narrow spiral staircase.

Stanley, a Harvard-trained lawyer, had worked in Hays' office until he had left to set up elsewhere in the city on behalf of Weil Gotshal & Manges. He would teach me to play the ping-pong machines in the *Royal Vendôme*; he explained this had been a distraction from his studies at Harvard. He would leave Paris for Hollywood but after spending some years with the motion picture industry he would return, dividing his time between his apartment off the Boulevard Montparnasse and his New York apartment in Park Avenue.

Michael Harrington had been an American socialist.

He had wanted to settle in Paris with his wife but she had a psychosomatic dislike of the city and they had returned to New York. He had written a book on poverty and when Lyndon Johnson became President of the United States he had invited Michael to the White House for a chat. Michael would write books on socialism, such as *The Next Left: The History of the Future*, and over the years, each time I visited New York, I would collect his latest work and nourish my own enthusiasm on the originality of his ideas.

Café de Flore had been popular because it had been off the Latin Quarter, because artists such as Jean-Paul Sartre and Albert Camus had met there; the American writer, Truman Capote, author of *Breakfast at Tiffany's*, had thought he would find artistic life in its salons; he would join the *Pouilly Club* and its members would meet around the tables to the left of the cashier, enjoying the white wine as much as the conversation; but all Capote would get would be snide obliquy because his second name was French for contraceptive.

Ernest Hemingway is also listed as one of the *Café*'s passing dignitaries, but he would prefer *Le Dôme* in the Montparnasse. Or as he would write: '*The people in the principal cafés might just sit and drink and talk and love to be seen by others'*. The French would describe this as *m'as-tu-vu?* Hemingway would also write: *'There were models who had worked and there were painters who had worked until the light was gone and there were writers who had finished a day's work for better or for worse'*.

I had called by *Café de Flore* with Malcolm, for the breakfast to be sure, but because we had been on our way to the theatre in the rue de Vieux Colombier where years ago I had seen Anton Chekhov's *Oncle Vania*. I recalled the typewritten sheet I had placed in the wall of my council house room, the words taken from one of Chekhov stories, of three young men sitting in a café not much different from the *Café de Flore*.

Forty years later the theatre is still there, not a hundred yards from the *Café de Flore*, a thoroughly modern theatre, its vestibule of marble and glass, with all manner of subscriptions to be taken out by friends. The words of Anton Chekhov placed on my wall in my council house ran still through my mind. What had I accomplished? Had I been bound by the inexorable law that of a hundred promising beginners only two or three rise to any position?

'Have I drawn a blank in the lottery?' I asked Malcolm.

'As a writer or a politician?'

'Or perished playing the part of flesh for the cannon?'

'Better ask Tony Blair,' Malcolm said. 'When you see him.'

Because we had first settled in Montparnasse rather than the Latin Quarter, our principle cafés, as Hemingway had described them, had been *Le Select*, *Le Dôme* and *La Coupole*. I had preferred *Le Select* because it had been warmer and cosier, and because when not working from his apartment above the sawmill Hemingway had written there, letting the saucers build up around him as the waiters left him to work undisturbed. The smoke and noise and condensation to the windows on cold days had not disturbed his concentration.

I recall a young woman sitting at the next table in *Le Select* writing a card to her parents, describing how she had met a painter not yet famous but who would be one day; and another evening seeing the young painter coming into *Le Select* to seek her out. He had been short with black hair and beard and black coal-like eyes, ferocious in their intensity. I do not know how well he painted, or what impression he might have made on the parents, but he frightened the life out of me.

Le Dôme had been frequented both by Ernest Hemingway and Henry Miller.

The artistic quarter of Paris had moved from Montmartre to Montparnasse, Gauguin would have his studio in rue de la Grande Chaumière where stood the Hôtel des Académies and *chez Wadja*; and as the artists moved in with their Bohemian hangers-on, so there developed around the *carrefour* between Boulevard Montparnasse and Boulevard Raspail the three famous cafes, famous that is for those artists and hangers-on who frequented them.

I would rarely set foot in *Le Dôme*, except possibly for a drink or rendezvous, standing at the bar, though I would often pass the stalls of oysters and king-size prawns in their ice buckets on my way to *La Coupole*; or if Margaret and I were eating at a modest restaurant in the rue Delambre because *chez Wadja* closed on a Sunday. When he visited *Le Dôme*, Hemingway would often take his *fine d'eau* on the Delambre side, sitting on the sidewalk looking across the wide Boulevard not yet encumbered with traffic.

Henry Miller would write of *Le Dôme* in his book *Tropic of Cancer*; the book would be described by Norman Mailer as '*one of the great novels of the century*'. Mailer was author of *The Naked And The Dead*, a war novel to rival James Jones' *From Here to Eternity*. *Tropic of Cancer* is no novel at all, rather an autobiography of Miller's time in Paris. He would spend thirteen years there, and in his book he would describe meeting one of his flames, each flinging themselves into the other's arms, settling on the sidewalk whilst others in *Le Dôme* were '*a thousand eyes, noses, fingers, legs, bottles, windows, purses, saucers, all glaring at us and we in each other's arms oblivious*'.

There had been pleasure in *La Coupole*.

One evening Margaret and I and American friends had been sitting behind the glass front overlooking Boulevard Montparnasse, sipping our coffee, not yet into *fine*, when an older man with balding head and wisps of grey hair walked by. He wore a shabby mackintosh and trudged rather than walked, his shoulders loose, but he paused to squint through the glass front. He did not need to raise his hands to shield the squint, for the light from *La Coupole* had been bright and enthusiastic.

'That's Henry Miller!' one of the Americans said.

'In that case,' I said. 'I'll ask him to join us.'

I left the round table and wicker seat and caught up with Henry as he was approaching *Le Dôme*.

'We're a group of young writers and artists,' I said.

Would he like to join us for a coffee?

Henry had been a Brooklyn boy, Brooklyn born, Brooklyn educated, Brooklyn accent. He had worked as personnel manager for a telegraph company but had walked out one day and taken a boat to France. He had settled in Paris. He made the entire journey on ten dollars, perhaps worth a great deal more in those days, the days of the Depression. *Tropic of Cancer* had been published in 1934 in Paris by *Olympia Press* but had been immediately banned.

This made Henry notorious if not famous.

When he came to England on a visit he was turned away at the port; he would be held in custody over-night. Yet if his days in Paris were lived without money or resources or without hope, as he himself would write in *Tropic of Cancer*, he described himself as '*the happiest man*' alive. George Orwell had picked this up and in one of his essays on Miller; writing of *Tropic of Cancer*, he would declare that the singularity of the book was that it had been written by '*a man who is happy*'.

George Orwell had been one of his early admirers; he had written his own book on being *Down and Out in Paris and London*. He would understand what it meant for a writer to reach the bottom of the pit, as he would describe it, yet emerge unembittered, laughing with the fun of it all. Orwell had gone to fight the Spanish Civil War and had met Henry in Paris on his way to the front. Henry had advised him not to go, and when I recalled this conversation to Henry over coffee at *La Coupole*, he replied:

'*That is one conversation that I prefer to forget.*'

Orwell had indeed continued his journey, he had been shot in the throat by a sniper and when his Trostkyist element of the Civil War movement had been dissolved by the Republican government he and his wife would escape back to France. The war had been a turning point in his writing career; he would become a dedicated socialist, notwithstanding he had been taught at Eton, and from such dedication would flow *Animal Farm* and *1984*.

Through his works, I had known Orwell better than I had known Miller, though *Tropic of Cancer* and *Tropic of Capricorn* I would buy in their uncut edition from Brentano's. Orwell's *Road to Wigan Pier* would describe the life of a mining community; he would describe conditions down the pit; and I would use a quote from this book as a frontispiece to my own mining novel. I would draw its original title – *Sons of Clay* – from an Orwell piece that described miners as 'caryatids' of the soil.

In a book written when he was eighty, Henry Miller would recall his life-long motto: *Always be happy, always be joyful.* Or as he had written earlier in his Paris days: '*Joy is like a river, it flows ceaselessly*'. *Tropic of Capricorn* would also be banned, described by the *Sunday Times* as peopled by '*eccentrics and nymphomaniacs*' and replete with '*fornication and anarchism*'.

Capricorn had been published in Paris before the outbreak of the Second World War, but by then Henry had returned to the United States to settle in Big Sur, on the Californian coastline between Los Angeles and San Francisco. Henry would call Big Sur '*the face of the earth as the creator intended it to look*'. Other writers would describe it as '*a state of mind*' not a place, an adopted Eden of sea and sky and mountain, of wild moods with chilly fog and rain as well as soft air and sunshine. There would be black cottonwoods, big-leaf maples, alders and willows, and a coast as lonely as it was beautiful.

Years later I would visit Big Sur in search of Henry Miller, driving up from Los Angeles, but by then he had left for Southern California, and Margaret and I and Ian and Yvonne would check in at the Big Sur lodge. I would write a short story on a log table from a log seat, sitting in the sun, writing with such concentration I would not notice that my right hand was burning. The flesh became raw and would not heal till we had left Big Sur and moved on to San Francisco.

On the day in Paris we had coffee with Henry, he had been to visit James Jones in his home on the Ile St-Louis. He had sat in the room where I had left my umbrella; he had seen the

354

guns but had not mentioned the silverware. He had been on his way to Majorca where he would receive a literary prize. He had not heard from his hotel confirming the booking and was getting a little anxious.

I grandly offered to send a cable to the hotel from my office in the Place Vendôme to ensure the booking would be in order and when I received the reply I sent it to his hotel in the Montparnasse. Henry would send me a postcard before leaving Paris. '*Dear friend,*' he wrote. '*I am most grateful and appreciative for your help. And good luck with the writing.*'

Henry had not been a *Café de Flore* man, but when last I had been there I had come to have an aperitif with Stanley Cohen. Henry Miller might wish me luck with my writing, but now I was written out; I had written of my past, of my pit village, of my life. Now like Hemingway and Orwell and Miller before me I had no money, with a wife and two children to keep, working again as a male secretary out of the Place Vendôme.

I sat silent and morose.

'What do you propose to do now?' Stanley asked.

I had seen little television in Paris, except a glimpse one evening of a children's programme in black and white. There had been *Nonourse*, a large brown cuddly teddy bear that would become a favourite of my son Ian; so much a favourite Alan Hays' wife would buy a model for him that he would keep till he reached his teens. He would bring *Nonourse* back to England in the car, falling asleep in the back seat, his dreams taking him back to his childhood, holding onto the teddy bear as he had then.

There had been a story on the children's programme recounted by a father to his children as they lay tucked in bed, a story that enthralled them as all stories should, rather like the stories still told by story tellers in the bazaars of the

355

East. At the end of the story the father closes the book and seeks to put out the light. The children grip the edges of the bedclothes, their eyes bright, their curiosity aroused.

This happened nightly and always one of the children would ask:

What happens next, papa?

And he would reply:

'Ça c'est une autre histoire.'

That is another story.

'It's like those children's TV programmes,' I said.

'What do you mean?' Stanley asked.

'It's another story.'

Malcolm and I had left Paris and returned to Middlesbrough to meet Tony Blair at the South Cleveland Hospital.

Tony had brought along his father Leo, he had been to his adoption meeting that morning in Sedgefield and as Tony did the rounds of the wards, television cameras at a respectful but fully-focused distance, he and I walked together down the long corridors, the light dull from the acrylic tiles. Leo had been brought up in Glasgow, he had left school at seventeen first to work as a clerk for Glasgow Corporation, before joining the Army in wartime. He had been demobilised as a major in 1947.

Yet the whole of his life had lain ahead.

He had enrolled at Edinburgh University to take a degree in law; he had read for the Bar and qualified as a barrister. In 1958, when his son Tony had been five years old, he had settled in Durham City where he and family would live for the next seventeen years. He had wished for a political career of his own but suffered a stroke at the age of forty and had spent three years without his speech.

He might have been an MP-manqué, but he had laid the foundations for his son's career.

It had not been surprising that for the adoption meeting within his Constituency Party, the last as an Opposition MP, the first before he became Prime Minister, Tony Blair would wish his father to be with him. His mother had died two weeks after he had graduated from Oxford, but had it not been for his own father's struggles, from a tenement council flat in Glasgow to doctor-at-law and barrister, his own school career might not have been so clearly defined, notwithstanding his own hard work, obtaining a scholarship to Fettes College in Edinburgh, graduating from Oxford and qualifying for the Bar in his own right.

His father might have cleared the way.

It had been Tony who made the run.

Would he be spending much time in the campaign?

'Tony wouldn't let me,' Leo said.

He was after all seventy-four.

Tony would further honour him, however, by naming his third son after him.

I did not try to keep up with Tony as he was marched along the various corridors, popping his head into the baby-care unit, the new-born children so small in their incubators, pausing too on the observation platform overlooking the cardiac unit where operations were performed. I did, however, manage to have a few words with him and tell him of my conversations with the Governor of the Bank of France and the Minister for Trade.

I explained that they had given me the up-to-date views of the French government both on the European Union and the single currency and completion of the single market. Tony had committed himself to early completion of the single market in a speech he had made at Party Conference and I had prepared for him a three-inch thick file of what needed to be done. I also told him that for the Governor of the Bank of France independence of the European Central Bank would be crucial and the rate for the single currency when it came would be set only a few hours before.

It would be a negotiated rate.

Only a few months earlier, when attending a course for would-be Ministers at Templeton College, Oxford, I had suffered a slipped disc and temporarily lost the use of my right leg. Now I suffered from sciatica which gave me a limp and I had trouble keeping up with Tony, mumbling my unsolicited briefing as television crews and Labour Party staff whirled around. There were too his own staff. Eventually, the hospital tour was over and we were swept out towards the campaign bus standing on the forecourt.

'The French,' Tony said. 'They're still keen aren't they?'

Though keen on what I never did ascertain.

Malcolm and I followed Tony onto the campaign bus that would take him to the airport. He would sit with his close staff behind a curtain at the back. He would complain as the bus made its way to the airport that it was taking a slower route, not a direct route, not a route to which he had been accustomed; but since it was under police escort the bus was required to take the route already mapped for the driver and at the speed set by the escort. The staff ate their sandwiches and drank their soft drinks, fretting and worrying how the visit to the hospital would play on the news bulletins.

They need not have worried.

The IRA threatened a bomb at Aintree, the Grand National was called off, thousands were turned away from the course, millions of television viewers were disappointed, bookies non-plussed: had stake money been lost, would the race be run another day? Tony visiting newly-born babies or standing on the observation platform of a cardiac unit, or shaking hands with nurses, or speaking with older patients in wards looking out upon green fields that unfolded all the way to the Cleveland hills.

They mattered very little.

Malcolm had waited for me in the Golden Gallery of the Bank of France when I had been in attendance of the Governor. The Gallery had once been the mansion of the Count of Toulouse. He had been the second legitimated son of Louis XIV and of Madame de Montespan. Though the original Gallery had been destroyed, it had been rebuilt in the original model, so that there were above you, as in the Cistine Chapel, painted upon the ceiling, scenes depicting fire, earth, sun, air and water.

There were too beautiful paintings upon the walls.

There were the Sabines fighting against the Romans, Corialanus vanquished by his family's tears raising the siege of Rome; there was Romulus and Remus taken in by Faustulus and Helen carried off by Paris. There had been gilded sculptures and vases and in the hearth a cast-iron plate bearing the coat of arms of the Count of Toulouse: the *fleur-du-lis* escutcheon of France with a bar betokening the Count's bastard origin.

All set in a decor of gold.

'Who needs a single currency?' Malcolm asked.

The following day, after visiting the Minister, Malcolm now up and about, we had walked to the Jardin du Luxembourg, and from the Jardin to Boulevard Montparnasse and *Le Select*. The day after we had walked across the Pont St-Louis, past the Notre-Dame Cathedral, its gargoyles as fierce as ever, chasing away devils, both interior and exterior; some of them would even be blown down in the hurricane that afflicted Paris on the eve of the millennium. We walked past the small park where I had almost slept out, towards Place St Michel and beyond its fountain into Boulevard St Germain.

We had kept walking to the *Café de Flore*.

359

Tony had known Malcolm since he was a child and they had last met at Darlington Station when Tony, as Leader of the Opposition, had been returning to his home in Islington from his Sedgefield constituency. Malcolm and Margaret had each been enjoying a hot-dog, unusual for them, settled on one of the benches awaiting the London train. Tony had come striding towards them. They had been somewhat discomforted when they had found the Leader of the Opposition bearing down upon them while they ate an unorthodox lunch.

Tony had talked of Malcolm's education and the nature of his curriculum, how he found mathematics, and since Tony planned to make education a major theme in the Election – education, education, education – perhaps talking directly to a teenage schoolboy he knew had helped. Tony had carried Margaret's bags onto the train and offered to give her a lift when they reached Kings Cross, except that his car would be going to Islington in the opposite direction to Dolphin Square.

Now Malcolm and I stood on the tarmac at Teesside Airport whilst Tony left the bus and boarded the plane.

'I told him about the Governor of the Bank of France and the Minister of Trade,' I said. 'I mentioned the single currency and the single market.'

Perhaps the hot-dog at the station still played on Malcolm's mind.

'Did you mention the hard-boiled egg at the *Café de Flore?*' he asked.

'I didn't offer him one either,' I said.

'Greater love hath no man,' Malcolm said.

Tony Comes to the Boro

Tony Blair had come to Middlesbrough the day before the General Election.

He had brought television actress Helen Mirren, who had played in a police series, and together they had met Detective Superintendent Ray Mallon who, having introduced zero tolerance in Hartlepool, was about to introduce this to Middlesbrough. The policy had been borrowed from cities in the United States where petty criminals were arrested for minor offences, cutting them off at the pass, as it were, before they became hardened criminals. The streets of New York had reputedly been made safe by this tactic and crime throughout other American cities had been steadily falling.

Mallon would vow to quit the police force if he was unable to reduce Middlesbrough crime by twenty per cent and there would be claims he had hit the target within half that time. He would become the country's 'most famous policeman' and gain massive support within the local community. Since Tony Blair had his own policy of being tough on crime and tough on the causes of crime he had wanted to meet Mallon first hand.

John Major had actually called for the General Election to be held on May Day, a national fête for workers. It had been an odd choice unless he had wanted to remind the electorate of the hammer and sickle, overweening trade union power, workers on the march, unfurling their banners, Tony Blair not New Labour but Old, not on his way to his constituency in Sedgefield after his hour or so in Middlesbrough, but to march at the head of a political Dad's Army, white shirt open around his neck, coat hooked by his thumb over his shoulder.

Or perhaps John as Prime Minister had called the date because it had been politically expedient, the last date it could feasibly be called within the constitution. 'I'll be sure I get you a sprig of *muguet*,' I said. 'For Election Day.'

'What is that?' he had asked.

'Lily of the valley,' I said.

'Why on Election Day?'

'It's a symbol of friendship among workers.'

'In France,' he said. 'If I recall.'

I had been making my way to the strangers' dining room in the House of Commons when I had passed John Major. He and I shared another attribute: we were both in *The Other Picture* that hung in the strangers' dining room. I had settled quietly and alone in the dining room, members already making their Election preparations, but when I looked up there was Richard Crossman standing at the entrance, a tall man in a morning suit, taller than I had imagined, his silver hair plastered to his skull, with odd tufts sticking out, his hair like his personality, irrepressible and ill-disciplined.

He had been Secretary of State in Harold Wilson's Labour government.

And there, at the next table, sitting directly before me, was Jeremy Thorpe, Leader of the Liberal Party; he entertained two or three others, a small man perched on his seat, his face thin, his hair and complexion dark, his eyes as dark as his hair, moving around the room as he talked, seeing who else might be around him.

'He's a bloody Liberal!' Tim Fortescue shouted.

Jeremy heard the dismissive tone and looked up, discomforted, aware that the Conservative MP was talking of him. I do not know whether Richard Crossman found himself a table, or whether he and his party had sidled off, if you can sidle anywhere when you are six-feet-two inches tall; but he was not there any more, nor was Jeremy Thorpe or Tim Fortescue; and I realised all this had happened thirty-one years ago.

I had relived it in my mind's eye.

I had come to the House of Commons for dinner in this very room, at this very table, as a guest of Tim Fortescue, Member of Parliament for Garston. I had driven down from Birmingham with my boss, Alan Hays, and we had met with Tim who was not only a Liverpool MP but who specialised in aviation matters. We had a putative client – Seaboard World Airlines – who were interested in landing rights at Liverpool Airport.

This would be the first time in thirty-one years that I would find myself at the same table and in the same seat, the reason being simple. The large members' dining room next door for the exclusive use of MPs had been underused at lunch-times, whereas the smaller strangers' dining room where MPs could entertain their guests had been overbooked. A swop had been the obvious solution, but such are the susceptibilities of MPs, the respect for tradition, that it had taken some years for the Catering Committee to achieve this simple transfer.

'I remember Tim Fortescue well,' Gerald Kaufman MP said. 'He used to be managing director for Nestlé. He worked out of Vevey, Switzerland. He fought his last election in 1970.'

Gerald would often have lunch in the members' dining room; he would advise me on the quality of the soup and the ice cream; and he had an encyclopaedic memory when it came to films and MPs. At the time of my dinner in the

House, he had worked in the Cabinet Office as a confidante of Harold Wilson; he would enter the House in his own right in 1970, and had headed the Shadow Cabinet lists in many of our years in Opposition.

He was now Chairman of the Select Committee on Heritage.

'Tim's political career remained unfulfilled,' Gerald said. 'And you won't find him in *The Other Picture*.'

The then Speaker of the House, Bernard Weatherill, now Lord Weatherill, had commissioned a portrait of the House of Commons. The original had been placed on the wall in the strangers' dining room to the left of me. The House, however, had six-hundred-and-fifty members, not all of whom could get into the portrait. Some of those, including myself, who were not in the original, commissioned *The Other Picture*. This had the Speaker's approval and would become even more popular than the original.

This was because the first painting depicted an orthodox House at Prime Minister's Question Time; but with deference and respect for the painter it was a House without atmosphere, without feeling; Margaret Thatcher lumpen at the Dispatch Box, Neil Kinnock disinterested, leaning forward as if there were no room for him; few order papers on the floor, few reporters in the Press Gallery, the House decorous and formal.

But not the House that I knew.

The second painting had more animation, more vibrancy, set not in a formal setting but in the smoking room and library of the House; even the lights that hang from the chandeliers appear vivacious and there is a warmth and camaraderie reflected in MPs of all parties chatting and sipping together, with librarians looking down from the upper floor. And John Major, too, a future Prime Minister smiling and talking, his arms folded.

I would explain *The Other Picture* to Penny.
She had come to dine with me at the House.
'I prefer *The Other Picture*,' I said.
'Because you were on the committee.'
'Because I'm in the picture.'
'Like John Major?'
'But not Tony Blair.'

Penny had worked with me in Paris at the time I had come to London with my boss to attend the Commons and meet Tim Fortescue. She had not changed with the years, small and blonde with short-cut hair, and if we would talk of Paris she would tell me what she had done with her life since our days together as secretaries. She had married a banker and spent some years in Singapore; she had raised two children, one in law, the other in banking; and now the family had settled in London where she worked for a Jewish charity.

'Do you remember the *muguet?*' she asked.

The French loved their national holidays, their fête days, either religious or civil, and the three I would remember most were the Fourteenth of July, All-Saints' Day and May Day. The first Fourteenth of July would see my brother and sister-in-law staying with Margaret and me at the Porte de St Cloud, and not only would we visit the military parade on the Champs-Elysées we would see the end of the *Tour de France* as the cyclists raced through the streets of Boulogne-Billancourt.

The fire brigades – *les sapeurs pompiers* – would open their casernes to the public; they would become the true popular places for the people to celebrate. There would be dancing to accordions and drinking and Chinese lanterns strung across the barrack square, the huge doors thrown open, *les sapeurs pompiers* serving drinks; young couples dancing so close whilst the moon and stars shone through the chestnut trees, their elders looking on through a haze of wine and spirits and beer.

One year there had been a firework display and Margaret and I had brought our son Ian and daughter Yvonne, parking the car in rue de Rivoli and ensconcing ourselves on Pont Neuf. We had settled in early, as part of the hoi-polloi, keeping the children occupied, sitting on the balustrade or pavement, the heat gone from the air, a chill growing around us, but waiting as patiently as one could with two children for the fireworks.

All Saints' Day would be a sombre national holiday, the dead commemorated, and I recall our first *Toussaint* at Carpantras in the Vaucluse, where Margaret and I had picked grapes at Chateauneuf-du-Pape and afterwards settled in Cavaillon. We had taken the bus to Carpantras for a day out. I cannot recall Carpantras, other than that the weather was cold and dull, no festive spirit to the air; it had grown dark early, clouds low and ominous, and we had been glad to be back to Cavaillon, its light as bright as a Van Gogh painting.

May Day, too, was a brighter occasion.

Flower sellers would offer sprigs of *muguet* for a franc a time, Lily of the Valley, neatly-cut, with dark-green leaves and spikes of white and yellow flowers, a dry light scent pleasant to the nostrils. They would sell them on street corners, not flower sellers really, young girls out to contribute to May Day, and you would put the Lily of the Valley in your buttonhole and wear it throughout the day.

I cannot recall that we did much in Paris on those fête days, other than take the Métro to the Champs-Elysées and see an English film in its original version; we did not have money for restaurants; but in the country they still danced around the maypole in village squares and chose May Day Queens, the contestants daintily pulled through the cobbled streets on floats of primula and primroses and bluebells and Lily of the Valley.

'Do you remember *quatre-vingt-et-un?*' Penny asked.

After lunch in the canteen in the basement of *Huit* Place Vendôme, we would go to *Le Blason* in the Faubourg St Honoré, near the small church pock-marked with grapeshot that Napoleon as an artillery officer had pumped into it in the days of the French Revolution. The phrase whiff of grapeshot had passed into the language, but we had played our *quatre-vingt-et-un* over a coffee and a *fine* under the eye of Lucien, the tall *garçon* who ran the café.

'*Bonjour, mon grand,*' Lucien would say.

I can see Lucien now, with his dark hair and pleasant smile and blue eyes, working in the café from morning to night, a family back at home whom he must have rarely seen but who must have been proud of all the hours he put in. He worked without ceasing, making the coffee, pouring the drinks, cleaning after the customers, wiping the top of the bar as clean as if it had never been used, his hands large, the backs thick-veined, the fingers white like stalks. He wore a black smock and neat shirt open at the neck so that the arms to the elbows rippled with muscle.

I would go back to *Le Blason* twenty years later to find Lucien still there, still dark-haired, no flecks yet of grey, the eyes as blue and sparkling as ever, the smile constant, pouring and clearing and wiping the top clean with his cloth, wearing the same coloured smock, pausing only to look at me, straightening to his full height, holding out his hand, the hand not using the cloth, and saying:

'*Bonjour, mon grand!*'

'What are you up to now?' I asked.

367

'Retiring soon,' he said.

And when last in Paris, stopping at *Le Blason* again, this time for an orange juice and a coffee, asking after Lucien, to be told that he was indeed in retirement, enjoying himself, the new garçons at the bar looking at me curiously, spanning now as I did some thirty years. And still I think of Lucien when I wash the dishes in my Pimlico flat, when the week is over, and I am due to return to Middlesbrough; Lucien with his cloth and his smock and his ever-ready smile and his good cheer and his bonhomie; and I say to him as well as myself:

'Bonjour, mon grand!'

Penny and I had enjoyed Paris as work-mates together, and now we could talk of those spring days when the phlox was out on the chestnut trees, white and fluffy, and when the sun had climbed high, benevolent, magnanimous, parching the dust in the Tuileries Gardens, its rays shining back from the cobbles of the Place Vendôme, the tops of the trees in the Tuileries a feathery green beyond rue Castiglione, already the sun reflecting back from the fountains in the gardens.

But not only would I remember the dinner at the House of Commons with Tim Fortescue and Alan Hays, I remember the drive back to the airport. I had hired a car at Birmingham airport and driven Hays to the House of Commons. He liked to cut things fine and we had to rush back to Heathrow, my driving so fast we missed the junction. I would have to go another fifteen miles up the motorway before I was able to turn and make my way back, suffering the disapproving silence of my boss as I drove.

We had made the flight anyway.

I would see Alan Hays for the last time seventeen years later, when I had returned to Paris shortly before the 1983 General Election, and after I had been nominated Prospective Parliamentary Candidate for Middlesbrough, with the certainty of a seat in the Commons. I had been walking from Place Vendôme down rue de Rivoli towards Place de la Concorde when I met Hays outside Smith's bookshop coming the other way.

'Mr Hays,' I said. 'Soon I shall be entering Parliament!'

He replied without a moment's hesitation.

'That trip we made to the House of Commons to see Tim Fortescue. It would stand you in good stead.'

And after all those years that was all he said.

I had not heard that Tony Blair was coming to Middlesbrough to meet Detective Superintendent Ray Mallon the day before the Election. His office had not told me nor had the Labour Party. The campaign was running so fast now it had no time for such courtesies. I had heard the news on one of my housing estates where I had been delivering leaflets; it had been passed to me by one of my campaign workers; but later I would reflect that Tony had visited the police station only a stone's throw away from the old courthouse converted to a canteen where we had first had lunch.

It had all seemed a long time ago.

Tony had met Mallon in his office in Dunning Street and had his photograph taken beneath a poster taken from *The Shawshank Redemption*, a book by Steven King which had been made into a successful film with Tim Robbins playing the leading role. Beneath the poster was a coffee tray on which stood a model Saab car and where Mallon would place memorabilia which he felt either important or significant to him in his journey through life. The wording of the poster entitled *Shawshank* must also have had significance:

Fear Can Hold You Prisoner
Hope Can Set You Free.

Tony, however, was not looking at the poster but rather relaxing with his left hand in his trouser pocket, coat open, revealing his white shirt and neatly-knotted tie, listening attentively to Mallon as he enumerated points on his policy of zero tolerance, in the manner that Tony himself often used on the floor of the House, that is using his left index finger and striking the points from the fingers of his right hand, the right thumb upraised straight as a lighthouse.

Zero tolerance, of course, was not the policy of a single individual but rather a policy of the Cleveland force; crime went down in nearby Redcar and Cleveland in the same percentage figures as it had in Middlesbrough. Stockton had not been far behind. Where Mallon had been successful was in inculcating into the minds of the people of the town that crime was indeed falling consequent upon zero tolerance and that the streets were safer.

Tony would meet other police officers in Middlesbrough this day, seven of whom would be suspended from duties because of allegations of corruption and malpractice, and though the investigations would drag on for two-and-a-half years none of the officers would be charged with criminal offences. The eighth officer suspended had been Ray Mallon, though Mallon would not be the subject of a corruption enquiry, nor would it be alleged that he took back-handers, or that he took drugs or dealt in drugs. The only criminal allegation, of which he would be cleared, had been whether he had covered up the alleged wrong-doing of other officers, or whether he had allegedly perverted the course of justice.

When Mallon left the force on his suspension the *Shawshank* poster went with him. For him the poster reflected the elderly and vulnerable in society who needed protection. Often he would speak of the fear of victims of crime. He believed the policy of zero tolerance gave them hope. As he loaded the poster into his car, Mallon would remark: 'I have nothing to fear and lots of hope'.

The poster would return with him should his suspension end.

Two days after Tony visited the Middlesbrough police

station a boiler said to be worth twenty pounds had allegedly been stolen from the crime property store. One of the officers who had briefed Tony would be charged with the alleged theft. The officer would be suspended and brought to trial, another officer would be charged with him, this case too would drag on for two-and-a-half years before being brought before Hull Crown Court. The twenty-pound boiler would be converted into half a million pounds in legal costs, two chief superintendents, two Assistant Chief Constables, a senior Crown Prosecution Service lawyer and the Director of Public Prosecutions would become involved.

To whom had the boiler belonged in the first place? What had it been doing in the crime property office? Who had valued the boiler at twenty pounds? Was its real value not closer to two hundred? How could it be stolen if it was already stolen? I had twice sat my criminal law examinations for the Bar, having failed the first exam; Parliament had changed the law in relation to theft prior to the second exam and I had to learn my criminal law all over again.

The Theft Act 1968 would never be far from my thoughts.

Had the central heating boiler allegedly been stolen with the intention of permanently depriving the owner thereof? What kind of boiler was it anyway – gas or electric? Did it have a thermostat? And what did a police officer who allegedly had the boiler installed in his home want with a boiler? Did he not have central heating? Like the Lambton worm of Durham county fame, the saga of the boiler had grown and grown. The only thing certain about the boiler was that it had been on the premises when Tony Blair had made his visit. The case would collapse at Hull Crown Court, perhaps under the weight of its own absurdity, an 'angry' judge Richard Henriques reaching the conclusion that he could only stay proceedings against the two officers charged.

Tony had indeed come to the Boro.

~

Election Day would dawn bright and clear, a warmth to the air, the sun gentle to the face; rather like those days in Paris, when winter is behind, the cloud has lifted and with it the greyness; when the people begin to smile and there is colour to their dress; reds and blues and yellows, as bright and as homely as the parasols above the pavement cafés.

I could almost feel myself again walking from the Place Vendôme, Napoleon's column before me, the oxydised iron from the cannon of his victories hopeful in the sunlight, wondering if I should turn left towards *Le Blason* or right towards the *Royale Vendôme* in rue Danielle Casanova. Either way the phlox would be out on the chestnut trees in the Tuileries Gardens.

The postman had come early on Election Day.

He delivered a recorded delivery from a constituent who threatened not only to kill herself but her young child too. I spent the morning, not visiting polling booths, nor making a final round with a loudspeaker, but sorting out the plight of the woman and her child, with the police and social services, before returning to the campaign.

The postman rang a second time.

He delivered a small parcel.

I opened the parcel to find a sprig of *muguet*, carefully laid out in cellophane, the elongated leaves slim and narrow, the nodules white and yellow, the faint perfume of the flower seeping through the cellophane. I placed the sprig in my button hole close to my red rosette, the rosette of the Candidate, the rosette of the Labour Party, the rosette of New Labour. I looked at the note still in the cellophane.

'All the very best,' Penny wrote. 'For the Election.'

It was also, of course, May Day.

Renvoi

'Take me back,' I said.

'You really want to go back,' God asked. 'I shall take you back – if you really want to go.'

'Yes, Lord. Indeed, yes. I want to go back. If it is possible.'

'All is possible.'

'Even the past?'

'Even the past.'

'I want to go back, Lord.'

'Very well,' God said. 'Close your eyes and take my hand. Settle yourself down. Contemplate upon the holy spirit. The holy spirit that I cast upon the waters. Let my goodness fill your mind and your soul. Let it permeate your being as a golden light. When you have achieved this perpetual peace I shall take you back.'

'I am settled, Lord.'

'And you are at peace?'

'I am at peace.'

'You accept your past with its unhappiness, its upset, its misery, its regret; its joy and its exhilaration and its wonderment? For in your life you have known things – the shadows and the sunlight of a great existence.'

'Written of Victor Hugo.'

'You are a writer and a politician and a barrister. You

are a human being. Your feet are of clay. Yet you wish to return to the past; you want to live it all over again. Do you still hold to your wish?'

'I hold to it, Lord.'

'And your eyes are still closed? And you hold my hand? And you are at peace with yourself and the world? You have a certainty of all such things?'

'Yes, Lord.'

'Very well. You may open your eyes and release my hand. And when you open your eyes you must tell me what you see.'

'Nothing.'

'You see nothing?'

'I see a pen. And I see paper.'

'And you see your past.'

'But where God?'

'You must write if you wish to relive the past,' God said. 'You must find it in your memory and your recollection. In your thoughts and in your imagination. And when you have found it you may commit it to paper so that others will read and understand, if they so wish; and you will be liberated. You may now release my hand.'

' "Take up thy bed and walk," Jesus once said.'

'And now I tell you,' God said. 'Take up thy pen and write.'

'So be it, Lord,' I said.